The Natu...

HEART OF THE LAND

The Nature Conservancy is an internationally recognized conservation organization headquartered in Arlington, Virginia. Its royalties from *Heart of the Land* will be used for the conservation program "Last Great Places: An Alliance for People and the Environment," which is protecting outstanding ecosystems in the United States, Latin America, and the Pacific.

❖

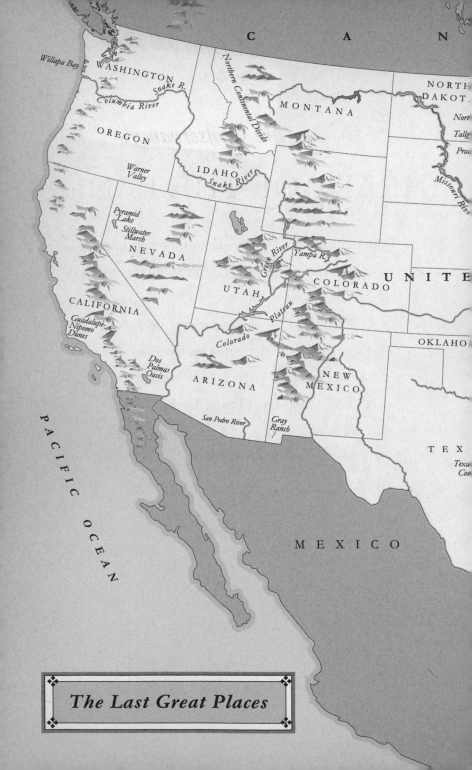

The Last Great Places

HEART
OF THE LAND

ESSAYS ON THE LAST GREAT PLACES

❖ ❖ ❖

Edited by Joseph Barbato and Lisa Weinerman

of The Nature Conservancy

Foreword by Barry Lopez

VINTAGE BOOKS

A Division of Random House, Inc. New York

The following essays have been previously published:

"Winter Solstice at Moab Slough" copyright © 1993 by Terry Tempest Williams,
"Wild Again" copyright © 1993 by Bill McKibben, and "Upon This River" copyright
© 1993 by William Least Heat-Moon all appeared in *The Nature Conservancy Reader*.
"On the Henry's Fork" copyright © 1993 by Thomas McGuane appeared in
Audubon magazine. "Promises" copyright © 1994 by Dorothy Allison
appeared in *Skin*, published by Firebrand Books.

*Grateful acknowledgment is made to
the following for permission to reprint previously published material:*

Blue Heron Publishing, Inc.: Excerpt from "Extinction" by Lynda Sexson from *Left Bank,*
vol. 2, edited by Linny Stovall. Reprinted by permission of Blue Heron Publishing, Inc.
Pantheon Books: "Time" from *Memory of Fire*: vol. 1, *Genesis*, by Eduardo Galeano, translated
by Cedric Belfrage. Translation copyright © 1985 by Cedric Belfrage. Reprinted
by permission of Pantheon Books, a division of Random House, Inc.

**The Nature Conservancy is grateful to the authors
for their generous donation of original work. The views expressed in their essays
are their own and do not necessarily represent the opinions of the organization.**

"Wilderness can be a means of reassuring
ourselves of our sanity as creatures, a
part of the geography of hope."

Wallace Stegner,
"Coda: Wilderness Letter," from *The Sound of Mountain Water*

CONTENTS

❖❖❖

PREFACE

❖❖❖

Recently, while cross-country skiing deep in the Adirondacks of upstate New York, I stopped for a breather at the top of a small rise. Stretching behind me were the twin tracks of my skis; ahead, the trail snaked down through the forest before disappearing into the snowy vastness of the great north woods.

Standing in that special place, I suddenly felt quite alone, humbled by its power and majesty. And then I remembered how the writer Bill McKibben described the Adirondacks: "You see what the world must once have looked like."

Of course, there are few such places left. But those that remain still retain the ability to inspire, to awe, and to fire our collective imaginations. They move us in ways that we all intuitively understand but cannot adequately explain.

In *Heart of the Land*, some of today's finest writers, both new and established, shed light on this mystery by giving voice to the wonders of biologically diverse areas that The Nature Conservancy is helping protect in a conservation effort called "Last Great Places: An Alliance for People and the Environment." Many contributors are well-known for their writing about the outdoors. But others will surprise you with their passion for the environment. Clearly, protecting our natural heritage is a value that transcends categorization.

Each essay is an original piece of writing. The authors have donated their work to help us spread the message about protecting these places, with proceeds from the collection benefiting conservation efforts at these sites.

In asking the contributors to visit these special places as our guests, we placed no constraints on their writing. Perhaps inevitably, some authors formed views different from our own. But differing opinions are part of what makes "Last Great Places"—and this anthology, for that matter—special. Fostering common goals out of diverse interests has always been the key to The Nature Conservancy's conservation efforts.

The words of these writers will resonate with anyone who has been touched by the natural world, who has felt what I felt on that snowy day in the Adirondacks. It is their gift to us, and for that, we are deeply grateful.

John C. Sawhill,
President and Chief Executive Officer,
The Nature Conservancy

FOREWORD

❖❖❖

When I was a boy of eight or nine, living amidst orchards and hayfields in southern California, I was given a copy of *Hammond's Illustrated Library World Atlas* (1949). It became a watershed book for me. I pored over its descriptions of other states and countries and carefully scribed in it (in pencil, on tracing paper) overland journeys I wanted to make—up to the so-called Iron Range of Minnesota and through more obviously exotic places like Brazil; but I also marked out a journey from northern Italy, Ravenna, to Warsaw.

A yearning to experience different parts of the world, to see and touch and smell them, was acute in me; in time, though, I forgot about the atlas, the book that had precipitated and shaped this desire. One day many years later, when I was forty-two or so, I happened to pull the atlas down from the shelf. I paged through it. Tears brimmed in my eyes when I came upon the gray sheets of tracing paper . . . from the Red Sea southwest to Cape Town, down the long coastal reach of Chile . . . the routes plotted earnestly in a child's hand. In the intervening years I had made many of these journeys. What I had longed to do I had been able to do.

I'm more struck now by the exceeding fortune, the privilege, in this coincidence than by any sort of heroic determination, which I do not believe is there. I had a longing that never abated, that amounted to a kind of love. When I looked around all these years later, I'd become a writer who traveled, a man who wanted to be tutored by these landscapes and their occupants. I was thrilled by the subtlety and variety of both and had come to believe wisdom was resident in all these places. I wanted to bring home what I had learned, to speak of it clearly and to convey the hope it made me feel. I knew my own people, like every people in the world, were troubled, sharply desirous of hope.

These thoughts—traveling away from home, a literature of hope—were on my mind when I deplaned one balmy March afternoon at Corpus Christi, Texas, with the manuscript of this book in my satchel. I was headed for a barrier island on the state's Coastal Bend called Matagorda, the name likely a reference in Spanish to thick oak groves, or mottes, that once marked the place. Now a Nature Conservancy preserve, it is country I'd long wanted to visit, as one might for years anticipate the pleasure of reading a book somehow missed in school—*Don Quixote* or *Middlemarch*—knowing it would hold one in its depths.

Sitting on a spacious, windblown veranda at Wynne Lodge, at the southern end of this thirty-eight-mile-long sand island curved like the rachis of a feather, I experienced a pleasing conjunction of thought and geography. My admiration for the writers in this book, for the moments of brilliance in their prose and its range, was elevated by the insistence of Matagorda's beauty. A mackerel sky exaggerated the fetch of the island's flatness. A steady onshore breeze drew and smacked the porch screens, a petty thunder. Birds' reel buzz and fiber creak, their bell strike and trill notes, their blunt hack and siren pitch, came from a perimeter thicket of salt cedars and a scatter of Washington palms, and from small flocks grubbing on a crabgrass lawn before me—red-winged blackbirds, eastern meadowlarks, boat-tailed grackles, mockingbirds, and bobwhite quail. I sat comfortable with the manuscript in a white wicker chair; below me thin layers of Holocene sand and lagoon muds overlay a foundation of 130,000-year-old yellow-orange Ingleside sand, spread over an older Pleistocene coastal plain. I felt situated and, despite my task, incorporated.

As I read, reaching for my binoculars occasionally to study hunters perched—a loggerhead shrike, a black-shouldered kite—or to follow the distant crossing of a flight of gannets, I knew I'd come here for more than two, very obvious reasons: to read what my colleagues had to say about thirty other landscapes; and to immerse myself in country I'd never seen, to feel again the exhilaration and bafflement that come with that. I'd traveled here hoping to discern how in modern landscape writing a new language was emerging.

In my generation some writers are looking, as Linda Hogan says in her essay, for a language to express love of the land, expression the poet W. S. Merwin has called a "forgotten language." It is not just words my colleagues are after but ways to make love clear, to adumbrate a moral relationship with the land, often through vulnerability rather than blindness to the divine. Such a language would make it possible to speak of reciprocity and tenderness, of the accommodation and respect conspicuously absent in our current dealings, our all-too-frequent Judas relations, our manipulative marriages, with natural landscapes.

If anything really new is developing today in the shadow breach between nature and culture, it is our courage in acknowledging imperialized landscapes of the past for the battered remnants they are; and our seeking to establish in their stead commensal landscapes, ones distinguished by an equity of being among resident species. Such places are marked not so much by conventional scenery or striking animals but by a reduction in the scale of human impact; by nurturing, by attempts to restore elements of the ecosystem as we found it; and by compassion, by our own forgiving acceptance of the damage we have inflicted.

Few things seem more fulfilling now, or psychologically more necessary for long-industrialized peoples, I think, than these endeavors, redemption through an expression of love.

In the book you hold, that expression, and the sense of hope that is its bound companion, are revealed in diverse ways. You will no doubt linger to reread, as I did, as one essay or another speaks more directly to you. We are in a time of wakefulness about our relations with the land, reacting to an inattentive and sometimes abusive human past; each one of us, awakening, understands this shift of consciousness and the dilemmas it presents somewhat differently. And, whatever our efforts, they are all shot through, we can see, with enduring paradox and moral complexity. The same economic entities, for example, that continue to create havoc in the natural world are sometimes a primary source of funding for the mitigation of that havoc. And, as almost any traveler outside the United States will tell you, most rural peoples in South America, in Africa, in India, are in search of niches in cash-based economies, not protection from development. They want protein first, not biological preserves. And their desire to own and to exploit land with destructive, short-term farming strategies is spurred on, in part, by North American television programs, by alluring images of astonishing wealth found in the hands of ordinary people.

If we are incapable of addressing these conundrums, which call on the courage inherent in abiding love, and upon social justice, then land conservation in our era will prove to have been only a fashion and not a profound cultural revision, one that could easily bring with it a far greater chance for human biological survival than what we face without it.

These difficult thoughts, imposing and nettlesome, are raised by some of the essays before us. They loom offshore like ships from a strange and dangerous country—insistent and undeniable. It was not so much to avoid them as to rest from their implications that, morning and evening, I would borrow a truck and go off somewhere on Matagorda to walk and look around. No matter where I went during the daylit hours, I remained within a sonic landscape described by birds' voices and by the sibilant pressure of the onshore wind, rolling over a pampas of cordgrasses and paspalum, a billow that incorporated bluestem, windmill, love, and panic grasses. These grasses dominate the shallow ridge-and-swale corrugation of the island's interior, which itself abuts a low, nearly continuous spine of coastal dunes on the Gulf side and tapers into tidal marshes on the bay side. Growing among the grasses is an array of elusive and intriguingly named plants: woolly honeysweet, spotted horsemint, fragrant boneset, slender snakecotton.

And within this mostly knee-high, humid thatch live creatures as be-
guiling: emerald-jawed jumping spiders, bird grasshoppers, dog-faced
sulphur butterflies. The mere existence of such obscure creatures—
and whatever we infer from an hour's witness to their confounding
enterprises—is often antidote to any persistent disaffection. Animals
pull us beyond ourselves, which is to say they draw us back into the
land, where we are their companions, not their owners, their stewards,
or their gods.

Harm, certainly, has found Matagorda Island. It is impossible,
walking its beaches and driving its oystershell roads, not to reflect on
it. The beaches themselves are strewn with plastic jetsam and with
shipping and fishing refuse from the Gulf. For nearly forty years,
beginning in 1940, much of the island served as a bombing range and
aerial gunnery target. At its southern end, diking and excavation originally done to hold and channel water for a cattle operation is still in
evidence. And a population of some sixty feral hogs continues to
severely disrupt Matagorda's natural ecology. They devour wild birds,
reptiles, and crabs, foul water holes, and contend energetically with
raccoons, coyotes, jackrabbits, and other creatures for the same food.
But the dramatic harm done by the military—the catfish, bass,
sunfish, African guinea fowl, and wild turkey they imported to improve fishing and hunting for personnel stationed at the island's air
base shifted the island's balance, as did the salt cedar and Macartney
rose they planted as shelter for introduced (as well as native)
bobwhite—that harm, even the bombing, cannot compare over time
with the natural change wrought by Gulf hurricanes. Terrific storms
in 1875 and 1886 virtually ended a relatively short, optimistic period
of farming and ranching; in 1961, storm surge from Hurricane Carla
inundated 95 percent of the island. Too, written everywhere on this
elongated barrier where geology plays such a quick hand are the
effects of high astronomical and wind tides.

The marauding hogs, vilified by the island's caretakers, are a
prompting presence. The mark of their intrusion is the insignia of
our own peculiar natural history. Somehow we must make not simply
peace with who we are but clear sense of the ways we obtrude. We
must begin to compare our economies, artificial and natural, with

those of others with whom, in this instance, we share an island; we must see what equitable arrangements we can make. How, for example, does a need for "open space" as it figures in the economy of the whooping crane, crowd the desire of *Homo sapiens* to reduce that space, to closely observe these wary, endangered birds? How do the complicated financial demands of the local shrimping economy affect the ecological economies of the island's wild residents? How, as Tom McGuane wonders in his essay, can we adjust for the way "human lives are swept along by fear and need and creaturely habit," while allowing, in his example, trout their economy? How, in short, can we infuse these restorative situations with wisdom and justice?

During the days I read on the veranda, I would sometimes see the island's two resident ecologists coming and going, often on their bicycles. I found the testament of their daily devotion to the place as invigorating as the torrent of birdsong. Like others you will read about here, however—Tom Wood hand-pollinating lemon lilies in Arizona or Carlos Méndez Montenegro being ambushed in southern Guatemala—they are more than ecologists or custodians. They are the active historians of these ecosystems. Without their interpretations and chronicles, without this history—our own as well as that of the wind, of wild creatures and tectonic forces—the land stays empty to us, a stranger. The essays here include some, such as those by John Jerome and William Least Heat-Moon, in which the authors are clearly visitors to strange places, writing in praise after having had, as it were, conversation and a meal with the landscape and its human companions. Other writers, such as Peter Matthiessen and James Welch, reflect on the cultural and natural history of places they've known all their lives. Reading either sort of history makes clear that we also require some kind of spiritual structure in which to examine and engage a new geography. Otherwise the land remains an object, a commodity.

You will feel, I hope, a sense of companionship with the writers as they search for a right language, for metaphors and a situation to convey what they variously mean by allegiance to the land, a wish at some level to come home to it. A desire to recapture from its subtle arrangements the sense of a more virtuous life. And how to be forgiven our trespasses and presumptions. These consequential themes are sustained by the most elementary phrases and moments—Victor Perera's description of the "gorgeous and inoffensive tenancy" of orchids in the Sierra de las Minas; Camille Kingsolver's influence on her mother, Barbara's, thoughts about Kentucky's Horse Lick Creek; Carl Hiaasen's rhetorical question about repeated visits to his favored Florida Keys: "Why does one sit with a dying relative?" The vase of wild flowers Rick Bass brings his mother from the Texas hill country; Linda Hogan's reflection on "disappeared" species; Jim Harrison's self-effacing humor.

Together, these writers form a blessing. Their personal predilections are a kind of collective wisdom; and you feel in certain places something often missing in American writing—the belief of the writer in a shared fate with the reader. It is not possible to draw these essays neatly together; the work varies so in character, as do the tallgrass prairies, coral reefs, riparian harbors, and rosemary balds described. But perhaps it is fair to say that taken together they suggest a line of thinking: that land *Homo sapiens* cannot survive without is critically threatened. The threat is mean. We must ask provoking, even infuriating questions about the impact our culture is having on our biology. And acknowledge that beyond Europe's and North America's shores a terrifying conflagration of biological life, invisible to us, is taking place. And that in this larger world, words like "conservation," "biodiversity," "biophilia," and "restoration" are arcane.

One evening when I was reading I saw a tiny flash of light in the dark, moist air beyond the veranda. It could have been a moving reflection from my pencil on the inside of my glasses or a burst of starlight coming through the low overcast. But what I thought of immediately was a revealed heartbeat. I imagined the intense dot of blue-white light as the distant heart-blink of an animal. A short-eared owl sliding over the barrier flats, a badger paused on a dune ridge in search of ghost crabs. I imagined the clustered heart-blinking

of gadwall and teal asleep at the rims of shallow ponds, heart-heave
in the breasts of sandhill cranes standing in the cordgrass, the heart-
wink of a western diamondback gliding dewberry brambles. I saw the
blue-white pin burn of killifish in the brackish inlets, of tarantulas
and assassin bugs, of rice rats and cicadas and slumbering doves. I
saw a dense twinkling hovering in the dark under cloud cover, the
nimbostratus overhead that masked another universe.

The veranda was so still. I shifted papers in my lap. I returned
to my reading. I heard coyote whimpersong, the night sigh and single
yips of animals in their sleep, punctuating the middle tones of the
wind, the steady seethe of surf from the beach.

I thought if our endeavor—the protection of natures other than
our own—is to succeed, it will require more than mind and hand can
bear. It will require the summoning-toward-magnanimity we feel
watching stormlight ignite a line of roseate spoonbills in lugubrious
flight, their bold eyes glistening, the spotless white bellies and the
pink wash of the wings blazing in the shuttered sunshine. It will
require that we reimagine our lives. It will require a frame of humbler
mind, one preserved the world over in various human cultures by
elders and passed along increasingly to outsiders—a wisdom about
life that Euro-Americans once largely set aside in pursuit of other
things that seemed more worthy. It will require of many of us a
humanity we've not yet mustered, and a grace we were not aware we
desired until we had tasted it.

I understood this from the language in these pieces.

The morning I left Matagorda Island I drove out toward Ayers Point
on the San Antonio Bay side to look for whooping cranes. I and a
companion saw three mated pairs. This protected island is the most
logical territory for whooping cranes to expand to from their wintering grounds at Aransas National Wildlife Refuge, five miles away on
the mainland—it's less visited by humans than any other area nearby.
I'd known about these cranes, the largest in North America, since
childhood, since a time of wondering with an atlas in my lap what it
might be possible to see, what could be hoped for. But it was only

now that I could pay my respects, that I could admire the simple and patient way the cranes searched for food, and observe how much more carefully I placed my feet as I walked away.

BARRY LOPEZ
April 1994

Barry Lopez won the 1986 National Book Award in nonfiction for *Arctic Dreams*. His short stories, which have received a Pushcart Prize and a PEN Syndicated Fiction Award, appear regularly in *The Paris Review, American Short Fiction, The North American Review, Mānoa*, and elsewhere. His other books include *Of Wolves and Men, Winter Count, Crossing Open Ground*, and *Crow and Weasel*.

HEART OF THE LAND

TERRY TEMPEST WILLIAMS

Colorado Plateau, Utah

Winter Solstice at the Moab Slough

❖❖❖

It is the shortest day of the year. It is also the darkest. Winter Solstice at the Moab Slough is serene. I am here as an act of faith, believing the sun has completed the southern end of its journey and is now contemplating its return toward light.

A few hundred miles south, the Hopi celebrate Soyálangwul, "the time to establish life anew for all the world."

At dawn, they will take their prayer sticks, páhos, to a shrine on the edge of the mesa and plant them securely in the earth. The páhos, decorated with feathers, will make prayers to the sun, the moon, the fields, and the orchards. These prayer feathers will call forth blessings of health and love and a fullness of life for human beings and animals.

And for four days, the Hopi will return to their shrine and repeat the prayers of their hearts.

My heart finds openings in these wetlands, particularly in winter. It is quiet and cold. The heat of the summer has been absorbed into the core of the redrocks. Most of the 150 species of birds that frequent these marshes have migrated. Snowy egrets and avocets have followed their instincts south. The cattails and bulrushes are brittle and brown. Sheets of ice become windowpanes to another world below. And I find myself being mentored by the land once again, as two great blue herons fly over me. Their wingbeats are slow, so slow they remind me that, all around, energy is being conserved. I too can bring my breath down to dwell in a deeper place where my blood-soul restores to my body what society has drained and dredged away.

Even in winter, these wetlands nourish me.

I recall the last time I stood here near the solstice—June 1991. The Moab Slough was christened the Scott M. Matheson Wetland Preserve. The Nature Conservancy set aside over eight hundred acres in the name of wildness.

A community gathered beneath blue skies in celebration of this oasis in the desert, this oxbow of diversity alongside the Colorado River. A yellow and white tent was erected for shade as we listened to our elders.

"A place of renewal . . ." Mrs. Norma Matheson proclaimed as she honored her husband, our governor of Utah, whose death and life will be remembered here, his name a touchstone for a conservation ethic in the American West.

"A geography of hope . . ." Wallace Stegner echoed. "That these delicate lands have survived the people who exploited this community is a miracle in itself."

We stood strong and resolute as neighbors, friends, and family witnessed the release of a red-tailed hawk. Wounded, now healed, we caught a glimpse of our own wild nature soaring above willows. The hawk flew west with strong, rapid wingbeats, heartbeats, and I squinted in the afternoon sun, following her with my eyes until she disappeared against the sandstone cliffs.

Later, I found a small striated feather lying on the ground and carried it home, a reminder of who we live among.

D. H. Lawrence writes, "In every living thing there is a desire for love, for the relationship of unison with the rest of things."

I think of my own stream of desires, how cautious I have become with love. It is a vulnerable enterprise to feel deeply and I may not survive my affections. André Breton says, "Hardly anyone dares to face with open eyes the great delights of love."

If I choose not to become attached to nouns—a person, place, or thing—then when I refuse an intimate's love or hoard my spirit, when a known landscape is bought, sold, and developed, chained or grazed to a stubble, or a hawk is shot and hung by its feet on a barbed-wire fence, my heart cannot be broken because I never risked giving it away.

But what kind of impoverishment is this to withhold emotion, to restrain our passionate nature in the face of a generous life just to appease our fears? A man or woman whose mind reins in the heart when the body sings desperately for connection can only expect more isolation and greater ecological disease. Our lack of intimacy with each other is in direct proportion to our lack of intimacy with the land. We have taken our love inside and abandoned the wild.

Audre Lorde tells us, "We have been raised to fear the yes within ourselves . . . our deepest cravings. And the fear of our deepest cravings keeps them suspect, keeps us docile and loyal and obedient, and leads us to settle for or accept many facets of our own oppression."

The two herons who flew over me have now landed downriver. I do not believe they are fearful of love. I do not believe their decisions are based on a terror of loss. They are not docile, loyal, or obedient. They are engaged in a rich, biological context, completely present. They are feathered Buddhas casting blue shadows on the snow, fishing on the shortest day of the year.

Páhos. Prayer feathers. Darkness, now light. The Winter Solstice turns in us, turns in me. Let me plant my own prayer stick firmly in the mud of this marsh. Eight hundred acres of wetlands. It is nothing. It is everything. We are a tribe of fractured individuals who can now only celebrate remnants of wildness. One red-tailed hawk. Two great blue herons.

Wildlands' and wildlives' oppression lies in our desire to control and our desire to control has robbed us of feeling. Our rib cages have been broken and our hearts cut out. The knives of our priests are bloody. We, the people. Our own hands are bloody.

"Blood knowledge," says D. H. Lawrence. "Oh, what a catastrophe for man when he cut himself off from the rhythm of the year, from his unison with the sun and the earth. Oh, what a catastrophe, what a maiming of love when it was made a personal, merely personal feeling, taken away from the rising and setting of the sun, and cut off from the magical connection of the solstice and equinox. This is what is wrong with us. We are bleeding at the roots. . . ."

The land is love. Love is what we fear. To disengage from the earth is our own oppression. I stand on the edge of these wetlands, a place of renewal, an oasis in the desert, as an act of faith, believing the sun has completed the southern end of its journey and is now contemplating its return toward light.

Terry Tempest Williams is Naturalist-in-Residence at the Utah Museum of Natural History. She is the author of *Refuge* and *An Unspoken Hunger*, among other books. She is the recipient of a Lannan Literary Fellowship, and serves on the Great Basin advisory board of The Nature Conservancy.

On Willow Creek

❖❖❖

I don't know how to start, but perhaps that's no matter. I am only thirty-five years old, and the land is over a billion; how can I be expected to know what to say beyond "Please" and "Thank you" and "Ma'am"? The language of the hill country of Texas, or of any sacred place, is not the language of pen on paper, or even of the human voice. It is the language of water cutting down through the country's humped chest of granite, cutting down to the heart and soul of the earth, down to a thing that lies far below and beyond our memory.

Being frail and human, however, memory is all we have to work with. I have to believe that somewhere out there is a point where my language—memory—will intersect with the hill country's language: the scent of cedar, the feel of morning mist, the blood of deer, glint of moon, shimmering heat, crackle of ice, mountain lions, scorpions, centipedes, rattlesnakes, and cactus. The cool dark oaks and gold-leaved hickories along the creeks; the language of the hill country seems always to return to water. Along the creeks is where most of the wildlife is found. It is along a creek that the men in my family built a hunting cabin sixty years ago. We have lived in Texas for a hundred and twenty years, and the men in my family have always hunted deer—hunting them in Tennessee before that, and Mississippi, and perhaps all the way back to the dawn of man, to the first hunter—perhaps that link across the generations is completely unbroken, one of the few unfragmented systems remaining in this century—*The Basses hunt deer*—a small thing, but still whole and intact.

It is only for the last sixty years, however, that we've hunted deer—once a year, in November—on this thousand acres deep in the hill country.

Sixty years. The land changes so much more slowly than we do. We race across it, gathering it all in—the scents, the sounds, the feel of that thousand acres. Granddaddy's gone, now; Uncle Horace, John Dallas, Howard, gone too: already I've lived long enough to see these men in my family cross that intersection where they finally learn and embrace the real language of the earth—the language of granite, and history—leaving us, the survivors, behind, still speaking of them in terms of memory.

We have not yet quite caught up with the billion-year-old land we love and which harbors us, but as we get older, we're beginning to learn a word or two, and beginning to see (especially as we have children) how our own lives start to cut knifelike down through all that granite, the stone hump of the hill country, until we are like rivers and creeks ourselves, and we reach the end and the bottom, and *then* we understand . . .

Water. The cities and towns to the south and east of the hill country—Austin, San Antonio, Houston, La Grange, Uvalde, Goliad—I could chart them all, thousands of them, for they are all my home—these towns, these cities, and these people drink from the heart of the hill country. The water in their bodies is the water that has come from beneath the hills, from the mystical two-hundred-mile-long underground river called the Edwards Aquifer. The water is gathered in the hill country by the forces of nature, percolates down through the hills and mountains and flows south, underground, toward the ocean.

That water which we don't drink or pump onto our crops or give to our livestock—that tiny part which eludes us—continues on to the Gulf Coast, into the bays and estuaries, where delicate moisture contents, delicate salinities are maintained for the birds, shrimp, and other coastal inhabitants that at first glance seem to be far away from and unrelated to the inland mountains.

A scientist will tell you that it's all connected—that if you live in Texas you must protect the honor and integrity of that country's core, for you are tied to it, it is as much a part of you as family—but if you are a child and given to daydreaming and wondering, I believe that you'll understand this by instinct. You don't need proof that the water moving through those shady creeks up in the wild hills and mountains is the same that later moves through your body. You can instead stand outside—even in the city, even in such a place as Houston, and look north with the wind in your face (or with a salt breeze at your back, carrying your essence back to the hill country like an offering), and you can feel the tremble and shimmer of that magic underground river, the yearning and timelessness of it, just beneath your seven-year-old feet. You can *know* of the allegiance you owe it, can sense this in a way that not even the scientists know. It is more like the way when you are in your mother's arms, or your grandmother's, that you know it's all tied together, and that someday you are going to understand it all.

Of course that's the point of this story, that I was one of those children, and that I am here to say thank you to the country in which I was birthed, and to ask "please" that the last good part of it not be divided into halves and then quarters and then eighths, and on, then, further divided into the invisibility of neglect or dishonor . . .

The men would go north in the fall—my father and his brother Jimmy, driving up to the hill country from Houston, while Granddaddy—only barely a granddaddy then, which now seems unimaginable—came down from Fort Worth.

They would meet up in the high hills and low mountains, in the center of the state. I'd stand there on the back porch in Houston with my mother and watch them drive off—it would often be raining, and I'd step out into the rain to feel it on my face—and I'd know that they were going to a place of wildness, a place where they came from. I'd know it was an act of honor, of ritual, of integrity. I was that boy, and knew these things, but did not seriously believe that I would ever be old enough to go in the fall myself.

Instead, I sought out those woods I could reach. We lived out near the west edge of Houston, near what is now the Beltway, a few hundred yards from the slow curls of Buffalo Bayou. While the men in my family went up into the hill country (and at all other times of the year), I would spend my time in the tiny de facto wilderness between outlying subdivisions. Back in those still-undeveloped woods was a stagnating swamp, an old oxbow cut off from the rest of the bayou; you had to almost get lost to find it. I called it "Hidden Lake," and I would wade out into the swamp and seine for minnows, craw-dads, mud puppies, and polliwogs with a soup strainer. In those woods, not a mile from the Houston city limits, I saw turtles, bats, skunks, snakes, raccoons, deer, flying squirrels, rabbits, and armadillos. There were bamboo thickets too, and of course the bayou itself, with giant alligator gars floating in patches of sunlit chocolate water, and Spanish moss hanging back in the old forest, and wild violets growing along the bayou's banks. A lot of wildness can exist in a small place, if it is the right kind of country: a good country.

That country was of course too rich to last. The thick oaks fell to the saws, as did the dense giant hickories and the sun-towering, wind-murmuring pines. It's all concrete now; even the banks of the bayou have been channeled with cement. I remember my shock of finding the first survey stakes, out in the grasslands (where once there had been buffalo) leading into those big woods along the bayou's rich edge. I remember asking my mother if the survey stakes meant some-one was going to build a house out there—a cabin, perhaps. When told that a road was coming, I pulled the stakes up, but the road came anyway, and then the office buildings, and the highway, and the subdivisions.

The men would come back from the woods after a week. They would have bounty with them—a deer strapped to the hood of the car, heavy with antlers (in those days people in the city did not have trucks), or a wild turkey. A pocket of blackjack acorns; a piece of granite. An old rusting wolf trap found while out walking; an arrowhead. A piece of iron ore, red as rubies. A quartz boulder for my mother's garden. And always, they brought back stories: more stories, it seemed, than you could ever tell.

Sometimes my father or uncle would have something new about him—something that I had not seen when he'd left. A cut in the webbing of his hand from where he'd been cleaning the deer. Or a light in his eyes, a kind of *easiness*. A smell of woodsmoke. Beard stubble, sometimes. These were men who had moved to the city and taken city jobs, who drove to work every morning wearing a suit, but they came back from the hill country with the beginnings of beards. There was always something different about them. The woods had marked them.

Because my parents could see that I had an instinctive draw to the animal world—to be more frank, because they could see that I was aflame with the wild—they did their best to keep me nourished, there in the city. My mother took me to the zoo every week, where I'd spend hours looking at the animals with a joy and an excitement, looking at exhibits which would now crush me with sadness. We went to the Museum of Natural History every Saturday. I heard lectures on jumping spiders and wolf spiders. I breathed window fog against the aquarium panes as I watched the giant soft-shelled turtles paddle slowly through their underwater eerie green light. I bought a little rock sample of magnetite from the gift shop. The little placard that came with the magnetite said it had come from Llano County, Texas. That was one of the two counties my father and uncle and grandfather hunted (the thousand acres straddled Llano and Gillespie counties). This only fueled the fire of my love for a country I had not even seen—a country I could feel in my heart, however, and could feel in my hands, all the way to the tips of my fingers: a country whose energy, whose shimmering life-force, resonated all the way out into the plains, down into the flatlands.

All that sweet water, just beneath our feet. But only so much of it: not inexhaustible. We couldn't, or weren't supposed to, take more than was given to us. That was one of the rules of the system. My father, and the other men who hunted it, understood about this system, and other such systems; for them, the land—like our family itself—was a continuum. Each year, each step hiked across those steep slickrock hills cut down deeper into the rocks, deeper into memory, gave them more stories, more knowledge, and at the same time, took them ever closer to the mystery that lay at the base of it.

I'd grip that rough glittering magnetite like a talisman, would put my fingers to it and try to feel how it was different from other rocks—would try to feel the pull, the affinity it had for things made of iron. I'd hold it up to my arms and try to feel if it stirred my blood, and I believed that I *could* feel it . . .

I'd fall asleep listening to the murmur of the baseball game on the radio with the rock stuck magically to the iron frame of my bed. In the morning I would sometimes take the rock and place it up against my father's compass. I'd watch as the needle always followed the magnetite, and I felt my heart, and everything else inside me, swing with that compass needle, too.

When we run out of country, we will run out of stories.

When we run out of stories, we will run out of sanity.

We will not be able to depend on each other for anything—not for friendship or mercy, and certainly not for love or understanding.

Of course we shouldn't protect a wild core such as the Texas hill country because it is a system still intact with the logic and sanity that these days too often eludes our lives in the cities. We should instead protect the hill country simply for its own sake, to show that we are still capable of understanding (and practicing) the concept of honor: loving a thing the way it is, and trying, for once, not to change it.

I like to think that in the sixty years we've been hunting and camping on that rough, hidden thousand acres—through which Willow Creek cuts, flows, forks, and twists, with murmuring little waterfalls over one- and two-foot ledges, the water sparkling—that we have not changed the humped land one bit.

I know that it has changed us. My grandfather hunted that country, as have his sons, and now we, my brothers and cousins, hunt it with them, and in the spring, we now bring our young children into the country to show them the part, the huge part, that is not hunting (and yet which for us is all inseparable from the hunting): the fields of bluebonnets and crimson paintbrushes, the baby raccoons, the quail, the zonetail hawks and buzzards circling Hudson Mountain, the pink capitol domes of granite rising all through the land as if once here lived a civilization even more ancient than our parents, grandparents, and great-grandparents.

A continuous thing is so rare these days, when fragmentation seems more than ever to be the rule. I remember the first time I walked with my daughter on the thousand acres, on the land our family calls the "deer pasture." The loose disintegrating granite chat crunched under her tiny tennis shoes and she gripped my finger tight to keep from falling, and the sound of that gravel underfoot (the pink mountains being worn away, along with our bodies) was a sound I'd heard all my life at the deer pasture, but this time, this first time with my daughter gripping my finger and looking down at the loose pink gravel that was making that sound, it affected me so strongly that I felt faint, felt so light that I thought I might take flight . . .

A country, a landscape, can be sacred in an infinite number of ways. The quartz boulders in my mother's garden: my father brought her one each year, and I thought, and still think, it was one of the most romantic things I'd seen, that even while he was in the midst of wildness that one week each year, he was still thinking of her.

Other families had store-bought Doug fir or blue spruce trees for Christmas; we had the spindly strange mountain juniper ("cedar") from the deer pasture. Even though we lived to the south, we were still connected to that wild core, and these rituals and traditions were important to us, so fiercely felt and believed in that one might even call them a form of worship. We were raised Protestants, but in our hearts' and bodies' innocence were cutting a very fine line, tightroping along the mystical edge of pantheism. When Granddaddy was dying, just this side of his ninetieth year, and we went to see him in the hospital room in Fort Worth, I took a handful of arrowhead fragments from the deer pasture and put them under his bed. It seemed inconceivable to me that he not die as he had lived, always in some kind of contact with that wildness, and the specificity of that thousand acres.

When Mom was sick—small, young, and beautiful, the strongest and best patient the doctors had ever had, they all said—and she was sick a long time, living for years solely on the fire and passion within, long after the marrow had left her bones and the doctors could not bring it back, and when she still never had anything other than a smile for each day—my father and brothers and I would take turns bringing her flowers from the deer pasture.

One of us would walk in through the door with that vase from the wild. There would be store-bought flowers, too, but those splashes of reds, yellows, and blues, from lands she'd walked, lands she knew, are what lit up her face the most. The specificity of our lives together, and of our love: those colors said it as well as the land can say anything—which is to say, perfectly. Indian paintbrushes. Bluebonnets. Liatris. Shooting stars. I'm certain those flowers helped her as much as did our platelets, the very blood and iron of ourselves, which we also shared with her. She really loved wildflowers, and she really loved the hill and brush country of Texas, and she really *loved us.*

My mother loved to drink iced tea. Sometimes she and my father and brothers and I would go up to the deer pasture in the dead sullen heat of summer, in the shimmering brightness. We'd ride around in the jeep wearing straw hats. We'd get out and walk down the creek, to the rock slide: a stream-polished half-dome of pink granite with a sheet of water trickling over it, a twenty-foot slide into the plunge pool below, with cool clear water six feet deep, and a mud turtle (his face striped yellow, as if with war paint) and two big Midland soft-shelled turtles living in that pond. An osprey nest, huge branches and sticks, rested up in the dead cottonwood at the pool's edge.

My brothers and I would slide down that half-dome and into the pool again and again. A hundred degrees, in the summer, and we'd go up and down that algae-slick rock like otters. We'd chase the turtles, would hold our breath and swim after them, paddling underwater in that lucid water, while our parents sat up in the rocks above and watched. What a gift it is, to see one's children happy, and engaged in the world, loving it.

We'd walk farther down the creek, then: a family. Fuller. My mother would finish her tea; would rattle the ice cubes in her plastic cup. She'd crunch the ice cubes, in that heat. She always drank her tea with a sprig of mint in it. At some point on one of our walks she must have tossed her ice cubes and mint sprig out, because now there are two little mint fields along the creek: one by the camp house, and one down at the water gap. I like to sit in the rocks above those little mint patches for hours, and look, and listen, and smell, and think. I feel the sun dappling on my arms, and watch the small birds flying around in the old oak and cedar along the creek. Goshawks courting, in April, and wild turkeys gobbling. I like to sit there above the mint fields and feel my soul cutting down through that bedrock. It's happening fast. I too am becoming the earth.

Seen from below as it drifts high in the hot blue sky, a zonetail hawk looks just like the vultures it floats with, save for its yellow legs. (Vultures' legs are gray.) The zonetail's prey will glance up, study the vultures for a moment, and then resume nibbling grass. Then the zonetail will drop from that flock of vultures like a bowling ball.

Afterwards, if there is anything left of the prey, perhaps the vultures can share in the kill.

Golden-cheeked warblers come up into this country from Mexico, endangered, exotic blazes of color who have chosen to grace the hill country with their nests in the spring. They place their hopes for the future, for survival, deep in the cool shade of the old-growth cedars, in only the oldest cedars whose bark peels off in tatters and wisps like feathers, the feathery old bark which the warblers must have to build their nests. But as the old-growth cedar is cut to make way for more and more rangeland, the brown cowbird, a drab bully that follows the heavy ways of cattle, lays its eggs in the warblers' delicate nests and then flees, leaving the warbler mother with these extra eggs to take care of. The cowbird nestlings are larger, and they outclamor the warbler babies for food, and push the beautiful gold-cheeked warbler babies out of the nest.

Why must the ways of man, and the things associated with man, be so clumsy? Can't we relearn grace (and all the other things that follow from that: mercy, love, friendship, understanding) by studying the honor and integrity of a system, one of the last systems, that's still intact? Why must we bring our cowbirds with us, everywhere we go? Must we break everything that is special to us, or sacred—unknown, and holy—into halves, and then fourths, and then eighths?

What happens to us when all the sacred, all the *whole* is gone—when there is no more whole? There will be only fragments of stories, fragments of culture, fragments of integrity. Even a child standing on the porch in Houston with the rain in his face can look north and know that it is all tied together, that we are the warblers, we are the zonetails, we are the underground river: that it is all holy, and that some of it should not be allowed to disappear, as has so much, and so many of us, already.

Sycamores grow by running water; cottonwoods grow by still water. If we know the simple mysteries, then think of all the complex mysteries that lie just beneath us, buried in the bedrock: the bedrock we have been entrusted with protecting. How could we dare do anything other than protect and honor this last core, the land from which we came, the land that has marked us, and whose essence, whose mystery, contains our own essence and mystery? How can we *conceive* of severing that last connection? Surely all internal fire, all passion, would vanish.

Stories. On my Uncle Jimmy's left calf, there is a scar from where the wild pigs caught him one night. He and my father were coming back to camp after dark when they got between a sow and boar and their piglets. The piglets squealed in fright, which ignited the rage of the sow and boar. My father went up one tree and Uncle Jimmy up another, but the boar caught Jimmy with his tusk, cut the muscle clean to the bone.

Back in camp, Granddaddy and John Dallas and Howard and old Mr. Brooks (there for dominoes, that night) heard all the yelling, as did their dogs. The men came running with hounds and lanterns, globes of light swinging crazily through the woods. They stumbled into the middle of the pigs, too. My father and Uncle Jimmy were up in the tops of small trees like raccoons. There were pigs everywhere, pigs and dogs fighting, men dropping their lanterns and climbing trees . . . That one sow and boar could have held an entire *town* at bay. They ran the dogs off and kept the men treed there in the darkness for over an hour, Uncle Jimmy's pants leg wet with blood, and fireflies blinking down on the creek below, and the boar's angry grunts, the sow's furious snufflings below, and the frightened murmurs and squeals of the little pigs. The logic of that system was inescapable: *don't get between a sow and boar and their young.*

The land, and our stories, have marked us.

My father and I are geologists. Uncle Jimmy and his two youngest sons manufacture steel pipe and sell it for use in drilling down through bedrock in search of oil, gas, and water. Our hunting cabin is made of stone. We have a penchant for building stone walls. Our very lives are a metaphor for embracing the earth: for gripping boulders and lifting them to our chest and stacking them and building a life in and around and among the country's heart. I've sat in those same boulders on the east side and watched a mother bobcat and her two kittens come down to the creek to drink. There used to be an occasional jaguar in this part of the world, traveling up from Mexico, but that was almost a hundred years ago. Granddaddy would be ninety this October. He and the old guy we leased from, Howard, were born in the same year, 1903, which was the number we used for the lock combination on the last gate leading into the property.

It's one of the last places in the world that still makes sense to me. It is the place of my family, but it is more: it is a place that still abides by its own rules. The creeks have not yet been channeled with concrete. There is still a wildness beating beneath the rocks, and in the atoms of every thing.

Each year, we grow closer to the land. Each year, it marks us deeper. The lightning strike that burned the top of what is now called the Burned-Off Hill: we saw firsthand how for twenty years the wildlife preferred that area, but finally the protein content has been lowered again, and it is time for another fire.

The dead rattlesnake my cousin Rick and I found out on the highway two years ago: we put it in the back of the truck along with the wood for that night's campfire: put it down there in the middle of all that wood. That night Russell and Randy unloaded the wood, gathering great big armloads of it. Rick and I shined the flashlights in Russell's face then, and he realized he'd gathered up a great big armload of rattlesnake. We yelled at him to drop that snake, but he couldn't, it was all tangled up everywhere, all around his arms.

The land and its stories, and our stories: the time Randy and I were picking up one of what would be the new cabin's four cornerstones, to load into the truck. August. Randy dropped his end of the sandstone slab (about the size of a coffin) but didn't get his hand free in time. It might have been my fault. The quarter-ton of rock smashed off the end of his left pinky. No more tea sipping for Cousin Randy. He sat down, stunned in the heat, and stared at the crushed pulpy end of that little finger. I thought strangely how some small part of it was already mashed in between the atoms of the rock, and how his blood was already dripping back into the iron-rich soil. Randy tried to shake off the pain, tried to stand and resume work, but the second he did his eyes rolled heavenward and he turned ghost-white in that awful heat and fell to the ground, and began rolling down the steep hill, to the bottom of the gulch. All the little birds and other animals back in the cool shade of the oaks and cedars were resting, waiting for night to cool things off. What an odd creature man is, they had to be thinking. But we couldn't wait for night, or its coolness. We were aflame with a love for that wild land, and our long, rock-sure history on it: our loving place on it.

Granddaddy knew the old Texan's trick of luring an armadillo in close by tossing pebbles in the dry leaves. The armadillo, with its radar-dish ears, believes the sound is that of jumping insects, and will follow the sound of your tossed pebbles right up to your feet before it understands the nearsighted image of your boot or tennis shoe and leaps straight up, sneezes, then flees in wild alarm.

There is a startling assemblage of what I think of as "tender" life up there, seemingly a paradox for such a harsh, rocky, hot country. Cattails along the creeks, tucked in between those folds of granite, those narrow canyons with names like Fat Man's Misery and boulder-strewn cataclysms such as Hell's Half Acre. Newts, polliwogs, bullfrogs, leopard frogs, mud turtles, pipits and wagtails, luna moths and viceroys, ferns and mosses . . .

The old rock, the beautiful outcrops, are the power of the hill country, but the secret, the mystery, is the water, that's what brings the rock to life.

It's so hard to write about such nearly indefinable abstractions as yearning or mystery, or to convince someone who's not yet convinced about the necessity and holiness of wildness. It's hard in this day and age to convince people of just how tiny and short-lived we are, and how that makes the wild more, not less, important. All of the hill country's creatures had helped me in this regard. It was along Willow Creek where as a child of nine or ten I had gone down with a flashlight to get a bucket of water. It was December, Christmas Eve, and bitterly cold. In the creek's eddies there was half an inch of ice over the shallow pools. I had never before seen ice in the wild.

I shined my flashlight onto that ice. The creek made its trickling murmur, cutting down the center of the stream between the ice banks on either side, cutting through the ice like a knife, but in the eddies the ice was thick enough to hold the weight of a fallen branch or a small rock, a piece of iron ore.

There were fish swimming under that ice! Little green perch. The creek was only a few yards wide, but it had fish in it, living just beneath the ice! Why weren't they dead? How could they live beneath the surface of ice, as if in another system, another universe? Wasn't it too cold for them?

The blaze of my flashlight stunned them into a hanging kind of paralysis; they hung as suspended as mobiles, unblinking.

I tapped on the ice and they stirred a little, but still I could not get their full attention. They were listening to something else—to the gurgle of the creek, to the tilt of the planet, or the pull of the moon. I tapped on the ice again. Up at the cabin, someone called my name. I was getting cold, and had to go back. Perhaps I left the first bit of my civility—my first grateful relinquishing of it—there under that strange ice, for the little green fish to carry downstream and return to its proper place, to the muck and moss beneath an old submerged log. I ran up to the cabin with the bucket of cold water, as fresh and alive as we can ever hope to be, having been graced with the sight and idea of something new, something wild, something just beyond my reach.

I remember one winter night, camped down at the deer pasture, when a rimy ice fog had moved in, blanketing the hill country. I was just a teenager. I had stepped outside for a moment for the fresh cold air; everyone else was still in the cabin, playing dominoes. (Granddaddy smoked like a chimney.) I couldn't see a thing in all that cold fog. There was just the sound of the creek running past camp; as it always has, as I hope it always will.

Then I heard the sound of a goose honking—approaching from the north. There is no sound more beautiful, especially at night, and I stood there and listened. Another goose joined in—that wild, magnificent honking—and then another.

It seemed, standing there in the dark, with the cabin's light behind me (the *snap! snap! snap!* sound of Granddaddy the domino king playing his ivories against the linoleum table), that I could barely stand the hugeness, the unlimited future of life. I could feel my youth, could feel my heart beating, and it seemed those geese were coming straight for me, as if they too could feel that barely controlled wildness, and were attracted to it.

When they were directly above me, they began to fly in circles, more geese joining them. They came lower and lower, until I could hear the underlying readiness of those resonant honks; I could hear their grunts, their intake of air before each honk.

My father came out to see what was going on.

"They must be lost," he said. "This fog must be all over the hill country. Our light may be the only one they can see for miles," he said. "They're probably looking for a place to land, to rest for the night, but can't find their way down through the fog."

The geese were still honking and flying in circles, not a hundred feet over our heads. I'm sure they could hear the gurgle of the creek below. I stared up into the fog, expecting to see the first brave goose come slipping down through that fog, wings set in a glide of faith for the water it knew was just below. *They were so close to it.*

But they did not come. They circled our camp all night, keeping us awake; trying, it seemed, to *pray* that fog away with their honking, their sweet music; and in the morning, both the fog and the geese were gone, and it seemed that some part of me was gone with them, some tame or civilized part, and they had left behind a boy, a young man, who was now thoroughly wild, and who thoroughly loved wild things. And I often still have the dream I had that night, that I was up with the geese, up in the cold night, peering down at the fuzzy glow of the cabin lights in the fog, that dim beacon of hope and mystery, safety and longing.

The geese flew away with the last of my civility that night, but I realize now it was a theft that had begun much earlier in life. That's one of the greatest blessings of the hill country, and all wildness: it is a salve, a twentieth-century poultice to take away the crippling fever of too-much civility, too-much numbness.

❖ ❖ ❖

The first longing years of my life that were spent exploring those small and doomed hemmed-in woods around Houston sometimes seem like days of the imagination, compared against my later days in the hill country. It seemed, when I went to Hidden Lake, or to the zoo, or the arboretum, or the museum, that I was only treading water.

I fell asleep each night with my aquariums bubbling, the post-game baseball show murmuring on the radio. That magic rock from Llano County, the magnetite, stuck to the side of my bed like a remora, or a guardian, seeing me through the night, and perhaps filling me with a strange energy, a strange allegiance for a place I had not yet seen.

Finally the day came when I was old enough for my first hunting trip up to the deer pasture. My father took me up there for "the second hunt," in late December. I would not go on the first hunt, the November hunt, until after I was out of college, and a hunter. The "second hunt" was a euphemism for just camping, for hiking around, and for occasionally carrying a rifle.

My father and I drove through the night in his old green-and-white 1956 Ford—through country I'd never seen, beneath stars I'd never seen. My father poured black coffee from an old thermos to stay awake. The trip took a long time, in those days—over six hours, with gravel clattering beneath the car for the last couple of hours.

I put my hand against the car window. It was colder, up in the hills. The stars were brighter. When I couldn't stay awake any longer—overwhelmed by the senses—I climbed into the back seat and wrapped up in an old Hudson's Bay blanket and lay down and slept. The land's rough murmur and jostling beneath me was a lullaby.

When I awoke, we had stopped for gas in Llano. We were the only car at the service station. We were surrounded by a pool of light. I could see the dark woods at the edge of the gravel parking lot, could smell the cedar. My father was talking to the gas-station attendant. Before I was all the way awake, I grabbed a flashlight and got out and hurried out toward the woods. I went into the cedars, got down on my hands and knees, and with the flashlight began searching for the magnetite that I was sure was all over the place. I picked up small red rocks and held them against the metal flashlight to see if they'd stick.

When my father and the attendant came and got me out of the woods and asked where I had been going and what I'd been doing, I told them, "Looking for magnetite." How hard it must be, to be an adult.

We drove on: an improbable series of twists and turns, down washed-out canyons and up ridges, following thin caliche roads that shone ghostly white in the moonlight. I did not know then that I would come to learn every bend in those roads, every dip and rise, by heart. We clattered across a high-centered narrow cattle guard, and then another, and were on the property that we'd been leasing for thirty years—the thousand acres, our heart.

It was so cold. We were on our land. We did not own it, but it was ours because we loved it, belonged to it, and because we were engaged in its system. It dictated our movements as surely as it did those of any winter-range deer herd, any migrating warbler. It was ours because we loved it.

We descended toward the creek, and our cabin. The country came into view, brilliant in the headlights. Nighthawks flittered and flipped in the road before us, danced eerie acrobatic flights that looked as if they were trying to smother the dust in the road with their soft wings. Their eyes were glittering red in the headlights. It was as if we had stumbled into a witches' coven, but I wasn't frightened. They weren't bad witches; they were just wild.

Giant jackrabbits, with ears as tall again as they were, raced back and forth before us—leaped six feet into the air and reversed direction mid-leap, hit the ground running: a sea of jackrabbits before us, flowing, the high side of their seven-year cycle. A coyote darted into our headlights' beams, grabbed a jackrabbit, and raced away. One jackrabbit sailed over the hood of our car, coming so close to the windshield that I could see his wide, manic eyes, looking so human. A buck deer loped across the road, just ahead. It was an explosion of life, all around us. Moths swarmed our headlights.

We had arrived at the wild place.

Rick Bass is the author of several books, including *Platte River*, *Winter*, *The Ninemile Wolves*, and *In the Loyal Mountains*. He lives in northwestern Montana's endangered Yaak Valley and is working on a book about the search for grizzlies in Colorado, and on a novel, *Where the Sea Used to Be*.

BILL McKIBBEN

(The Adirondack Mountains, New York)

Wild Again

❖❖❖

Up along the side of an old low mountain, we kept coming across big trees: spruces a hundred feet high, birches and hemlocks twelve feet around at the base. The mist hung in the upper branches and slickened the mossy nurse logs scattered through the woods. We had wandered into a few hundred acres of old-growth forest, one of a fairly small number of tracts that had escaped the lumberjack's saw when this region was cut in the nineteenth and early twentieth centuries.

"Big" is, of course, relative. These trees had not grown big in the same way redwoods and Douglas firs sucking the warm mist off the Pacific grow big. These trees survive seven-month winters—no one is going to build a road to one, and carve a hole in it, and let you drive your car through. But they are big enough, worn old survivors. Big enough like these mountains are big enough, four- and five-thousand-foot peaks pushing up through rugged weather at the top of New York State. There are no snowcapped peaks in summer, but by October the winds will blast you off the summits.

And anyway, big and old are not precisely the right issues. Merging with these stands of old-growth are stands of new-growth, forests fifty and a hundred years old now protected by a unique provision in the state constitution, trees which will never again be cut, which will someday be indistinguishable from their larger cousins down the ridge. We canonize old-growth, but new wilderness is just as awesome—it testifies both to the beauty of Eden and the chance of redemption.

The Adirondacks, old-growth and new, cover an area larger than Glacier, Yosemite, Olympic, Yellowstone, and Grand Canyon national parks combined—about six million acres. Of that land, roughly one-half is public preserve, "forever wild" under the state constitution. The other half is in private hands, at present endangered by development but still more tightly regulated than backcountry anywhere in the nation. A hundred years ago, the bulk of this land was in the process of being razed by loggers. Photographs from every corner of the region prove the destruction—loggers standing stiffly in front of lakeshores stripped of trees, views from mountaintops of clear-cuts that cover ridge after peak after valley. But the state, in a fit of vision that presaged the environmental movement by seventy-five years, began buying land and passing laws. Now the spots where those photographs of clear-cuts were taken show forest again, and if the lakeshore pines are not as high as the ships' masts originally cut from them, they are high enough yet that eagles have begun to return. Roads weave through the woods, but not so many roads—moose, wandering over from New England, have begun to recolonize the park, joining the beaver and the bobcat and the otter and the fisher and the marten.

And when you climb most of the mountains now, you do not see clear-cuts. You see, from open tops, long rows of smaller mountains stretching off in every direction—six or seven or eight or nine lines of ridges, disappearing into the twilight. You see what the world must once have looked like. Since this place was preserved for essentially ecological reasons (primarily a fear that further deforestation would silt up the Hudson River) and not because of its grandeur, the forest preserve encompasses hundreds of thousands of acres of the kind of land that has been cut, drained, filled, developed everywhere else in the East and most places in the West. The spectacular High

Peaks region, a fairly small portion of the park, inhales hikers; the rest of the park effortlessly absorbs the few that wander in. And it's that rest that really defines the park. This is not rocks and ice and wildflower-meadow wilderness—this is swamp and spruce thicket and mile upon mile of hardwood forest and hemlock-height wilderness, thousands of mountains too short to be bare on top, never climbed by people because there's no reason, except maybe venison, to climb them. Even the hunters don't reach a lot of places—someone killed a bear last season that the biologists said was forty-two years old. It had been hiding out since the Truman administration. It's the kind of country where no one got around to naming a lot of things—there are whole small ranges of anonymous mountains, and pond after pond called "Mud" or "Round" or "Fish." Where instead of sweeping views you get strained glimpses through the lattice of bare branches. It's all curves and circles, dimples and bulges, woods that just go on and on and on. *You see what the world must once have looked like.*

You look down, not up. We've just come through a rainy, cool summer, and you can spend days in a mushroom trance, connecting dots of traffic-cone orange and slickly obscene brown as you wander through the woods. Fall is on us, and already the leaves are dropping the hills are returning to their normal aspect, covered with their seven-month coat of skeletal hardwood puffs. Geese: gone, honking. Loons: gone. Tourists: gone, except for the ski areas. But in the woods everything subsides back to quiet, the fever of short lush summer just a rustling layer underfoot.

Not all the woods, of course—half the park is public land, but the other half is private, and here the skidders are straining logs across the frozen muck. It would be pleasant to simply write of the natural history of this place, page after page of loon and lynx, but to do so would miss the point. The Adirondacks is as much idea as place. It's a great experiment, more important than Yellowstone: can people live in the same place where nature lives? Are we as a species compatible with real, large wild wilderness? *This place looks like the world looks now* —the Third World, the vast expanses that are neither park nor suburb but somewhere in between. For a century now, with more care than any other place in the world, people have been trying to coax a coexistence out of these mountains. Tough zoning, careful review— a place where there are actually limits on human behavior, the sort of limits all humans will embrace in the not-distant future if it matters to them to keep the world in somewhat the shape they found it.

The experiment has yielded some exasperating results. Poverty remains high in these mountains, higher than in any other of New York's counties. (And if you consider what else is in New York, that's saying something). Some of the poverty is simply the result of living where the air's too cold and the soil's too thin to yield ease: the growing season in a great year is ninety days, and at least one derivation of the word "Adirondack" claims it is a Native American insult aimed at the Indians who lived among these mountains and hence were so poor they became "Bark-Eaters." But there's also the trouble common to all residents of resource-extracting areas, where wealth is daily shipped away—all those logs that could be turned into furniture here. And the poverty helps pave the way for developers, who pave the mountains once they find the loopholes in the state's zoning laws. More and more the richest private lands—the lakeshores, the mountain views—are under siege, and a fiscally strapped state has done very little to expand its holdings.

Saddest of all, and most threatening to the experiment, many Adirondackers have stopped living as much in the mountains as in the matrix of human desire that spreads out from Hollywood and Manhattan and makes it nearly impossible to be pleased with the real world that sustains and suffices. Fewer local people hike and hunt; more and more their sense of being "Adirondack" is nourished mainly by their anger at "government regulations" restricting their "property rights."

All this threatens to stall the Adirondacks short of their potential, both as a wild place and as a beacon. The existing protected lands need to be augmented, creating the kind of core wildernesses large enough to support the wolf and the mountain lion, to name two of the most conspicuous absentees from these hills. If the park's private land is slowly developed instead, it will turn into a resort range, crisscrossed with the roads that cut up the rest of the East. And "slowly" in this case may well mean the next ten years. Either it's carved up, or it is preserved as a place big enough and intact enough to weather climate change and acid rain and the thousand other sadnesses that drift across its boundaries. And if it is preserved, and if the communities meet with some success in healing themselves—what an example. America's own bioreserve, a living lesson to the rest of the East. If, on the other hand, we can't make it work here, what chance have they in Africa or Ecuador?

These mountains, sleet gray as the fall wanes, can be inventoried: hemlocks, pines, maples, tamarack, tax troubles, mink, beaver, otter, lousy education, great individual competence, weakening communities, southwest winds, rime ice, birch blowdown, grosbeak, coyote, demagogue, cattail, bog, hardwood draw, granite, white water, eagle, stillness, canoe, gun, puffball, oak, spruce, bear-clawed beech. They are not—just—ancient, virgin, pristine, big, new, endangered, saved. The Adirondacks are deeply real, profoundly *actual*, penetrated and penetrating. God they matter.

Bill McKibben, a frequent contributor to the *New Yorker,* is the author of *The End of Nature* and *The Age of Missing Information.* He lives in the Adirondack Mountains of New York.

DAVID JAMES DUNCAN

Stillwater Marsh and Pyramid Lake, Nevada

Lake of the Stone Mother

*One Fly-fisherman's Impressions of a Landlocked
Great Basin Drainage*

On January 14, 1844, Captain John C. Frémont and twenty-four other white men were searching the deserts of western Nevada for a river reputed to flow east to west from the Rocky Mountains to San Francisco Bay—a river reputedly large enough to be navigable, at least by large canoes. What Frémont found instead, at the terminus of the unnavigably small, swift river now known as the Truckee, was a huge, landlocked, saline lake. On this lake's eastern shore, miles away across the water, Frémont spotted a four-hundred-foot triangular rock that reminded him of an Egyptian pyramid. In his journal he wrote:

> We've encamped on the shore, opposite a very remarkable rock
> in the lake, which had attracted our attention for many miles.
> This striking feature suggested a name for the lake, and I called
> it Pyramid Lake.

There is just one problem with Frémont's journal entry: the lake already possessed a name. Resident Paiutes had long ago named it after a little tufa-rock formation just behind Frémont's grand pyramid, a formation called Tupepeaha, which translates "Stone Mother." Unprepossessing though she was, the Stone Mother's legend was the Paiute people's origin myth—their three-dimensional Book of Genesis, if you will—and for centuries the tribe had told stories and sung songs that gave her real presence in their lives. It was her tears that had created the lake and its life-giving bounty (and when you taste the water, sure enough, it's salty). According to Joe Ely, the tribe's ex-chairman, the Stone Mother and her legend "set our identity, and forever fix the components that make up our way of life." In the tradition of Great White Explorers the world over, however, Captain Frémont was not interested in indigenous tongues, mythic names, or mysterious presences. Frémont desired a navigable east-to-west river, not a navigable inner life. And most of our forebears have inherited, by choice or by force, the tongue and mindset of Frémont, not that of the Paiutes. So the Stone Mother continues to be an ignored matriarch of knowledge lost or forgotten. And the lake continues to bear a trivial name.

How important is this loss of meaning? Does it matter who names a lake, or any other body of water? Does it matter *what* they name it?

I believe that it may. It rains an average of five inches a year in west-central Nevada. The wettest year on record here is nine inches, and the dry year's record is no measurable rain at all. In a land this arid, H_2O ought to be measured in karats, not acre-feet. Water here is the essence of life, the only possibility of it. And to be careless in the way one handles life's essence can be fatal.

Four years after Captain Frémont "discovered," denamed, and renamed Pyramid Lake, gold was discovered in California. In the ensuing cross-continental rush of "forty-niners," an estimated 45,000 would-be millionaires crossed, or attempted to cross, the nameless forty-mile-wide soft-sand desert just south and east of Pyramid Lake. By the end of that year (see George B. Stewart, *The California Trail*, McGraw-Hill, 1962), that little no-name desert contained 9,771 dead domestic animals; 3,000 abandoned wagons; and 963 fresh human graves. Yes, there were precious metals in California. But on the trail through Nevada, water proved even more precious.

Nevada is a strange state for many reasons. High on the list of strangenesses is the fact that 82 percent of the state isn't even the possession of the state: it's public land owned by every single citizen of the United States. Equally high on the strange list is the legal gambling, which has created a multi-billion-dollar tourist business, which has in turn created Las Vegas, Reno, Tahoe, and other casino cities, which have in turn created dire water shortages, extinct species, traffic gridlocks, foul air, high crime, mafia corruption, environmental devastation, and all the other urban amenities. But even stranger, and more crucial, than either of these things—especially juxtaposed to these two things—is that five annual inches of rain. A "Fun Nevada Fact": there are more than twice as many people employed full-time by the Mirage Casino in Las Vegas as by every farm and ranch in the entire state. Another Fun Nevada Fact: there are only eighty-six fewer security guards working for the Mirage as highway patrolmen working the entire state. An UnFun Nevada Fact: the Mirage Casino, the 800,000 residents of greater Las Vegas, and the city's 20 million annual casino-bound visitors are dependent not on Nevada's own rivers, rainfall, or mountain runoff, but on the state's entire portion of Colorado River water, *and* on the eons-old, nonreplenishable underground reserves the city is sucking at a no-tomorrow pace.

In "Living Dry"—his definitive essay on the American understanding, and misunderstanding, of the arid inland West—Wallace Stegner pointed out that the syllable *pah*, in the Great Basin's Shoshonean tongues, means "water, or water hole." This is why so many Shoshone place-names (Tonopah, Ivanpah, Pahrump, Paria) contain this syllable. It's also why the region's prevalent tribe are called Paiutes: Pah-Ute means, literally, "Water Ute."

The Paiutes of Nevada, accordingly, lived in small, highly specialized, lake-dwelling, marsh-dwelling, or river-dwelling bands, most of which were named after the prevalent food of their small ecosystems. The Paiute word for cattails, for instance, is *toi*, and the word for eating is *dokado*, so the band that lived on Stillwater Marsh was known as the Toidokado—the cattail eaters. Trout, similarly, are *agai*, so the trout-eaters of the Walker River region were the Agaidokado. And the endemic (and now endangered) food fish of Pyramid Lake were the cui-ui (pronounced "kwee-wee"), so the band that lived here were the Kuyuidokado—cui-ui eaters. Cattails, trout, cui-ui—*pah* foods, water gifts, all.

Stegner wrote:

> The West is defined by inadequate rainfall [and] a general deficiency of water. . . . We can't create water or increase the supply. We can only hold back and redistribute what there is. . . . Aridity first brought settlement to a halt at the edge of the dry country and then forced changes in the patterns of settlement. . . . It altered farming methods, weapons, and tools [and] bent water law and the structure of land ownership. . . . In the view of some, it also helped to create a large, spacious, independent, sunburned, self-reliant western character. . . . Of that, despite a wistful desire to believe, I am less than confident.

Sipping scotch on the rocks in an air-conditioned casino while pumping one's paycheck into a slot, one feels infinitely removed from the natural laws of the desert. But the fact remains—sorry, gamblers—that the rocks in those scotches come to us compliments of a *pah*, a place of water. This is why, minor or moot as the point may seem, I'm serious about my refusal to accept Frémont's offhanded renaming of the Kuyuidokado's desert lake. Four inches of rain per annum is not a viable climate, it's a perennial crisis; 963 graves just south of the Stone Mother demonstrate that to be careless in the face of this crisis is fatal. And a cavalier naming of a desert body of water is a form of carelessness.

There was a culture that lived with quiet grace beside these waters for tens of centuries. There is another culture that's left devastation, dreck, and dead bodies strewn all along the path of its half-cocked arrival. The Kuyuidokado, the Agaidokado, the culture that considered water to be the Stone Mother's tears, has nearly vanished. The culture of the gold rush and the Mirage has begun to feel the desert heat. In this land of constant, critical aridity, who can we trust to properly name and care for the precious springs, hidden seeps, and rare bodies of water? What should the inland sea known as Pyramid really be called? I don't pretend to know. But I do know that we must soon find out; that we must ask the water questions unselfishly; that we must dig deep, and listen to the earth, and each other, very closely.

Where, exactly, to begin?

Were it up to me, I'd ask the Stone Mother.

Fly-fishing Atlantis

On April 28, 1993, a battered American pickup empties an expedition of four white guys—me; a sculptor friend, Frank Boyden; The Nature Conservancy's Graham Chisholm; and the Paiute tribe's fisheries biologist, Paul Wagner—onto the shore of a large saline lake at the terminus of the Truckee River. Maps, road signs, countless books, and the local populace all refer to this body of water as "Pyramid Lake." But scattered along the beach upon which we've parked are fishermen—fly-fishermen, most of them; eighteen, at a quick count. And each of them has carried an aluminum stepladder out into the lake, which they are now using as casting platforms as they ply the wide waters for trout. Watching them cast—and still obsessing on Captain Frémont—I pop open a beer, reach for my pen, and make a journal entry of my own. I write:

We've encamped on the shore, opposite a very remarkable row of men in the lake, which row had attracted our attention for many miles. This striking feature suggested a name for the lake. I have therefore decided to hell with the maps, road-signs, books and native populace, and have renamed the whole shit-a-ree "Aluminum Stepladder Lake."

This beach has a name. It's called "The Nets." And it was not, I am happy to say, named by Captain Frémont. It was christened just recently, Paul tells me, by the local Paiutes, after a failed attempt to raise Lahontan cutthroat trout in net-pens right off the beach here.

Graham has fixed us chips and salsa. He's watching birds now. And he's spotted two kinds of warblers I could have added to my life list if I'd been looking. But—typical fly-fisherman—I was watching a cloud of mayflies hovering over the hood of the pickup.

We've seen five or six hundred white pelicans, many at close range, a few still in sight on the lake. Also mallards, great blue herons, coots, grebes, many doves, Graham's warblers. My favorite sighting was a raven, alone on a big tufa formation over near the Stone Mother, madly croaking at the jet trails in the sky above. Low-flying black god calling out to high-flying white ones. Be careful who you worship, Raven. (But maybe he was cursing . . .)

The hills are pale pink, the sagebrush pale green, the lichen on the rocks brilliant yellow. The white snow patches high up on the Pah Rah Mountains seem precious in this clime: next month's water. If we stayed on this beach and kept eating these chips for a couple of decades, perhaps we'd become known to local Paiutes as the Chips&Salsadokado. Maybe the Stone Mother would begin to speak to us. Hope so. My wife sure wouldn't.

In digging out my notebook I found a tourist brochure about the lake. Not the sort of thing I normally read, but it's amusing, with the lake right here, to compare the purple brochural rhetoric to the bright blue evidence before my eyes. Pyramid, the brochure assures me, is "a magnificent lake; a lake remarkably different from any you've ever seen. It's enchanting, a primeval lake where the weathering forces of wind and water have carved one of nature's bold statements: timelessness."

Something about this "timeless" prose makes me want to glance at my watch and note that it is 5:30 P.M. But I do agree that the lake is a "bold statement" of some kind. It's twenty-six miles long, four to ten miles wide, up to three hundred fifty feet deep, and its waters range, as the brochure promises, from turquoise to copper green to deepest blue. The wide beach upon which we've parked is one of "more than 70 miles of sandy beaches that make picnicking and camping ideal." A beach-feature the brochure neglects to mention, though, is the cow pies. We had to displace an entire herd of impending hamburger in order to park our trucks, and there are cow calling cards everywhere. Not that I'm complaining. It's an occasion for added sport, actually: the desert air dries the pies so fast that I find (after my second beer) that I can take a little run, hop onto the dried top of a pie, and "skimboard" three or four feet along the beach, leaving a fragrant green streak (another "one of nature's bold statements"?) on the sand behind me.

Swallows dip low over the pelican-tracked and tire-tracked sand. Sound of waves, sound of gulls, sound of fly-reels cranking. But the predominant sound here at The Nets is the human voice: deep male voices, most of them; calm for the most part, and conversational; but now and then broken by the weird grunts, hoots, and laughter of men hooking and playing trout.

Pyramid is famous for its Lahontan cutthroat; "world-famous," the brochure proclaims—and at any rate famous enough to create a boom in local stepladder sales. In 1925, a world-record forty-one-pound Lahontan was caught in the lake. During that same era commercial fishermen were netting fifteen tons of trout from the lake each week. Broken down into Fishing Fantasy terms, this means the lake was producing an average of *six thousand individual five-pound trout per week*. The big cutthroat, on their Truckee River spawning runs, looked more like Chinook salmon than trout. They traveled like salmon, too, up rapids and over falls, all the way up the Truckee to Lake Tahoe and its tributaries. The ranger station at Pyramid, where I stopped to buy a fishing permit, has a nice framed photo of Clark Gable holding up two big trout he'd just caught in the lake. There's a photo of Ronald Reagan's favorite president, Calvin Coolidge, giving the big cutts a try as well. But—no political innuendo intended—Coolidge got his wide ass skunked.

Four buffleheads land on the water just out of casting range. A twenty-four-inch fish (by his estimate) follows Frank's fly right in to his rod tip. Then Paul hooks one. I wade over, once it starts losing the war, to give it a look. It's sixteen inches long, very slender, very silver, and healthy: it gives him a good fight. But I can see that Paul's no predator. His life's work, after all, is the breeding and rearing of these fish. As he lets the cutthroat go he wears the haunted look of a kindergarten teacher who's just paddled one of his pupils for no reason.

I wish I could keep the story simple and just go catch a fish, but Paul's profession raises a question. In a lake and river system so prolific that it naturally produced fifteen tons of trout per week, why does the Paiute tribe feel compelled to contribute hatchery-reared trout at all?

The depressing answer is that if Paul and the tribe did not contribute trout, there would be none in the lake.

The culprit, as in so many Post-Western Blues sagas, was the federal Bureau of Reclamation. The "Bureau of Wreck the Nation," as it's sometimes known locally. It was the bureau that took it into their heads to erect a crude, turn-of-the-century dam on the lower Truckee River, the purpose of which was to divert Truckee water into a canal, over a ridge, and down into the neighboring Carson River valley, where it would turn desert into farmland, coyotes into dairy cows, dust into agricultural dollars, and the sleepy town of Fallon into a wide-awake fast-foods strip.

To an extent, that's exactly what happened. But there were a few unpredicted costs. In keeping with its reputation, the bureau did no soil surveys, no environmental studies, no study of possible impacts on the Pyramid trout, no study of impacts on the Paiute people, resident flora or fauna, or the nearby Stillwater Marsh. According to a later *Reno Gazette-Journal* account:

When the Truckee River was abruptly diverted during the dam's inaugural celebration, thousands of cutthroat trouts were left flopping in the mud. Cheering spectators, rolling up pantaloons and pant legs, wallowed in the slime and clubbed the fish to death.

By 1938 the Truckee-dependent Winnemucca Lake National Wildlife Refuge had become uninhabitable hardpan desert, so its refuge status was hastily removed. By the same year Pyramid Lake had dropped forty feet, the Truckee River delta had become permanently impassable to spawning cutthroat, and the Lahontan trout remaining in the lake were forced to live out their life-spans, unable to spawn. Sometime in the 1940s or '50s the last of these lunkers sank unseen to the lake's bottom, and the great Pyramid cutthroat strain was extinct. Only their unusual longevity has kept the endangered cui-ui from extinction. But—Fun Nevada Fact—they're growing cantaloupes, and other crops that already existed in surplus, just over the hill in Fallon.

The cutthroat we're now fishing for, Paul tells me, are actually a Summit Lake strain, raised in hatcheries here at Pyramid by the Paiute tribe, then released into the lake once they're big enough to survive. And, despite everything, trout still thrive in this desert lake. The largest cutthroat Pyramid has produced since they were reintroduced was a thirty-six-inch, twenty-three-pound monster. Ten-pounders are common. And the word is out: the sport fishery generates between five and nine million dollars a year for the city of Reno and the Pyramid Paiute tribe.

Paul Wagner's own cautious words on the Pyramid sport fishery are worth remembering. He told us, "One generation took something wonderful and turned it into nothing. We've turned it back into something. If we're careful—and lucky—maybe one day it'll grow back into something wonderful again."

We've left The Nets behind, driven to a quieter, much more beautiful beach, and as the sun drops behind the Pah Rahs I'm wading out, rod in hand, intent on experiencing the "something."

Paul's name for this quiet cove is "Atlantis." Back in the eighties, his explanatory story goes, the boosters of Reno and Washoe County decided to sink some money into a campground in hopes of luring more spendthrift fishermen to the lake. To that end they built eight concrete picnic tables with permanent metal sunshades, several deluxe outhouses, and a large, all-weather concession building to purvey hot food and drink. Demonstrating the booster's unwavering fondness for both anachronism and cliché, they dubbed the place "Warrior Point." But happily, almost the day the job was finished the record rains of the mid-eighties began, the lake rose twenty feet, the concession, outhouses, and tables were flooded, and Warrior Point, for Paul anyway, became "Atlantis."

In the drought of the past seven years the waters dropped and the campground reappeared. But the risen Atlantis seems to have been discovered by no one but the ubiquitous cows, who, judging by the ample evidence, are experiencing serious confusion about the respective functions of the picnic area and the outhouses. Graham's begun making barbecued veggies and chicken while the rest of us fish. I'm happy to report that he's cooking on the beach, not in the picnic area.

Lahontan cutthroat are famous for feeding right on the bottom, so I'm a little surprised, after a few fruitless casts, to see a fish rise nearby. I point out the rise-form. "Tui chub," Paul speculates. A trash fish. But I cast to it anyway—with a no-name nymph a friend sent in the mail. It's covered with peacock feathers, like a dancer in an MGM floor show—feathers that imitate no insect known to man but do sometimes generate the same iridescent confusions in trout that the dancers do in humans. The nymph hits the water while the rise-form rings are still expanding. I start it strutting across the sandy bottom. The fish takes it. I set the hook. But as the rod bends hard I know before I see it that this is no kind of chub: it's one of Paul's Lahontan pets. It's not a leaping fish, but it makes several strong runs. Its fighting tactics remind me more of brown trout than of the cutthroats I'm used to catching on the Oregon coast.

All through the long dusk and into the darkness the cutthroat keep rising. And casting to those rises I hook, and further educate, eight of Paul's bright pupils. Fourteen to nineteen inches, if anyone's wondering. All rock-hard, moon-silver swimmers, reluctant to let me touch them in order to let them go. No trout I take compares to the two bloodied lunkers Clark Gable was holding in the photo. But— no political innuendo intended—I didn't get my ass Coolidged, either. And every trout with whom I danced at Atlantis is still living in this once-ruined lake, slowly growing—if we're careful, and lucky—back into something wonderful.

I am, however, a fly-fisherman. And "It is not fly-fishing," wrote my neighbor, Norman Maclean, "if you are not looking for answers to questions." So let me ask: *how wonderful?* How wonderful can a man-ufactured lake fishery ever really be? Isn't this lake, divorced by dam from its river, a bit like a body divorced from its head? I come from the Pacific Northwest—land of migrating salmon—and I've felt the wonder that passes, at the salmon's annual coming, between the fish-people and the two-leggeds. Something crucial, two mysterious messages—one from mountains, rain, and snowmelt, another from the sea—crisscross in the heart of a waiting human when the great salmon runs pour in each fall. So I can't help but remember the Lahontan trout's ancient spawning runs. Will the big cutthroats ever again climb the Truckee to Lake Tahoe and beyond? Am I being absurdly neolithic to even consider such a question? Or is there some-thing worth yearning for here? I have lived my life on the shores of little rivers where, each fall, enormous, ocean-fattened, exotic-colored creatures suddenly appear on beds of gravel to circle, dig, and dance their species to life even as they batter their own bodies to death. That's the biological truth of the salmon's life-cycle—but also a spir-itual example that changes the way a lot of us Northwesterners choose to live. So what about the cutthroat? Will the guardians and users of this small inland sea and river one day yearn to see their trout set the same beautiful example?

I don't pretend to know. In the climate of our time it's just a dream to me, or prayer. Were I ever to require an answer, though, you'd find me rod in hand on the vast, salty lake there, close by the Stone Mother.

Five percent of the rivers in North America empty, not into an ocean, but into inland deserts and lakes. Nearly all of these "closed drainages" are in the Great Basin region of the West. The Truckee and its Pyramid Lake terminus are one such drainage. The Carson and its Stillwater Marsh terminus are another. Yet whenever a Nature Conservancy staff member here refers to these two drainages, they take a deep breath and rattle off both names: "The Pyramid Lake/Stillwater Marsh project," they usually call it. The reason for the deep breath and the compound name is the same reason the cutthroat were wiped out in the Truckee and Pyramid Lake: the Bureau of Reclamation's Derby Dam. I just had to fortify myself with the tale of an evening's fishing before going on to describe more of the havoc this dam has created.

The Nature Conservancy's principal claim to fame has been land acquisition. It's an organization whose reputation was built by identifying crucial habitat, buying it, and protecting it forever. The world's most altruistic real estate firm, you could call it. But here on the Carson and Truckee rivers the Conservancy has been playing a difficult, volatile new game—and it's here that my admiration for it has jumped a level. What it's doing on these two rivers is buying water rights from farmers, then retiring those rights, and letting marginal farmland return to desert, in order to pass the water downstream into the troubled lake and marsh. *Genuine* reclamation, in other words: that is, genuine restoration of critical wetlands, after the so-called Bureau of Reclamation has done its sorry work.

It's an unprecedented conservation tactic—and the unconventionality has caused the Conservancy some problems. Admirers of its traditional land acquisitions have voiced concern over the water purchases. Water rights on these rivers don't come cheap, and some Conservancy backers feel there's something less satisfying, or less substantial, about purchasing a substance that eventually evaporates in the desert air. I don't want to sound as though I'm stumping for the Conservancy, but in its defense I feel it's crucial to remember that the mere acquisition of land has never been the motivating factor in any Conservancy land purchase: *preservation of life* and of biodiversity has always been the motivating factor. And here in the desert, water *is* life. In the desert, vast tracts of land can be purchased for virtually nothing—for why should it cost to buy real estate that can do little but kill you? Nevada land, without water, offers virtually no nature for the Conservancy to conserve. And the Stillwater Marsh, sans water, is not a marsh.

With water, the Stillwater supports fully 50 percent of Nevada's waterfowl, including 200,000 ducks; 1,000 geese; 3,000 avocets; 1,000 black-necked stilts; 1,000 Wilson's phalaropes; 800 snowy plovers; and many, many more species. It supports the largest white-faced ibis colony in North America. It is a major staging area for hundreds of thousands of shorebirds, including as many as 275,000 long-billed dowitchers alone. It has been designated as one of just fourteen Western Hemispheric Shore Bird Reserves in North and South America. But these are just statistics. Let me try to stress the marsh's importance in a storyteller's way:

Imagine running in one of the great American marathons. Or, if you're in the kind of shape I'm in, imagine jogging, then walking, and in the end possibly crawling to the finish of an American marathon. Whatever your condition, by the time you reached the finish line you would be in dire need of fluids, food, and rest. Stillwater Marsh—for waterfowl and shorebirds enduring the marathon we call migration—is one such crucial finish line. But now imagine that, after giving your all for twenty-six miles, you were greeted at the finish by a sign that read:

SORRY. WE'RE FRESH OUT OF FLUIDS, FOOD, AND REST AREAS HERE.
YOU'RE GOING TO HAVE TO RUN ANOTHER TWENTY-SIX MILES TO
ANOTHER FINISH LINE. HOPEFULLY THEY CAN HELP YOU THERE.

If this were to happen to me, I have little doubt about the result: a short distance into the second marathon I would lay down and die. And Norman Saake—the State Department of Wildlife's resident expert on birdlife in the Stillwater—told me that migrating birds react no differently than you or I. Norm has seen large flocks of migrating ducks, geese, and shorebirds fly into the Stillwater at dusk during the recent low-water and no-water years; has seen them circle, circle, and circle the marsh again—finding no place to land, no edible vegetation, no predator-safe place of rest. The sun is setting. They've been flying all day. And where is the next place of refuge? Hundreds of miles north, in the Klamath or Harney or Malheur lake basins. Hundreds of miles east, in the troubled marshes around Salt Lake. Seven hundred miles south, in the heavily hunted wetlands of Mexico. Or due west, in the Sacramento Valley—not such a great distance: but to reach it they've got to climb clear over the Sierras. Norm believes this is often what they attempt to do. He's seen them set out in near darkness. And he's certain that any bird even slightly injured or weakened, any bird too old or too young, will drop from the sky in the mountains and never be found.

Nevada, in this century, has lost over 85 percent of its wetlands. The Stillwater Marsh, in the recent drought years, shrank by 82 percent. After four decades of life in this bewildering time and country, I've become a pretty thick-skinned old campaigner. But the thought of a little curve-billed avocet falling out of a night sky high in the alien Sierras still brings Stone Mother tears to my eyes. The purchase of desert water is buying these beautiful little marathoners the water, food, and safe haven they need to remain among us. I wish long life, and sweet water, to the birds, the Conservancy, and the marsh.

David James Duncan is the author of two novels, *The Brothers K* and *The River Why*, both of which won the Pacific Northwest Booksellers' Award. *The Brothers K* was also a 1992 *New York Times* Notable Book, but "that doesn't necessarily mean it's no good." He lives with his family in western Montana.

Clinch Valley, Virginia

The Most Patient of Animals

❖❖❖

Before I tell you about the cows pooping in the river in southwest Virginia I want to mention an article that just came in the mail, titled, "Is human culture carcinogenic for uncontrolled population growth and ecological destruction?"

The author, Warren M. Hern, of Boulder, Colorado, writing in the journal *BioScience*, argues that human beings are a cancer upon the planet. This is not a particularly original thought, except that Hern isn't just being metaphorical. He's not waxing poetic. He's an M.D. and this is literally his diagnosis: Earth has cancer, and we are it. You can tell he's serious because he includes, as illustration, maps showing population density increases around London between 1800 and 1955, and, on the next page, photographs of metastatic malignant melanomas in the human brain. (He's right, by the way: brain tumors *do* look like London.)

Hern's thesis is a nasty little corollary to the Gaia Hypothesis. It's lovely to visualize the planet as a living organism, but what if the organism has a fatal disease? My own feeling is that humans-as-cancer doesn't entirely make sense on its own terms; would you say the cancer is in remission in cities where population is decreasing?

But if we're not cancer, what are we? Hern's way of looking at things is at the very least useful. In the old days we liked to pose as "stewards" of the environment. "Steward" is certainly a dignified-sounding occupation, especially in comparison to "metastatic malignant melanoma." We saw ourselves as the benign overseers of flora and fauna. Bird got a broken wing? We'll fashion a splint! Thorn in your paw? Here comes a human with tweezers! The problem with this paradigm is that it seems contradicted by certain human tendencies and hobbies, such as the practice of going into the woods, locating a deer or other large furry creature, and shooting it in the head. It's hard to find an excuse for that when you realize that it is mostly done purely for the entertainment value. If we're the stewards of the environment, how come we always carry a gun, saw, axe, or fork? There ought to be a way to interact with nature without so many damn utensils.

So: we are not cancer, we are not stewards—perhaps we can say we are farmers. Clad in overalls, we cheerfully plow the planet, controlling the chaos and untidiness of biodiversity. I am not ashamed to admit that I once called up the great E. O. Wilson and asked him why we couldn't sustain the planet as a huge farm with about ten species, the really useful creatures and plants, such as pigs, cows, chickens, some lambs if we were feeling sentimental, corn, wheat, soybeans and maybe asparagus for the upper classes. The animals would be given hearty daily allowances of feed, so that they would not have to resort to the barbarism that is predation. Why, I asked Professor Wilson, wouldn't this work just fine? (The wonderful thing about being a reporter is that you are not only allowed to ask dumb, insensitive, crudely conceived questions, but are expected to.)

Wilson explained, patiently, kindly, that my Earth-farm would be hell to operate, for the very reason that it wouldn't have enough species. The least stable ecosystems on the planet are the ones with the fewest species. The Arctic is the classic example: one minute you're standing there happily fishing through a hole in the ice, the next you're up to your keister in lemmings. It is a sickening fact that during a Lemming Year it is not safe to drive in some northern climes, because of viscera on the road. Likewise, as you reduce the number of species on Earth, the ecosystems become less stable, and certainly no farmer could control and regulate what survived. You'd have Parasite Years, Staphylococcus Bacteria Years, not to mention the dread Skeeter Years. It would be long hours, low pay, no fun. Also it would be wrong, but let's not complicate things worse than they already are.

I apologize for all this throat-clearing but this was the intellectual context of my trip to southwest Virginia where the cows are pooping in the river. Normally I try to deal with the environmental issues without ever going to any actual environments; this time I was inspired to seek direct visual contact, because I had heard that the Clinch River had a great diversity of freshwater mussels, and because I wanted to get out of Washington, the City of Lies.

Bill-the-naturalist drove the car across the field and parked it in high weeds. We were going to see the mussels and that involved getting wet. The river was right there on the edge of the field, with only a narrow strip of trees guarding the bank. One might have expected a more grandiose buffer—a few hundred yards of woods, or a cliff, or a parallel canal, or a fence, or an interstate highway, or something to prevent random people, total strangers to the river, from walking right into it. But this is part of the problem with the Clinch: there's not much of a "riparian zone," as a biologist would put it.

The Clinch runs northeast to southwest between mountain ridges in a part of the Appalachians far from any major city. It's six hours of very speedy driving from Washington. Short of the Maine woods it probably has more rural territory than any other place east of the Mississippi. Not even the glaciers have been through here, which is why there's so much biodiversity: nothing's been scraped away.

Some might call this Appalachia, but that's not quite right; the poverty is not so omnipresent, and this is several counties south and downstream from coal country. The land is rugged, with knobby hills popping up between the long linear mountain ridges. The land is too rough to cultivate but there are cattle farmers, and some of the people work in furniture factories, or in the executive offices of upstate mining companies, or at the big chemical plant downriver in Tennessee.

This is Honk if U Love Elvis country; June Carter Cash, Johnny's wife, is from this area. You will see a church along the highway with a sign out front saying Independent-Fundamental-Premillennial, and a grocery with a sign saying Night Crawlers–Coins–Indian Relics–Beer.

But what you most notice is the absence of large numbers of people. There are lovely, long, newly paved country roads, no doubt the work of some energetic congressperson, but there are hardly any cars. There are people here, of course—a lot of them tucked back in the hollows, descendants of the original Scottish mountain people. But a few homes here and there aren't sufficient to destroy the life in a river. Humans are managing to have an impact far beyond their number, in part because we bring other exotic species with us, like those cows, and in part because the ecosystem itself is fragile.

Mussels have only one weakness: they are slow. They are not quick afoot. For one thing, they have only one foot, a little extension that comes out of the shell and can haul the critter along a millimeter at a time. They are what you would politely call sedentary and what you would rudely call a river potato. For the most part a mussel sticks to one spot, filtering the water, letting the food come to it. A mussel will live for fifty years that way, hunkered down. They've been doing this for millions of years. In mussel time, humans are a blur, a shock, a kudzu outbreak, an asteroid impact.

Bill Kittrell is The Nature Conservancy's point man in saving the mussels of the Clinch. He's twenty-nine, tall, soft-spoken. He was raised on a farm in North Carolina and educated at the university in Chapel Hill, so he can both "talk dirt" with local farmers and code-switch to talk environmental policy with econerds. "One minute you're talking to a dairy farmer who has forty head of Jersey cattle and the next you're talking to a businessman who's worried about the consequences of signing the NAFTA agreement," he says.

Bill wanted to show me the mussels up close and so we tromped down into the cool, slow-moving water. The river bottom was covered with round stones and, as Bill pointed out, mussels. I am ashamed to admit that their appearance surprised me: I had expected snails, or something. I had expected something that could easily be imagined as part of a French meal. Instead, I discovered that a mussel is what people where I come from would call a clam. It lives in a clamshell. Big old thing.

Bill pointed out the different types: the sheepnose, the shiny pigtoe, the pink heelsplitter, the pocketbook, the three-ridge. There seemed to be a lot of sheepnoses.

Had we searched we might have also found the purple wartyback, the monkeyface, the rabbitsfoot, the kidneyshell, the pheasantshell, and the unprepossessingly named pimpleback. The river braids into several streams here, and the islands in the middle are collectively known as Pendleton Island, home to something like forty-five species of mussel, there's no place like it on the planet, it's the New York City of freshwater musseldom.

But we're changing all that! We are extirpating these mussels as fast as we humanly can. We kill them with dams, siltage, coal-mine runoff, chemical spills, fertilizer bleeds, dredging, channeling, and garbage dumping. Arnold Edward Ortmann, a great naturalist of the early twentieth century, found sixty species of mussels in this area, at least ten of which are now extinct. The green blossom pearly mussel? Gone! The acorn shell mussel? Gone! The narrow catspaw mussel? Gone! Of the ones that survive, fourteen are listed as endangered species.

"They're the first animals to go when streams become degraded," says Dick Neves, a biologist with the National Biological Survey. "Then we start losing the fish fauna and the other invertebrate fauna that sustain the food base."

Humans screw things up even by accident: small zebra mussels from the Caspian Sea stowed away aboard a European tanker a few years ago and have already smothered the indigenous mussels of the Great Lakes. They'd love to find their way to the waters of the Clinch and stomp on the monkeyfaces and sheepnoses.

As we waded in the river a small creature appeared in the water about fifty yards away and Bill opined that it was a muskrat. The muskrats eat mussels. In the past, humans hunted the muskrats and sold the fur as "mink." Wearing fur is now viewed as a social atrocity, so there are fewer muskrats being captured and killed to supply the fake mink, and thus the muskrats are eating more mussels. I report this with trepidation, knowing that somewhere out there a smug fur-wearing person is going to start going around saying, "I wear fur to save the mussels."

Of course the real danger to the mussels is the water quality, not predation. This is where the cow poop comes in. The cows, having no barrier in the riparian zone, cool themselves in the river, and drink of its waters. Naturally they relieve themselves as well, and the organic matter eats up much of the oxygen in the water. There are other sources of pollution: fertilizer runoff, siltation from mining operations far upstream, and just human garbage dumped in the river.

Now you would think that there would be some government agency with irrefutable authority over something as simple as the water quality of a certain river. Not so. One of the great achievements of the environmental movement has been the creation of an environmental bureaucracy. Probably you'd want to start out by talking to the people at the State of Virginia Department of Game and Inland Fisheries. If the pollution came from a single source you could call the U.S. Environmental Protection Agency. For advice on species protection you would of course contact the U.S. Fish and Wildlife Service or perhaps someone at the new National Biological Survey or some other official within the Department of the Interior or maybe an employee of the state of Virginia's Natural Heritage Program, though ultimately you would probably be frustrated because all the pollution from the mines upstream is governed by the state of Virginia's Division of Mine Land Reclamation. And although the cow-poop problem is monitored by the Virginia Division of Soil and Water Conservation, it's not really regulated, because it's "nonpoint" pollution, and no one does anything about pointless pollution.

Except the polluters themselves, maybe. Bill Kittrell introduced me to Jim Cox, a dairy farmer who let The Nature Conservancy fence off the river along his property.

"The river is not the river it once was," Cox said. "I can remember it clear enough to drink."

Cox has 40 cows. To fence his land is a worthwhile endeavor. But then you have Zan Stuart, who had 1,300 cows when I called him up and who usually has about 3,000, plus as many as 2,400 sheep, spread along 8.5 miles of the Maiden Spring Fork of the Clinch River. Stuart's family has been farming for more than two centuries.

"We've had the land since 1774. It was a colonial grant given to my great-great-great-whoever-he-was who built an Indian fort on the farm. It's been used as a farming operation ever since."

Would he put a fence between his cattle and the river?

"We have thought about it. I can see both sides of the question. I just really don't know. Too much of that could impact some people down the river. On the other hand, if you own land and you've grazed it and you've watered the cattle there for two hundred years, it makes it difficult to say we've got to find another source of water for the cows."

He said, "A lot of farmers would like to do better and they have some fears that maybe they are doing the wrong thing, but they can't afford to do anything else. Here I am, worrying about having enough money to pay off the bank this year."

Zan Stuart struck me as a fundamentally decent man who'd probably like to do the right thing. And he's the kind of person the environmental movement might co-opt: at the age of seventy, despite having six children and thirteen grandchildren, he's got no offspring with any real zest for the farming life. One son, Sandy, spent some time on the farm but finally said, "Daddy, the bright lights are calling. I can't stand this any longer."

Sandy became a commodities trader in Chicago.

I will remember always two things about that little jaunt to southwest Virginia. The first is the air. Usually the Appalachians are misty, atmospheric, but I hit upon a shockingly clear couple of days, the hills yanked into sharp focus. As a flatlander from birth I have always worshiped three-dimensional landscapes, and this one, with its folds and ridges and hillocks, is perhaps more aesthetically perfect than even the grander Smokies farther south or the lovely Shenandoahs to the north.

And I'll remember the blackberries. Bill and I found them along a dirt road leading up to Brumley Mountain. The species, *Rubus al-legheniensis*, is opportunistic. When man chops a path through the forest, the blackberries sprout in the sun. We gorged ourselves. I don't know what blackberries represent but somehow they gave me hope.

Perhaps the ultimate problem with the steward or farmer paradigms is that they imply that humans are apart from nature, superior to it, above it. It denies our status as animals, as a breeding population whose habitat has been extended by technology to almost every inch of the planet. Maybe that's why I sort of like the cancer model—because it is internal, part of the host. Because it destroys in a way that seems so senseless.

We think often of saving the natural habitats of endangered species, but clearly Earth itself is our habitat. Maybe the secret to saving the environment is helping people like Zan Stuart realize that fencing the river is a way of protecting the human species, not just ol' sheepnose.

And maybe we could learn something from the mussels. They have a nice humility. They have great powers of patience. They have a nice pace.

❖❖❖

Joel Achenbach works for the *Washington Post* writing feature stories and the weekly column "Why Things Are," which is syndicated nationally. His commentaries appear regularly on National Public Radio's "Morning Edition."

Snake River, Idaho

On the Henry's Fork

❖❖❖

Our history is understood by riverine chapters, and it is impossible to know American life without constant reference to rivers, to the Shenandoah, the Suwannee, the Missouri, the Mississippi, and the Rio Grande. It is still to them we look for restoring some poetry to our national life in the face of an increasingly platitudinous present.

We are all, rich or poor, downstream. There is almost always a waterway nearby in American life that nourishes and binds communities together. It is the very last thing a thinking people should pollute or pointlessly obstruct.

Our assault on North America has relied on rivers as corridors of travel and communication, as well as settlement zones and cultural neighborhoods. We have used them as a junkie uses his veins. The substances titrated into the riverine systems of America have become systemic. As we look to the preservation of our wild lands and even to their healing and recovery, river conservation offers some of the same advantages it offered the settlers.

Here in the West it is heartening to see the Missouri wandering through various habitats and states, or to see the Milk wandering in and out of nations. Rivers *are* the real nations. A river like the Missouri certainly deserves sovereignty based on what it is from its source to its mouth. The average American is two-thirds river water and ought to have more sense about these things than he has shown. Obviously, a creature that is itself made mostly of rivers would do well to offer itself to the exaltation of rivers in good works and ceremonial acts of worship like fishing and contemplative floating in poetic watercraft such as canoes and jonboats.

I went to Idaho to fish the Henry's Fork of the Snake River. I was interested to see what could happen to a great river that had been nominated for the Wild and Scenic system but for political reasons had failed to achieve designation.

I spent a couple of days with Mike Lawson, fishing and driving around. Mike is a fly-shop operator and outfitter at Last Chance on the Henry's Fork. He and his wife, Sheralee, have lived in the area all their lives. Mike grew up in Sugar City, one of the sacrificial hamlets in the pathway of the burst Teton Dam, one of those dubious waterworks that not only swindled the American taxpayer with a lousy cost-benefit ratio but also was built in such a bad place that it gave way in 1976 and killed people as predictably as Uzis in the hands of crack dealers.

Mike took me to a small tailwater fishery downriver. As we passed the small farms and ranches on our way, well kept by an industrious people, Mike said with real feeling, "I grew up with these folks. I don't want anything bad to happen to a single one of them. But if they don't learn to negotiate and compromise, they're going to lose it all." Mike is right in the middle of it, as an angler, as a conservationist, as a native son, and as a Mormon. Mike is serious about his faith, an elder in his church, a truly great angler, and as perfect an angling companion as God ever made, relaxed and persistent and informed about his immediate natural world. He is also an active conservationist on behalf of his beloved rivers, and this has put him in direct conflict with many in the communities in which he has always lived. One would have to have spent substantial time in these close-knit western farm and ranch towns to understand what personal

toughness this requires. That Mike Lawson has acquired this toughness without losing his love of the native people of his area is absolutely remarkable.

One of the unpleasant subcurrents of the conservation movement
is a generic categorizing of Mormons as dam builders and irrigators,
people who have controlled or subverted the Bureau of Reclamation.
It is naïve not to understand that Mormons are the irrigation pioneers
of the arid West or to fail to see some heroism in their survival against
persecution and the poor gambler's odds of desert life. But now they,
and their practices, are entrenched, and the appropriateness of these
practices is dimming. The West is finite and its bounty more diverse
than previously imagined. The slogan on Idaho license plates, "Famous Potatoes," has come to seem some obsolete farmer joke instead
of what it is, the merest insinuation of the power of Idaho's all-
powerful water lobbies, as well as of her many nature-hating legislators, with their string of zeroes from the League of Conservation
Voters.

Still, it was no small thing to bring this region into agricultural
productivity. I am often astounded at how lightly western historians
toss around notions of how farming and ranching should have been
done, how miners should have mined, how cavalry officers should
have realized, how starving or surrounded people should have taken
a longer view, and so on; I am astounded at the facility of their
judgment and their lack of feeling for the way human lives are swept
along by fear and need and creaturely habit. Some of the new historians, looking over the shoulders of the pioneers, are unable to see
why the West seemed so imposing, so vacant, and so fear inspiring.

There were several rapid channels deflected by a narrow, wooded
island. Mike picked a place to cross. It looked like a tough crossing
to me, but this was Mike's river, so we locked arms and set out. I
soon felt the strength of the river and the erosion of gravel under
my feet as the current sped by. "I'm going," said Mike, a remark
which at first seemed redundant, as we had already set out. Just before
he was swept into a crablike grasp over the top of a submerged
boulder, I got what he was trying to tell me. But by then I was already
floundering downstream. We wallowed back to shore, reconsidered,
started out again, and this time, made it.

Now we could look around from the gravelly midriver shallows. "All kinds of birds winter in here," said Mike. "Some of them, like robins, stay the whole winter. And waxwings. I've seen a great gray owl in here." The little canyonlike enclosure did seem protected in every direction, with its tall, stately rock walls and its floor of twisting river currents.

We caught a few trout and then, fishing upstream, I hooked another on a nymph, a most delicate take and a rather measured reaction by the fish as I set the hook. When the fish eased out of the current into the slack water it rolled once, and I saw that it was an enormous rainbow. It fought at first, as large trout sometimes do, like an annoyed dog, shaking its head in the current and planing off at a leisurely angle to turn and shake once again. I had enough of a sense of the fish's size that I hated to make him mad. Then with one sand-filled boil he turned and ran downstream. Where the channels rejoined each other, the river deepened too much to wade after him. I pushed my fingers through the arbor of the reel and tried to slow the spool down. I got nowhere. As the line peeled off and the diameter of the spooled line decreased, everything got faster. The reel's clicking ran together in a little screech as the hog trout roared off.

By now, Mike had passed me and was trying to find a path downstream to follow the fish. Thirty yards below me, the backing passed over his head, parallel to the riverbank. As I watched the hundred yards of line shrink, the last look I'd had of the fish, a big, dull-red stripe wider than my hand, seemed to hang before me as I acknowledged that this was the largest resident trout I'd ever hooked. I thought of the fish I'd stared at on restaurant walls in northern Michigan as a boy. Most of them would have seemed like *cuisine minceur* to this fish.

Then the trout stopped. There was one single turn of backing wound around the spindle at the center of my empty reel. The fish stopped right then and there. It was like literature! He stopped long enough to let me think about how wonderful life could be when it had great literature-style items in it, like coincidence and fate and elegant ironies. Then in that moment of antimagic when literature is converted to the far more familiar land where we actually live and breathe and spend our days, the great trout turned and straightened my hook. I had so much line downstream that its sheer weight continued to bow my rod. I had to reel it all in. I had to salute the absence of the great fish who had made such short shrift of me. With nothing to commemorate the fish except the whispering river around my knees, my rod was now a straight, dead stick. There was a terrific, evangelical silence.

In the long ago when I decided to release every fish I caught, the encounter itself began to consume my consciousness, and I am doubtless not alone. We no longer look to the product, the slab with the stilled fins, that was so recently hovering in the racing current to inspect a mayfly or to ease off under a shady bank at the sound of gravel under a wading shoe. It is a fact that we are almost entirely made of river water ourselves; but the flesh that remains organizes this spectral borrowing from riparian valleys and, rod in hand, blesses our origins by counting coup.

The next day I fished the slower water upstream to see the outcome of severe drawdowns and to see which, of the diversity of values represented by the Henry's Fork, had been honored. The Bureau of Reclamation, now world famous as a welfare program for corporate and millionaire irrigation farmers, had taken a strict-constructionist view of its duties and went on insisting that its only responsibility in the management of its Island Park Dam was to supply irrigation water from the Henry's Fork. Idaho Fish and Game, pointing to its limited budget for a proposed trash-fish kill, collaborated in the drawdown of the dam's reservoir pool to catastrophic levels: The bottom sediment was disturbed, and more than fifty thousand tons of silt headed into the finest piece of trout water in the nation. It shot through the Box Canyon and upper Last Chance area; but when it reached Harriman State Park, site of the august Railroad Ranch, the water slowed down and the silt dropped to the bottom.

It had been fifteen years since I fished here, but I quickly saw that it had gone badly downhill. The silt was bermed up around boulders on the bottom, and as I waded through the priceless waters the Harriman family had entrusted to the state of Idaho, huge, vague clouds of muck spread out before me. Where were those hundreds of big, surface-feeding rainbow trout of not so very long ago? Grossly reduced, to put it mildly. This was the corpse of the old Railroad Ranch and a monument to the short memories and hit-and-run management techniques of many public agencies.

So the slug of silt headed downstream; the resident trout of the reservoir pool were captured, more or less, and replanted into the Henry's Fork, where by my visit, they were silvery and gaunt and not at all the vaunted river fish of yore. The trash fish were offed, and the pool was refilled and replanted with rainbows supplied at the lowest cost. There are important genetic differences within trout species, and this approach often results in populations of fish mutts like the Skamania strain of steelhead that has seemed such a panacea to fisheries agencies throughout the Northwest. Many people around the Henry's Fork thought that there should have been other criteria besides cheapness in such an important job of work.

It ought to be enough to say that the Idaho Department of Fish and Game sufficiently disgraced itself that I made certain I bought the shortest-term license, three days, that they could force me to own. It would be bad karma for me as an Irishman to give up potatoes, but I have found that other states produce them too. Responsibility for the steep decline of this great fishery must be shared by the supervisor and staff of the Targhee National Forest, who have abetted the clear-cutting of this fragile region.

At present, The Nature Conservancy is trying to buy a ranch on the Henry's Fork, and one would hope that it might use its water to help with critical winter flows. But in this part of the West, the doctrinal heartland of "prior appropriation" of water, the subject of instream flow is both controversial and ambiguous. The "use it or lose it" approach to water seems to invade even the sacred precincts of private property, an astonishing lapse in an area fetishistic about individual rights: the owner of a decreed water right cannot sell it, nor can he give it to the stream itself. His rights as an owner are restricted. Parts of the West, dominated by the church of irrigated farming, seem willing to accept this abrogation of individual rights. State or federal property condemnations to accommodate the movements of the automobile are acceptable to most westerners, but they are considered "unconstitutional" when they are on behalf of protecting the natural world.

This spell of fishing, rambling, and philosophizing with Mike Lawson took place in the Island Park caldera, the mouth of an ancient volcano, one of the largest and oldest in the world. The impression on the ground is of a broad, level, circular area with a surrounding rim of low mountains—quite low really, when viewed against the Tetons to the east, in my view the more impressive way to see them. Through the old lava floor, through the porous and mineral-rich basalt, bubble substantial volumes of water that, emerging into streams and rivers, are eyed sharply by farmers and trout fishermen. They are eyed even more sharply perhaps by migratory creatures like the trumpeter swan, which staged a comeback at the eleventh hour of extinction from this glorious region.

Not completely discouraged by the condition of the Railroad Ranch, Mike and I traveled along the Henry's Fork and were soon so submerged in its glories that I began to forget its troubles. We visited Upper Mesa Falls, a blizzard of vertically dropping mountain water, wonderfully tall, between steep forest walls. A plume of mist climbed into the blue Idaho sky, striped with rainbows and drifting slowly into a tall curve.

Mike pointed to a place far below us where nearly invisible water raced across slabs of basalt. When he was in high school, he and friends used to work their way out onto the rock to catch wild trout at the base of the falls. Once he was swept away toward Cardiac Canyon and lost his father's watch. I began to suspect that this river lover, probably like most river lovers, had been often swept away.

Mike and I had taken our chilly ride on the lower river. That evening we floated the Box Canyon through bird-filled shafts of declining light, cold, clear water racing through a gallery of boulders where trout took up their stations for passing food. When we pulled our boat out at the bottom of the canyon, he said that as a baby, guarded by an inattentive aunt, he had been, you guessed it, swept away by the Henry's Fork, to be recaptured through heroic effort by his mother as he floated through the rocks.

As we looked down into the wild gorge of the Henry's Fork,

where the railroad bed wound around above the river, Mike told me how his father had taken him along the tracks in the inspector's motorcar and dropped him here and there to fish. I was happy to think that the rivers that first carried me off my feet, literally and figuratively—the Pere Marquette, the Pine, the Black, the Manistee —were now in the Wild and Scenic Rivers system and receiving its imperfect benediction. I thought Mike's river ought to have that kind of care too.

Thomas McGuane is the author of *Nothing But Blue Skies, The Sporting Club, Nobody's Angel, Keep the Change,* and other books. He is a recipient of the Richard and Hinda Rosenthal Award of the American Academy and Institute of Arts and Letters, and was nominated for a National Book Award for his novel *Ninety-two in the Shade.*

WILLIAM W. WARNER

The Atlantic Barrier Islands, Virginia

Of Beaches, Bays,
and My Boyhood with the Colonel

❖❖❖

Very little in my upbringing seems to have pointed toward a love for our great Atlantic beaches, much less writing about them. I was born and grew up in New York City in a house that was without great books, without a father, and, for some periods of the year, without a mother. In *loco patris* I had only a highly irascible step-grandfather. Colonel George Washington Kavanaugh was his name, and he wanted to be known by all of it. His most frequent utterance to me, apart from constant reminders that I was no blood kin, went something like this: "Your father is a bum, your mother is running around with every gigolo in Europe, so I suppose the spring can rise no higher than its source."

So much for the Colonel, as my brother and I always called him, and the genetic malediction he constantly laid on us. But there was one thing the Colonel did for us for which we are both eternally grateful. Come June every year he took our family, such as it was, to a place called Spring Lake, a summer resort on the New Jersey coast. Not that we especially liked the place. Our school mates all went "to the country" on vacations, and Spring Lake with its kiosked board-walks, well-ordered streets, and great hotels with long porches and double rows of rocking chairs didn't seem very country to us. Reinforcing this impression was an institution known as the Bath and Tennis Club, where our contemporaries spent much of the day playing blackjack and sneaking cigarettes.

But at one end of the well-ordered streets, beyond the boardwalk and the great hotels, was an immense space. How immense I learned from my older brother, who at age nine or ten gave me my first taste for geography. "Look here," he said, showing me a world map and running his finger along the fortieth parallel, "there is nothing but the Atlantic Ocean between our beach and the coast of Portugal, four thousand miles away."

Suffice it to say that this bit of information, which was quite accurate, overwhelmed me. I soon began taking long walks along the beach, staring out at the ocean and dreaming of the day I might have a boat of my own to venture beyond the breakers and explore it. My brother shared this vision, although more in terms of a quest for better fishing. In due course we therefore built a crude box-shaped scow of heavy pine planking, painted it red, white, and green, and proudly named it the *Rex* after the great Italian ocean liner that was at the time the largest and most luxurious ship in the transatlantic passenger service. With the help of some of our huskier friends we grunted the *Rex* down to the beach. The chosen day was fine, with a sprightly land breeze that did much to calm the breakers. Our plan was alternately to fish and paddle down to an inlet at the south end of Spring Lake that led into a small bay known as Wreck Pond. But after we were successfully launched, our friends all laughing and cheering us on, we found the *Rex* to be something less than seaworthy and quite difficult to paddle. In fact, the sprightly western breeze that had made our passage through the surf so easy was now rapidly carrying us out to sea—straight for Portugal, I could not help thinking—with a strength against which our best efforts were no match. The reader can guess what followed. Alarms were sounded, authorities were summoned, and we were rescued. "One more trick like this and I'm cutting you out of my will," the Colonel said to us when we were brought home, humiliated, by the Coast Guard.

Nevertheless, before the summer was over, my brother and I

found we could explore the incongruously named Wreck Pond well enough by foot and bicycle. It was, in fact, what biologists call a complete estuarine system, in miniature. At its mouth was the tide-scoured inlet, constantly shifting its sandy course. Behind the inlet was a shallow bay, a labyrinth of marsh islands, and ultimately, well inland, a freshwater stream fed by a millpond bordered by pin oak and magnolia. Thanks to this complex we could do everything from netting crabs and small fish to stalking the marsh flats looking for shorebirds, muskrat, or an occasional raccoon. We could even catch small trout up by the millpond dam, graciously provided by the New Jersey state fish hatcheries. What a relief these occasions offered from the Bath and Tennis Club, what an escape from the Colonel! Wreck Pond, in short, became our private world.

But there were other worlds to conquer, as the saying goes, in particular a large blank space on maps of the coast which my brother and I had both noticed and wondered about. It appeared as a long finger of land pointing southward, a mere ribbon of land between the Atlantic Ocean and Barnegat Bay. Most remarkably, the southern part of the finger, below a cluster of closely spaced beach resorts, showed no signs of human settlement nor even a road, as far as we could tell. (The reader will understand how rare this was when I say that even in the 1930s, which is the time I speak of, much of the New Jersey coast was already a solid corridor of resort townships.) The blank space was called Island Beach. It had to be investigated, we agreed.

For this greater enterprise we borrowed a canoe, provisioned it with three days' worth of canned pork and beans, and left an ambiguous note concerning our intentions on the Colonel's pillow. But once again the Aeolian gods did not favor us. This time a wet east wind slammed us against the marshes of Barnegat Bay's western shore, so strongly, in fact, that we found we could only gain ground by wading in the shallows and pushing and pulling the canoe. There was one bright moment in this otherwise dismal effort, however. After rounding a sharp bend in one of the marsh islands we came upon a sheltered and relatively quiet cove. There to our amazement were four or five mink cavorting down a mud slide they had excavated in the marsh bank. Over and over they shot down the slide—head first, tail first, on their stomachs, on their backs—to splash into the water with splendid abandon. Well hidden by the tall cordgrass, we watched transfixed as the mink evidently scrambled up an underwater burrow, reappeared above on the marsh bank, shook their silvery wet coats, and repeated the process. Forever, it seemed, or what must have been at least ten minutes. I have never forgotten the sight, nor seen another mink slide since.

We passed what seemed like a sleepless night huddled under a tump of bushes in the cordgrass that offered little cover from intermittent rains. The next morning we set out again, very tired, under a hazy sun and on glassy calm waters. Island Beach seemed almost in sight on the far horizon to the east, although it was hard to be sure in the haze. Just as we began to ponder the wisdom of continuing our journey, a large and official-looking motorboat with a slanted red stripe on its bow came alongside bearing instructions to take us in tow. "That does it!" the Colonel said to us two hours later when we were brought home again, humiliated but grateful, by the Coast Guard. "I'm cutting you both out of my will."

A few years later, or when I was sixteen and my brother and I had gone our separate ways, I got to Island Beach. I got there in what today is known as an ORV, or off-road vehicle. But mine was quite different from current models. Mine was a splendid little ORV, in fact, for which I make no apologies. Unknown to the Colonel I had acquired a lightweight Ford Model-T beach-buggy prototype with a chopped down body, painted in salt-resistant aluminum and equipped with four enlarged wheel rims and tires, all for the sum of $50. My buggy was totally incapable of sustained driving in soft sand, having only the standard two-wheel drive and a weak one at that. It therefore could never charge up dunes or otherwise alter the beach topography. To operate it successfully on Island Beach it was necessary to travel at low tide, only, along the wet and more compact swash sand of the forebeach. This meant driving along close to the surf, constantly dodging the biggest waves, in what proved to be a thoroughly exhilarating experience. One could do this, moreover, for ten glorious miles, ten miles of wind-plumed breakers rolling in from the Atlantic, ten miles with seldom another human being in sight. Sometimes there would be schools of marauding bluefish just beyond the surf, marked by sprays of small fish breaking the surface and the screams of wheeling gulls and terns. In such event I would jam on the brakes (stepping on the reverse gear pedal worked even better), grab my cane surf rod, and heave out a heavy lead-squid lure as far as possible. If your cast went far enough, you got your blue. By the time you brought him in and unhooked him, you had to jump back into the buggy and race on to catch up with the fast-moving school. For a boy of sixteen these were moments of pure bliss, of feeling at one with the sea and the sand.

There were other attractions. Often I would leave my fishing companions to their patient pursuits and explore the back beach. The dunes of Island Beach were low, but with steep rampart-like faces on their seaward side. Behind the ramparts were small hollows of smooth sand marked only with the delicate circular tracings made by the tips of swaying dune grass. Then came beach heather and thickets of sea myrtle, stunted cedar, holly, and scrub oak. Gain the highest point of land, perhaps no more than twenty feet above sea level, and the small world of Island Beach lay revealed before you. On the one side were the choppy waves of Barnegat Bay at its broadest, bordered by salt marsh and tidal flats that attracted great numbers of both migrant and resident shorebirds. On the other were the dunes, the white sand, and the Atlantic breakers stretching away to a seeming infinity. It was a small world, easy to comprehend, and I loved it from the beginning.

New Jersey's Island Beach is what is known to geologists as a barrier island. (The fact that it is not now an island is merely a question of time; it once was and could be again anytime after a hurricane or winter storm washes over its narrow width to create an inlet.) Barrier islands are the dominant feature of our Atlantic and Gulf Coast shorelines and they are found there to an extent not matched elsewhere in the world. They are also the most fragile of our landforms, subject to constant change by wind and water. This is especially true of overwashes, as the storm incursions are properly called, which can both create inlets and move the islands landward. North Carolina's Outer Banks are probably champions in the former regard. The Banks have had at least twenty-five major inlets open and close—six are open today—in their known history.

The formation of barrier islands is complex and still a subject of some discussion among scientists. One of the most common origins, easy to understand, goes by the ungainly name of spit accretion. Picture a relatively straight north-south coastline with a large embayment somewhere along its length. Sand dredged up by wave action from offshore shallows to the north of the embayment will be carried south by a prevailing current. Some of this sand will be deposited when it reaches the slack where the coastline first curves into the bay. The sand so deposited will form a small spit in the same direction. The spit will in turn trap more sand and beach detritus, growing longer and longer in the direction of the current. It may even grow until it completely closes the bay mouth. (This is a common occurrence, incidentally, along the south shore of Massachusetts's Martha's Vineyard island, giving rise to some rather large landlocked bodies of water known locally as "ponds.") Or, what is just as likely, the spit may be intersected by inlets to form one or more barrier islands.

How then can sand dunes build up from what began as low-lying spit accretions? Here wind, not water, is the principal creative agent. Wind blowing sand across the beach will also bring seeds. To begin with, only a few seeds of beach grass need sprout along the beach's driftline. The blades of beach grass will then reduce the speed of the wind passing between them, causing more seeds to drop. More sand will be deposited as well, of course, in progressively greater quantities as the thicker beach grass slows the wind even further. Thus do the dunes grow in nature's form of compound interest. And thus are they rendered more stable, unless man interferes, as the grass roots bind together the sandy subsoil.

Lie down at the crest of a dune in a good thirty-knot offshore wind—enough, that is, to make the sand grains sting against your skin—and you may witness another phenomenon common to barrier beaches. Carefully squinting your eyes, you can see sand flying up from the dune's seaward face and raining down in its lee. What you are literally witnessing is the landward creep of a barrier dune. But here wind is a supporting player. Water—or better, storm-driven water—takes the major role, often generating something more than a creep. The storm overwashes that sweep over barrier islands inevitably add to their landward side by depositing large fans of sand and other sediments which kill the bordering salt marshes and tend to fill up the bays behind them. Some islands have been known to retreat as much as forty meters after a single great storm. Dramatic as such events may be, they do not on the whole contribute as much to landward migration as the ebb and flow, four times a day, 365 days a year, of the tides that race through the islands' inlets. The sand and other sediments carried by these tides are deposited in the form of a fan-shaped delta after passing through the inlets and gaining the quieter waters of the back bays. Thus do the bays fill and thus do islands creep toward the mainland. Some sand, but not as much, will also be taken back out to sea on the ebb tide, in some cases to form dangerous offshore bars. You will notice these dangers on nautical charts, wherever the Coast Guard places the stern warning "**CAUTION**: Entrance to Inlets: The channels are subject to constant change. Entrance buoys are not charted because they are frequently shifted in position."

Oh, that barrier-island beachfront developers were required to issue a similar warning to prospective clients! It might well read "**CAUTION**: The properties you are about to purchase are subject to constant attack by the sea. Domiciles built thereon cannot be insured because they are frequently shifted in position." Perhaps this will come in our lifetime, after more and more beach houses wash out to sea.

Such are some but not all of the ways the barrier beaches of our Atlantic Coast take shape. They are almost as various as the forces that create them. In the north are the wind-driven "walking dunes" of Cape Cod, or the tide-swept and relatively barren Monomoy Island. In the south are the quiet groves of live oak and palmetto of the "sea islands" of South Carolina, rapidly being lost to development, or

Georgia's Cumberland Island, mercifully spared by a combination of public and private sources. In between these is the lonely majesty of North Carolina's Hatteras Island, now part of the Cape Hatteras National Seashore. Fifty-five miles long and for the most part pencil thin, the island lies between the Atlantic Ocean and the broad expanse of Pamlico Sound. Drive down below Hatteras Light to the extreme tip or cusp of the cape (the Cape Point, as it is called, is a highly movable spit) and cast your eyes seaward. For as far as you can see the seas rise up in pyramidal crests and tumble against each other in wild confusion, even in a moderate breeze. But here there are no rocks or underwater reefs. Rather, what you are witnessing is the clash of the Atlantic Coast's two great current systems, or the cold and southward-trending Labrador Current and the warmer waters of a Gulf Stream gyre. Underneath them, extending twelve miles out to sea, are the shifting sands of the dread Diamond Shoals, known as the "graveyard of the Atlantic." So it was in the age of sail, for some eighty known shipwrecks. Little wonder the sailor's rhyme:

If the Dry Tortugas let you pass,
Beware the Cape of Hatteras.

Little wonder, too, that in this wild setting the Hatteras Lighthouse will soon be moved back from the sea's grasp. Or that the oak frames of old ships, once buried out on the shoals, are periodically exhumed on Hatteras's retreating beach.

Not far to the north of the Outer Banks are the barrier islands of Virginia's Eastern Shore. Starting with the Chincoteague National Wildlife Refuge on Assateague Island, these islands run eighty miles south to Cape Charles at the mouth of the Chesapeake Bay. They are eleven in number counting only the larger islands, and all but two of them are protected by a combination of federal, state, and private sources. At the north is the Wallops Island space-tracking center, whose NASA landords have at least kept it off limits to visitors. At the southern extremity is Fisherman's Island, a small national wildlife refuge at the tip of the Cape Charles corridor, where migrating hawks and falcons foregather in the fall before crossing the Chesapeake. In between, or at the heart of this system, are the twelve islands—Smith, Myrtle, Mink, Godwin, Ship Shoal, Cobb, Little Cobb, Hog, Revels, Parramore, Cedar, and Metompkin—that make up The Nature Conservancy's Virginia Coast Reserve. The islands and the adjoining back bay and salt marshes, totaling thirty-five thousand acres, are a meeting ground for northern and southern plant and animal species and thus have a rich biological diversity. For this reason they have been given world-class status, or designation as a United Nations' Biosphere Reserve.

For me the Virginia islands have long held a peculiar fascination. One reason, I am sure, is that getting to them is often an adventure in itself. There are no roads, bridges, or causeways to the Virginia barriers. Rather, you must go by shallow-draft boat and have some knowledge of the labyrinth of marsh creeks, tidal flats, broad bays, and deep-running ancient river courses that lie between the mainland and the outer islands. This area—the back bays, as they are sometimes called—literally pulsates with life. The mud banks of the marsh creeks come alive at low tide with *Uca pugnax*, or the feisty and well-named little fiddler crabs darting in and out of their burrows. Great blue herons or their lesser cousins wait for them at almost every bend in the creeks. Out on the broad marsh you will see marsh hawks circling the hammocks and tumps of firm land. Ospreys dive in the inlets, to compete in winter with loons and mergansers. In the fall there will be huge flights of snow geese and brant numbering in the tens of thousands, not to mention the ubiquitous Canada goose and a variety of tipping and diving ducks. Out in the broader bays you will find commercial fishermen dragging for the succulent hard clams and salty oysters these waters offer in profusion. At certain low tides the oystermen will snub their boats to the channel banks, step out onto the bordering tidal flats, and take their pick of the best oysters. These same flats offer prime feeding grounds for oyster catchers and a host of other shorebirds. Willets, yellowlegs, sanderlings, turnstones, glossy ibis, whimbrels, and marbled godwits are always present in season. Other species come in astounding number. Flocks of over a thousand dunlins may be seen in winter, and an estimated six thousand knots have been counted feeding on the larvae of blue mussels on Metompkin Island in the spring.

Summer will see large populations of black skimmers nesting on isolated sandbars, while great egrets and tricolored herons occupy their crowded nests in the shrubs and small trees of the marsh hammocks. Visitors from the south include the brown pelican, white ibis, and Wilson's plover, which nests here at the northern limit of its range. Summertime will also see great silvery tarpon rolling through the inlets, although not in great number, and loggerhead turtles lured from Florida by warming waters. Visitors from the north include the threatened piping plover, which finds the shell fragments of undisturbed beaches much to its liking for nesting materials. Terns—least common, gull-billed, royal, and sandwich—prefer to nest on the berm of the island beaches, not far from the dune line. But the swift-flying Forster's, which can hover like a small hawk, will build its nest from the wrack of the marsh islands. Beneath the shallow bay waters are wavy meadows of sea lettuce and other aquatic plants. These underwater meadows are a favored hiding place for the tasty Atlantic blue crab, which searches them out to moult, and a nursery and juvenile growth area for a great many fish, including valuable commercial species, that will return to the sea as young adults. The list could go on, the list, that is, of all the living treasures so carefully guarded and nourished in the lee of the barrier islands.

I like best to visit Parramore Island, the largest in the Virginia Coast Reserve, in mid-October. Starting from the reserve headquarters to the south, there is only a suggestion of what is to come. After passing through narrow tidal creeks, a thin dark line begins to appear far out on the horizon. This is Hog Island, seven windswept miles from the mainland across the reserve's broadest bay, now dotted with small flocks of old squaws and buffleheads. But soon there will be the shelter of more tidal creeks and salt marsh as Parramore's mid-island forest comes into view. Overhead are the long V's of Canada geese, flying south. The first snow geese may also have arrived, and ducks are everywhere, wheeling and turning in the clear autumn sky or dropping down swiftly to marsh potholes. After landing on Parramore's bay side one traverses a pond-studded salt marsh and enters a forest of loblolly pine, surprisingly tall for being so close to the sea. The air is cool and quiet, and the carpet of pine needles makes walking easy. An inquisitive deer may approach you, completely unafraid, as if wondering where you fit in the island's scheme of things. Migrating warblers flit overhead. But soon, very suddenly, you break out of the forest near the ruins of a Coast Guard lifesaving station. There is the ocean. And there is the beach, the broad and gently sloping beach, and the long rows of breakers rolling in from the Atlantic.

At this time of year you may want to look for the long wavy lines of scoters beating their way south just beyond the breakers. Or be on watch for the rare peregrine falcon rocketing down to Cape Charles. Or you may simply want to train your binoculars in either direction, as far as vision will carry, until there are only mirages where sand, sea, and sky come together in a common haze. To pause, that is to say, and gaze at Parramore's endless beach. There are not many like it. Pray God it may remain so.

Thinking back I sometimes wonder where or to whom one should express gratitude for the rich experience our national seashores and other coastal reserves so generously provide. In my case thanks would have to begin with New Jersey's Island Beach, scene of my boyhood awakening and still preserved, wonder to say, by the state's Department of Environmental Protection. Or perhaps even further back to Wreck Pond, Spring Lake, and, yes, even the Colonel. So I will say a word to him now, in a form of address I never used in his lifetime. Namely, thank you, Grandpa, for getting me into all this. And thank you, too, Grandpa, for getting me out, in another sense, at a very critical moment. On that day long ago when my brother and I were drifting rapidly toward Portugal in the *Rex*, it was you, after all, who called the Coast Guard.

William Warner is the author of the Pulitzer-winning *Beautiful Swimmers: Watermen, Crabs, and the Chesapeake Bay* and *Distant Water: The Fate of the North Atlantic Fisherman*, nominated for the National Book Critics Circle Award. A recipient of the Smithsonian Institution's Exceptional Service Award, he lives in Washington, D.C.

CARL HIAASEN

The Florida Keys

Last of the Falling Tide

❖❖❖

My father first took me to the Keys when I was six. He was a passionate deep-sea fisherman, and had decided that I was old enough to join the hunt for blue marlin and sailfish.

The invitation was thrilling, but I had secret doubts about my suitability for big water. I suspected—correctly, it turned out—that I had not inherited my old man's cast-iron stomach.

But I wanted fiercely to experience the Keys. I'd wanted it since the day I'd seen an old photograph of my father, struggling to lift an amberjack that seemed nearly as tall as he was. The picture was taken in Key West around 1938, when my father was thirteen. He wore a white shirt and khaki pants, and with long tanned arms hoisted the fish for the camera. He looked as happy as I'd ever seen him.

Over the years, my father and grandfather told me so many stories that the Keys had become in my young mind a mystical, Oz-like destination: a string of rough-cut jewels, trailing like a broken necklace from Florida's southernmost flank—the water, a dozen shades of blue and boiling with porpoises and gamefish; the infinite churning sky, streaked by pink spoonbills and gawky pelicans and elegant ospreys. This I had to see for myself.

On a summer morning we headed down U.S. 1, which was (and remains) the only road through the Keys. Although we lived in Fort Lauderdale, merely a hundred miles north, it might as well have been Minneapolis. The drive seemed to take forever. From the back seat I watched fruitlessly for evidence of paradise, but all I saw were trailer parks, gas pumps, bait shops, mom-and-pop diners, bleached-out motels, and palm-thatched tourist sheds that sold spray-painted conch shells. My restlessness took the form of whining, and from the front seat my father and grandfather instructed me to settle down and be patient. The farther south we go (they promised), the better it gets.

We passed the charter docks at Bud n' Mary's, where the great Ted Williams occasionally could be found, and suddenly blue water appeared on both sides of the Overseas Highway. To the distant east was the full sweep of the Atlantic, deep indigo stirred to a light, lazy chop. To the near west was Florida Bay, glassy and shallow, with knots of lush green mangroves freckled with roosting white herons. At the time I didn't know the names of these islands, but they were Shell Key, Lignum Vitae, the Petersons, the Twin Keys, the Gophers—places where I would spend, in coming years, hundreds upon hundreds of hours, none wasted.

The Keys never looked so enchanting as they did on that morning. As soon as we got to the motel, I grabbed a spinning rod from the car and made straight for the pier. Standing at the brim of those velvet horizons, gulping the sharp salty air, I understood what my father and grandfather meant. This was an honest-to-God wilderness, as pure and unspoiled and accessible as a boy could imagine. On my first trip to the Gulf Stream, I caught no marlin, only a bonito, but it pulled harder than anything I'd ever felt. It was a great day, made better by the fact that I'd managed to hold down my lunch.

The deep-running Atlantic was undeniably impressive, but the calm crystal flats of the backcountry intrigued me the most. To wade the banks was to enter a boundless natural aquarium: starfish, nurse sharks, eagle rays, barracuda, bonefish, permit, and tarpon, all swimming literally at your feet. The flats rippled with unique tidal energies—sweltering, primeval, seemingly indomitable.

This was around 1959, and nobody considered the possibility that the shoals of the Keys might be destroyed, and that it might happen within a single human generation. Unimaginable! Life flourished everywhere in this tropical embrace, from the buttonwood hammocks to the coral reefs. The sun was so warm and constant, the waters so wide and clear, the currents so strong. Destroyed—how? By whom? Over centuries the Keys had survived droughts, floods, and the most ferocious of hurricanes. What was there to fear from man?

The worst, as it turned out. The population of Miami exploded during the next three decades, and urban blight metastisized straight down Highway 1, bringing crowds, crime, garbage, and big-city indifference to the Keys. The quaint and casual opportunism of the islands was replaced by an unrelenting hunger to dredge, subdivide, pave, build, and sell. It was tawdry, sad, and probably inevitable. By the 1980s, southeast Florida was home to four million souls, increasingly frenetic and determined to recreate at all costs. Where else would they go but the Keys?

I was one of them. A few years ago I bought a stilt house in a hammock near Islamorada. It's significant to note that Ted Williams, his timing still flawless, had already sold his place and fled Monroe County. The stampede of humanity was too much for him. My own friends gingerly questioned why a person would move to the Keys at a time when smart people were bailing out. Maybe there was a sentimental component to my decision—why, after all, does one sit with a dying relative? Duty? Guilt? Nostalgia? Maybe there was more.

Certainly I had no illusions about what was happening. As a journalist, I've written plenty about the rape of the Keys and the fast-buck mentality that incites it. On Big Pine, for instance, the federal government is doggedly buying up land to save the diminutive Key deer from extinction. Pro-growth forces have retaliated with lawsuits, high-powered lobbying, and old-fashioned venom. Road signs that alert motorists to deer crossings are routinely defaced—crosshairs painted over the emblem of a leaping buck.

As dispiriting as such cretinous behavior might be, the Keys also breed a devoted and tenacious species of environmentalist. About ten years ago, the hardwood forests and coral shores of North Key Largo were in danger of being bulldozed and dynamited into a series of huge condominium resorts. If completed, the developments would have brought as many as sixty thousand residents (and their speed-boats) to a narrow belt of hammock situated between a national wild-life refuge and North America's only living barrier reef. You'd have been hard-pressed to find a more catastrophic location for a massive condo village. But local conservation groups banded together in op-position, and dragged slow-moving regulatory agencies into the battle. One by one, the seaside resort projects collapsed; today, much of North Key Largo has been purchased by the state for preservation.

That was a rare victory, but it made many of us believe that what was left of the Keys could be saved. To give up would be unthinkable, cowardly, immoral.

So I arrived to find the stores, tackle shops, restaurants, and high-way jammed, even in the deadening heat of summer. This depressing state of affairs also applied to the bonefish flats and tarpon lanes. Raging and cursing, I've managed to cope; friendly fishing guides generously help me avoid congested waters, and I've marked a few hidden spots of my own. There are still plenty of fine fish to be caught.

Of course it's not the same place I knew as a boy. The best of it is gone forever. But if one knows where to look, and which tides to ride, it's still possible to be the only human in sight, to drift along crescent banks while schools of bottle-nosed dolphins roll and play ahead of your bow. These luminous moments become more rare with each tick of nature's clock. The Keys are in desperate trouble.

Not long ago I drove south past Bud n' Mary's and, on both sides of the Overseas Highway, the water was the color of bile—algae, emptying from Florida Bay to the sea. A foul stain has settled around Shell Key, Lignum Vitae, the Petersons; on the falling tides it bleeds through the channels to the ocean. At the fishing docks, the talk is of little else. The old guides are sickened, the young ones are angry, and all of them are frightened for tomorrow. Wherever the cloud of algae appears, sea life vanishes. That which cannot flee dies. Already the baby lobsters have disappeared from Florida Bay, spelling future disaster for commercial crawfishermen.

Smaller blooms are not uncommon in the summer months, but the water ordinarily clears as soon as temperatures drop. Not in recent years. The chilliest days have failed to stop the spread of the milky green-brown crud. As I write this, about 450 square miles in the heart of the bay, Everglades National Park, is essentially dead. From the air, the sight is heartbreaking. If the algae continues to spill out to sea, it will smother the coral reefs, which require sunlight to survive.

For years, bureaucrats and politicians beholden to Big Agriculture have insisted that the "decline" of Florida Bay is unconnected to the egregious flood-control practices that have transfigured the lower Everglades. But this much dirty water was impossible to ignore. The algae bloom in Florida Bay became so vast and unsightly that tourists began to complain, prompting Florida's leaders to exhibit the first official signs of alarm. Assorted agencies, departments, and task forces are holding emergency sessions to discuss the crisis. A local congressman is asking that $3 million be set aside for more research. From Tallahassee to Key West, establishment voices are demanding swift action to replenish the bay, preferably before next winter's tourist season.

As if it was as easy as turning a spigot. It's not. Florida Bay historically was a brackish estuary, fed by a dependable, unimpeded flow of fresh water from the Everglades. As the state's population grew, the water from the glades was purloined and diverted through a network of deep man-made canals. This was done exclusively to benefit farmers, developers, and newborn cities, with no thought whatsoever to the profound long-term consequences. To this day, the golf courses of South Florida are more assiduously tended than the Everglades. Nature's plumbing has been rejiggered so that farms and cattle ranches can tap into the Everglades at will, use the water, then dump it back as waste. Florida's famous river of grass is being used not only as a fountain, but as a toilet.

The high-tech siphoning of the Everglades begins below Lake Okeechobee, at the sugarcane fields, and continues down to the tomato farms and avocado orchards of southern Dade County. The capture is so efficient that only 10 percent of the fresh water naturally destined for Florida Bay ever gets there. Many scientists believe this is why the bay is so sick. Without a seasonal flow from the East Everglades, the bay water has gotten saltier and saltier.

Several years of drought accelerated the transformation from estuary to hypersaline lagoon. By the mid-1980s, rich beds of turtle grass had begun to die and decompose, leaving bald patches on the bottom. The rotting grass became a nutrient for aquatic algae, which bloomed extravagantly in the salty, overheated pond. The algae, in turn, blocked so much sunlight that it killed the sponges and other marine organisms. The bay started turning to mud. Each year it looks worse.

Now it's early spring and the algae continues its spread. A steamy summer promises an eruption of new growth; airplane pilots and boat captains already report that bilious mile-wide puddles of the stuff have drifted out of the bay toward the pristine Gulf banks of the Lower Keys. Meanwhile, in the Upper Keys, floating clumps of dead sponges can be found from Flamingo to Long Key.

What can be done to save Florida Bay? Many experts say the most urgent priority is reviving the freshwater flow through Taylor Slough, which drains from the Everglades into the northeast part of the bay. A new trickle has been promised; getting more water will require taking it from Dade farmers and developers, who have powerful political allies in Tallahassee. And restoring flow is only part of the prescription—the water coming to the bay also must be free of phosphates and pesticides, and its arrival must be timed for the dry winter months. Too much fresh water can be just as lethal as too little, especially during the rainy season.

It doesn't take a marine biologist to know that tropical waters aren't supposed to look like bean soup, or smell like rotted mulch. These are not signs of a healthy ecosystem. Maybe the algae will die naturally, drowned by heavy summer rains, or blown out to the Gulf of Mexico by tropical storms. Yet even if we awake tomorrow and the stuff is gone, it's only a temporary reprieve. For the killer algae is but one symptom of many threats to the Florida Keys, each resulting from the uncontrolled invasion of man.

Runoff and sewage from high-density condos and hotels poison invisibly. Offshore, rusty freighters plow into the reef, while pleasure boats drag heavy anchors across the delicate corals. In the backcountry, manic water bikers and macho speedboaters frighten wading birds from their nests in the mangroves, disrupting centuries-old breeding patterns. Turtle-grass beds—a crucial nursery of the marine life chain—are gouged, shorn, and crisscrossed by propeller ditches.

This is not what I wanted to show my son.

I first brought him here when he was a youngster, and I probably spent too much time telling him how splendid it used to be, before the greedy bastards ruined it. My boy listened but he also kept his eyes on the water—and fell in love with the place, prop scars and all. He got his first bonefish at age seven, and a big tarpon on fly at age sixteen. He spends every spare moment here, including precious college vacations. On a recent spring morning when many of his classmates were slugging down Budweisers on the beach at Daytona, my kid was wading the flats of Long Key, scouting for tailing fish.

Battered, ragged, and long past their prime, the Keys continue to enchant and seduce. I can't blame my son for his weak heart, because there's still nothing as gorgeous as a calm dawn at Ninemile Bank, or a sunset in the Marquesas. The truth is, I always wanted him to love the Keys as much I did, and as much as my father and grandfather before me. But if my son was to grow up fighting to save this place, he also needed to feel the sorrow and anger that comes with watching something precious be destroyed.

He does feel these things, deeply, and that gives me a jolt of hope. The kid is damn angry about what's happening down here. Maybe even angrier than his old man.

Carl Hiaasen is a columnist for the *Miami Herald* and the author of several novels including *Strip Tease, Tourist Season, Skin Tight,* and *Native Tongue.* He was born and raised in Florida.

GIOCONDA BELLI

Journey to the Lost City of the Jaguar

❖❖❖

As I enter the jungle, a childhood memory suddenly surfaces. I see myself riding in my father's car, my face leaning on the back window. My imagination running faster than the wind. Ever since my grandfather had talked to me about the Indian tribes that once inhabited the Pacific coast of Nicaragua, the slopes and hills of the terrain had taken on a life of their own. I thought of hidden, buried temples: the dwellings of my ancestors.

Now, as we enter the jungle, leaving the four-wheel-drive vehicle parked at the end of the dirt road next to the wooden sign that announces "La Milpa Site. Programme for Belize," I feel as if I am about to knock on the door of my own past; I am, at last, going to be allowed to enter.

It is humid here, and hot. The trail goes up among some rocks and a profusion of palm trees, mahoganies, rubber trees, and other species I have never seen. I look up and around, overwhelmed by the exuberant greenery that surrounds me. All of a sudden, a rustling of leaves prompts us to stop.

"What was that?" I ask, turning to John, my Irish-looking Belizean guide. "It sounded like something big."

He looks around without moving. We stand quietly listening to the busy silence of the jungle. In my mind I have seen the jaguar springing into the undergrowth. Is it a warning, a sign? The jaguar was a sacred animal. According to the Maya, the sun at night hid inside the jaguar.

"It's nothing," says John, resuming his easy gait.

I follow him, alert, my adrenaline flowing. John seems to think that we would be very lucky if we saw a jaguar. He describes it as a "religious experience" and assures me that it would be very unlikely that the jaguar would attack us. According to him, they have no interest in humans. I am not sure that I agree with him. I associate the jaguar with death, with the faces of priests covering their heads and bodies with the jaguar skin, lifting beating hearts up to the sky to placate the gods.

I follow John deeper and deeper into the thicket, wondering when we will arrive at the site, not knowing what to expect.

According to him, La Milpa was a very important urban and ceremonial center for the Maya. Yet, in modern times, very few people knew of its existence. It had first been discovered in the 1930s by a *chiclero*, when the chicle tree was harvested for its thick, rosy sap to make chewing gum. Like many Mayan sites in Belize, it had been looted and abandoned again to the jungle. Now it is a part of the Río Bravo Management and Conservation Area, a natural reserve consisting of 229,000 acres of tropical forests and savannahs in the northwestern part of Belize. John Masson, my guide, works for Programme for Belize, the organization in charge of Río Bravo.

He talks nonstop, pointing to this and that tree, showing me the abundance of young mahoganies that now have been able to reproduce in the forest, protected from loggers. The jungle is magnificent, humid, sensual. I am drenched in sweat, dizzy from the smell of damp earth that fills my nostrils. The deeper we go, the more it feels as if we were entering the life-giving maternal womb again. It seems to me that at any moment we might come upon the secret cauldron where ancient spirits stir a primeval soup teeming with the seeds of creation. This is what the world was like in the beginning: untouched, wild, green, wet, beautiful.

All of a sudden, we come upon a clearing. There is a large stone lying on the ground. On top of it, a small, perfectly round stone ball sits in a puddle of water. I look around bewildered at the sight of an obviously man-made object, somehow expecting to find myself surrounded by masks and feathered headdresses. Palm trees scattered about the open space shudder in the wind, their leaves vibrating in succession, like a giant green exotic musical instrument.

John announces that we are at the first plaza of the site. I see nothing but jungle and high, strange-looking hills where trees grow at impossible angles. He enjoys my perplexity and, with the delight of one who unwraps a wonderful present, starts pointing deliberately, slowly, to the different hills.

"That is a temple," he says, "and that one, and that one. See how they form a square?"

It is my childhood again. This time, however, my imagination does not need to be summoned to assign the shapes of temples to indescribable mounds. This time, it only takes a few moments for the ancient blueprints to surface in my mind, and for me to see underneath trees and earth and underbrush and roots the pyramidal shapes, the rectangular platforms.

I am indeed standing at the center of a Mayan plaza. In front of me, a hill looking like an aspiring slim volcano hides the largest construction, not a perfectly triangular pyramid, but the Mayan pyramid, ending at the top with a small square building. There are two lower, longer mounds at both sides of the plaza. Another high construction stands opposite the largest temple. Like a mirage appearing and disappearing, shapes and volumes metamorphose before me. One moment I can almost see the inhabitants of the city dressed in bright clothes, going through the motions of their daily lives, or standing, curiously looking at us, the intruders from another time; and the next, it's the jungle again, the high pitch of the cicadas reverberating louder and louder, the sound of invisible birds setting in motion the canopy of the forest, enormous trees plunging their roots into the eyes of the ancient buildings, blinding them forever. Life and death inexorably intertwined. Men and nature fighting it out again, like warriors in eternal battle. The jaguar roaming near, hidden in the jungle, waiting for its prey.

"Come," says John, bringing me back. "Come and see this."

I follow him around the tallest building, the volcano-shaped mound, and find myself standing in front of a man-made tunnel, a straight line to the heart of the pyramid. John explains that it is a looter's trench. Looters had solved at least one of the mysteries of Maya civilization: they knew that the Maya used to bury important personalities, kings and priests, under the stairs, in the guts of their pyramids. The dead would have been dressed in royal regalia and accompanied by precious objects, jade and gold ornaments, to offer to the Nine Lords of the Night in Xibalba, the dark region of the Maya underworld. Little could they have known that their treasures would never reach the hands of gods; that instead, after many centuries, they would return to the living, probably their descendants, to be sold and traded in a different kind of underworld.

The funeral chambers are empty now. Nothing remains but the careful limestone construction, the perfectly square blocks giving us a glimpse of what's underneath so much earth, so many roots. There are several layers of construction, one on top of the other, and John explains that as kings and powerful personalities came and went, they would build their own structures on top of previous ones, to assert their greater glory over that of their predecessors.

It is still possible to see how smooth the walls of the chambers were. It is still possible to see, here and there, a splash of the red paint that once upon a time covered them. I go over the stones with my hands and the whitish powder of the limestone covers my skin, giving it a ghostly tone. A flock of parrots crosses the sky and I remember my grandfather saying that the parrots were souls in torment, condemned to repeat forever the sounds of human speech. Whose voices did these birds echo? What warnings are they chanting now, as they fly above our heads?

I would like to see beyond the stones, beyond time. I would like to hear the ceremonial chants, the funeral procession moving through the plaza, the pallbearers carrying the body. But only the the parrots interrupt the silence. The parrots repeating the undecipherable words of the dead.

We cross the plaza, weaving through trees that filter the light and swing lazily in the breeze. There is so much death here, and yet so much life. The abundance of palm trees amazes me. There are many varieties; some have slim trunks, while others have thick and solid bases that sprout in a multitude of arms, reminding me of graceful dancers on the walls of Oriental temples. Rubber trees, their leaves shiny and soft, spread their many roots, standing in a precarious equilibrium on the sides of the mounds. The *ji ocuago* with its shiny reddish bark shoots up into the canopy. John tells me that the natives call this tree the "tourist tree" because its bark, like the tourists' skin, becomes red under the sun.

Our steps resonate in the silence as we go through several plazas, all of them flanked by mounds of different sizes forming perfect quadrilaterals, many of them scarred with looters' trenches. Above our heads trees of many shapes and heights form a Gothic canopy of naves and architraves, while below there is a profusion of parasites, bromeliads, and lianas.

In one of the plazas John points to a ceremonial stele, a stone projecting out of the ground, intricately carved on all sides. "Look," he says, pointing to its lower left corner. "This is the signature of the artist, and this is the date: September 30, 628 A.D." Moss grows on the stone, into the carvings, as if in defiance of the human intent to track time, to record historical events. The Maya used stelae to sing the glories of the powerful, to indicate their lineage and important dates. One of the few ancient American civilizations to have a written language, they wrote obssesively about time, the movements of the stars. Yet their books were burned by the Spaniards in an effort to cleanse the natives of their beliefs. On July 12, 1562, a Franciscan monk, Diego de Landa, ordered the destruction of the Mani library, a deposit of hieroglyphic books found in Mérida, written on long strips made out of the bark of the fig tree. Nowadays only three Mayan codices remain.

John picks up from the ground a small red fruit. He offers it to me to smell. It's the fruit of copal, the tree whose sap provided the Maya with the incense for their sacred ceremonies. The aroma is sweet and intense, evocative of the rituals of life and death. The men of corn had to appease their gods with blood. Only when death joined life in the fluttering of the dying red heart did the worlds of spirit and matter, the worlds of above and below, come together. It was necessary to die, to placate the jaguar, so that life would be renewed, so that the sun would rise again and life, corn, could be nourished.

Again we hear the rustling of leaves. We stand still. I am sure it's the jaguar following us, watching us, guarding his treasures, guarding the ghosts that, at night, endlessly worship him, performing rituals in a futile effort to triumph over death and time. Fragile, sad ghosts of this jungle, a monument to nature's invincibility, to its eternal, patient persistence.

As if he could listen to my thoughts, John extends his arm to show me a strangler fig wrapping itself around a breadnut. The rays of the sun shine over their trunks, enveloping them in an eerie light. From the ficus family, the strangler fig, better known as the "tree-killer" in Central America, starts off like a vine twisting itself around large trunks. Once it reaches the canopy, its abundant foliage opens, taking up all the light from the host. Its weak branches start to grow and thicken, and soon its victim dies in a deathly embrace. Like tentacles of a mythical monster, a multitude of branches sprout from the strangler and close tightly around the tall breadnut, attesting to the strength and blind determination of the life-force. It doesn't matter that the host tree was, at the beginning, the strong one. Over time, it's been defeated, overpowered.

A perfect metaphor, I think, of Maya civilization succumbing to the jungle, its monuments strangled by the trees and the earth they once thought theirs to rule and command. It's said that the Maya mysteriously vanished, but anyone traveling through Belize or Guatemala will find that they are still a presence. One can see them sowing the land, tending gas stations, speaking Spanish and Maya in Belize, where English is the official language. One would have to speak of the Maya diaspora, the squandering of natural resources, the deforestation, the slash-and-burn of the land to plant corn and feed the ever-growing population. At some point the earth would have been exhausted and famine would have set in. The hungry population would have refused to work to build and rebuild more and more temples and cities for the theocratic aristocracy that thought its power divine and absolute. A peasants' revolt would have done away with the ruling class, and this would explain the signs of desecration noted by archeologists in temples and ceremonial buildings dating from the ninth century, the time when this great civilization perished. Free from their leaders, the population would have dispersed, forming small communities, abandoning the temples and ceremonial centers, the great palaces and buildings, to the ever-present, ever-patient jungle.

The cicada's song rises up again slowly, as if some unseen hand had decided to raise the volume to a deafening pitch that pierces through my brain, making me feel confused, vulnerable, unable to handle so many thoughts, so many omens, so many symbols.

I look up and see the ceiba tree. A sacred tree for the Maya. In their cosmogony, the world was thought to be a square, flat surface, suspended between thirteen succesive heavens and nine underworlds, each one of them ruled by a god. On the geographic center of the Earth a great ceiba tree grew, while four smaller trees stood on its four corners. Each corner had a separate color: white for the North, yellow for the South, red for the East, black for the West. They believed Earth stood on the back of a gigantic crocodile lazily floating on a lily lake.

As we come to the last large mound, and walk behind it to where the looters' work reveals a massive stone wall, perfectly erect, a soft, insidious sadness comes over me: I've come this close to my American, native past, only to discover that it's been forsaken. So much history, so many treasures are silently buried here. La Milpa in Río Bravo and so many other Mayan sites are our own, American, Valley of the Nile and yet there are not enough resources to unearth these secrets, to reveal these mysteries.

In other parts of the world, a site like La Milpa would have been sealed, enshrined, cleaned from the debris of time. Free of tangled branches, balancing trees and earth, these temples would be open for the world to see and admire. We could proudly bestow our indigenous heritage, the grandeur of an imposing past. And yet, if that should happen, the solitude and magic of this jungle would be forever ruined.

Paths would be opened. Little shops selling T-shirts and miniature scale models of the pyramids would line the trail we followed to arrive here. Trees, as monumental as the temples they covered, would be cut down.

John has said that their idea is to keep everything very much like it is. Programme for Belize owns these lands, and its plan is to protect the fauna and flora, and to protect these sites. Its research station is an obligatory stop for anybody wishing to visit La Milpa.

We retrace our steps, going through a ball court where the Maya used to play the popular sport known as *pok-a-tok*, a ball game that could be played for entertainment, and also to resolve political disputes.

As we go back, I think of the Maya abandoning these temples to the jungle. I think of a Maya equivalent to Lot's wife, a woman walking slowly, reticently, turning her head to look back, unable to bear the parting, thinking lovingly of an abandoned, adulterous lover whose voice she would never hear again.

I tell myself I will come back to these jungles and these temples, but when we come out again to the dirt road and the Jeep, I also turn my head back to see what was lost, to see the shudder of the palm trees, the green eyes of the jaguar shining in the dark woods.

❖ ❖ ❖

Gioconda Belli is a Nicaraguan writer who currently lives in Los Angeles. She has published four books of poetry and two novels. Her poetry collection, *From Eve's Rib*, and her novel *The Inhabited Woman* have been published in English.

Guadalupe-Nipomo Dunes, California

Natural History Crashes, Resurfaces

❖❖❖

Our little group changed shape with the fall of every wave, for the shoreline which we walked along shifted dramatically in breadth from one moment to the next. We must have looked like a flock of sandpipers, trying to follow the waterline, but scurrying wildly whenever a blockbuster wave surprised us.

It was no wonder we could hardly hear each other speak, for the gusty winds and roiling sea waters kept the background noise at high pitch. Terns and plovers, curlews and whimbrels whirred around us. The turbulent power of the Pacific was felt in the salty air, in the blowing sand, and in our wind-whipped bodies. This was California's Central Coast, and the power we felt was the same that had driven wild the likes of Robinson Jeffers, Jaime de Angulo, Edward Weston, John Steinbeck, Chester Alan Arthur III, and the lesser known, but no less colorful, Elwood Decker the Dunite.

Nancy Warner motioned me in from the shoreline, back fifty yards or so from where the ocean thundered and frothed on the beach. We were approaching Oso Flaco Creek, a swift-running corridor of brackish water flowing back and forth between the tides and a lake tucked in upon the leeward side of the Guadalupe-Nipomo

Dunes. To cross the creek, she had selected a spot where it was fifteen to twenty feet wide but shallow enough to ford without rolling her pant legs up too high. She was unlacing her shoes when I came to sit down next to her and do the same. While we were taking our shoes and socks off, Nancy pointed out a wading bird's tracks in the wet sand next to the creek. She tried to explain something to me, but the wind kept on roaring into the conversation:

"Ever since I moved down here to work for The Nature Conserv"—the wind carried her words away—"learning to read animal tracks from . . ." and another gust came up to swallow the story. "If you find a place where dry sand has recently blown over moist sand," I leaned closer to her, craning to hear her ephemeral words, "you can scrape away that dry layer and find perfectly preserved tracks underneath!" She motioned with her hands, as if pulling an imaginary squeegee across the wet surface. "How many layers are preserved like that, I don't know, but when I asked"—the wind again whisked away a few phrases—"maybe all the way back to Chumash Indian footprints hundreds of years ago, he said slyly!"

I had not followed all that Nancy had said, but perhaps I could ask her to fill in the blanks later, when we were out of the wind. For the moment, however, I plunged into the clear, cold current that connected the freshness of Oso Flaco Lake with the saltiness of the ocean. From stories I had heard previously, each of those two bodies of water held an animal on its side, an animal that was larger than life in my mind's eye.

In 1980, near where the creek meets the Pacific, a ninety-foot blue whale beached up here. I wondered if the imprints of its fins still lived beneath several strata of sand. . . . Likewise, Oso Flaco Lake was named for a skinny bear killed there in 1769 by Spanish explorers, on the very first day that Gaspar de Portola's crew arrived in the dunes. Perhaps its skull still lies buried beneath the sand. Stories of bears and whales, fragments now and then resurfacing to remind us what wildness is. This little effervescent stream held them together for me.

Nancy led us southward down the beach, with five-hundred-foot Mussel Rock Dune towering above the spray of blowing sand on the far horizon. Suddenly, pointing to a piece of driftwood not unlike dozens we had already passed, she shouted to us: "Here is where we turn for Hidden Willow Valley! Make a mental picture of this place, in case you come out to the beach by yourself later, and then want to find your way back to camp." I looked at the little blowout between two foredunes; it took me a while before I picked up on its peculiarities compared to other entranceways running back into the dunes. With eighteen miles of sandy ups-and-downs stretching along the Guadalupe-Nipomo Dunes complex, I wondered how long I could keep within my memory the image of this secret passage back to Hidden Willow Valley—a place so quiet, according to Nancy, that I might be able to hear complete sentences for the first time in an hour.

A few minutes later, when we climbed down from the dunes into the willows, poison oak, and shrubby lupines of Hidden Willow Valley, the quiet was punctuated by the pounding of a nail into wood. We rounded a corner, and found a man hammering penny nails into the door of a handmade plywood box perched up on a post. Norman Hammond, the oral historian of the dunes and spiritual descendant of the Dunite community of mystics and poets which settled here earlier in the century, looked a little embarrassed that we had found him with such a weapon of civilization in hand.

"Oh hello," he said quietly. "I've been having a running battle with a flicker here for years, and this is the latest episode."

He showed us his handiwork. Since 1987, Norman has kept a visitor's registry within this plywood box, but the flicker keeps on drilling through the plywood door on the box and damaging the sign-in notebook within the hutch. Three plywood layers and one aluminum sheet later, the profile of Norman's box has the bulge of a pregnant woman, and the flicker has shown no signs of retiring. No matter what Norman has done to close their friendly argument, the flicker has inevitably reopened it.

Norman stopped his futile effort against the flicker, smiled, and asked for our help bringing some precut kindling over to the fire pit. We made some tea, shared a light dinner, and listened to Norman pass on the stories of the dunes just as old-timers had passed them on to him.

And after a while, I noticed a common stream running through Norman's stories: no matter what any society has done to fix a future for themselves here, the dunes have remained unsettled over the long run, and their future is as unpredictable as the size and sound of the next wave.

We have no idea how many times bands of Chumash Indians came and went, but their shell middens lie half-buried on the dune slopes above Oso Flaco Creek. Their numbers became thinned by diseases that arrived with the missionaries at San Luis Obispo in 1772, so that Chumash visitation to the dunes was greatly diminished after 1800. Even after Spanish settlers decreed the dunes part of the Bolsa de Chamizal land grant after 1830, the dunes were looked upon as little more than unarable land, incapable of supporting forage enough for more than a few head of livestock.

It was not until the railroad arrived nearby in San Luis Obispo in 1895 that the dunes were first marketed as a touristic diversion. A beach pavilion was built in Oceano in that same year, and in 1907 developers tried a similar scheme in the midst of the dunes at Halcyon Beach. An ornate, three-towered pavilion went up in record time and hosted thousands of tourists for its Fourth of July opening. But when the developers failed to sell the eight thousand lots in the sand they had advertised, La Grande Pavilion fell into disuse. As Hammond discovered, "By 1915, the pavilion and its pier stood deserted and in ruins. . . . Wind whistled through the gazebo towers. Vandals had pushed the grand piano out the second-story dance-hall window. It lay broken in the sand, wood cracked and peeling in the rain, its broken strings flailing in the wind. . . ."

If that had been the only boom and bust that the Guadalupe-Nipomo Dunes suffered, their history would be unremarkable compared with that of the rest of the continent. But as soon as the dunes reclaimed one half-baked scheme, another entrepreneur or visionary would appear, oblivious to previous assaults on the integrity of the dunes complex. Hoboes, moonshiners, and hermits didn't change it much. But when poets, artists, and mystics spread the word among their friends that they had found *the* refuge of refuges," wave after wave of oddities occurred in the Guadalupe-Nipomo Dunes.

Theosophists arrived in the late twenties, and built themselves a temple as outlandish as the pavilions built by developers over the previous decades. Later, Lemurians came, and were seen on the beach trying to chant a lost continent up out of the fog-laden Pacific. The grandson of President Arthur decided to create a utopian commune in the dunes, so he built the Moy Mell community house and several guest cabins to be used by visiting gurus such as Meher Baba and Krishnamurti. And yet, all of these cultural enclaves were sooner or later swallowed up by sand, broken down by human greed, or burned up through internecine contentiousness. Their traces may not be entirely gone from the dunes, however, for the shifting sands reveal snapshots of past perturbations at their own pace.

Sand mines. Oil refineries. Hunters' camps. Dune-buggy pit stops. Off-road vehicle raceways. Parking lots. Farm junkyards. These little human endeavors have cut into the dunes here and there, whittling away at the mass of habitat that once attracted bears and even whales. And yet, somewhere within the remaining acreage of undisturbed ground, at least eight rare forms of plants persisted, and California least terns tenaciously stake out one of their last nesting colonies known along the beaches. By the 1960s, such living riches began attracting more and more attention from conservationists, much to the disgust of local businessmen who looked upon the barren dunes as a dumping grounds, a site for a nuclear-power plant, or a future industrial harbor.

"I ask you," eighty-year-old George Smith said as he scanned the place where conservationists would not let him build a $20 million harbor for the Central Coast, "is this what you call pristine? Maybe a hundred years ago you could call it pristine, but it sure isn't today."

Smith was right in the short run, but perhaps wrong over the long haul. The Guadalupe-Nipomo Dunes have been inhabited, their vegetation burned, and their hollows filled with trash middens for upward of eight thousand years. It is not virgin land, but father, mother, home, and haven to hundreds of offspring: two hundred kinds of birds; a couple dozen mammals, snakes, turtles, and lizards; the famous Pismo clam; and a not-so-famous water beetle that swims its way through the sand. It has spawned the whacky dreams of several bands of artists, intellectuals, and ne'er-do-wells. All have left their tracks buried in the sand. Many of those tracks might someday be squeegeed back to the surface, for the dunes have a memory that abandons little from the past. Forget the word "pristine," though, for what is of value here is not virginity, but a family of creatures emerging from sand.

Smith did not get to build his harbor, but a woman named Kathleen Goddard Jones has progressively seen parts of her own dream surface out of the sand. First she stopped plans for a nuclear reactor atop the dunes, then she helped friends put the skids on plans for the harbor. In 1980, the Nipomo Dunes were designated a National Natural Landmark, for the eleven habitat types remaining there gave it top preservation priority from the U.S. Fish and Wildlife Service. More recently, The Nature Conservancy has assumed the management of a 3,400-acre chunk from beach to lake just south of a barren off-road vehicle area, and renamed it the Guadalupe-Nipomo Dunes Preserve. More important, however, is the Conservancy's collaborative efforts with the California Coastal Conservancy, California Department of Parks and Recreation, Santa Barbara County Parks Department, and Vandenberg Air Force Base to co-manage certain rare organisms along this stretch of dunes, one of California's longest sandy coastlines.

These new designations and schemes may be no more permanent than those hatched in Halcyon, chanted by Lemurians, or meditated up into thin air by Theosophists. As dunes shift, so do human plans for them. But what attracts us to the dunes is not any sense of stability that we might gain from them; it is their dynamism, their ability to surprise us, to wipe the slate clean time and time again.

To touch such unpredictability, to my hand, is as much a rush as touching virgin land.

Gary Paul Nabhan is cofounder of Native Seeds/SEARCH, and a Science Adviser at the Arizona–Sonora Desert Museum. Author of five books, including *Songbirds, Truffles, and Wolves*, Dr. Nabhan is a John Burroughs Medal recipient, MacArthur Fellow, and Pew Scholar working in the Sonoran Desert.

LINDA HOGAN

Ría Lagartos and Ría Celestún, Yucatán, Mexico

Creations

❖❖❖

*We were told by the Creator; This is your land. Keep it for me
until I come back.*

THOMAS BANYACA, HOPI ELDER

We are traveling toward the end of land, to a place called Ría
Celestún, Estuary of Heaven. It is a place where clouds are born. On
some days they rise up above the river and follow water's path. On
those days, from across the full length of the land, Río Esperanza,
the River of Hope, can be seen as it is carried up into the sky. But
today, the late morning clouds have formed further out, above the
ocean.

It is the day after spring equinox, and as we near the ocean,
whiteness is the dominant feature. Salt beds stretch out at water's
edge. Beaches, made of sea-worn limestone and broken-down coral,
are nearly blinding in the early spring light. Water, itself, wears the
sun's light on its back, and near a road sign several young men are
at work, throwing buckets of salt-dried fish into the bed of a pickup
truck.

It has been a long, narrow road through the Yucatán. We have passed jungle, brush, and villages created from bone-colored lime-stone. A woman in an embroidered white huipil walks along the road carrying a bundle of firewood. Smoke from a household fire rises above the thatched roofs. Two boys with small rifles step into the forest in search of food. In spite of the appearance of abundance in the Yucatán, it is a world endangered, not only by deforestation but by other stresses to the environment, by the poverty some people's greed has created for others. It is a hungry place with dwindling resources.

In some villages, the few livestock—a single horse, a solitary cow—are bony of rib. People, too, in many towns, are thin with an evident hunger, a poverty that, as it grows, is left with little choice but to diminish the world about it.

Many of the people in and near Ría Celestún are new people. Previously, they were farmers of henequen, a plant used to make hemp rope, but since the introduction of plastic and nylon rope, the people have been relocated without consideration for what their presence would mean in this region, or how they would stretch a living out of the land. In order to build houses, swamps were filled in with garbage. There are sewage problems, contaminated water, and the cutting of trees has resulted in the destruction of watershed. With the close-in waters now overfished, the farmers turned fishermen are forced into the dangerous business of taking poorly equipped boats out to deeper waters in search of food. Subsistence, a thin daily scraping by of hunger and need, has taken its toll on the people and the land.

In geological history, as with that of the people, this is a place of rising and collapsing worlds. There is constant movement and transformation. Some are subtle changes—the way mangrove swamps create new soil, the way savannah grows from the fallen mangrove leaves—but most of the boundaries here are crossed in sudden and dramatic ways, the result of the elemental struggle between water and land, where a water-shaped cave collapses and new water surges to fill the sinkhole left behind, where water claims its edges from land, where swamp becomes ocean, ocean evaporates and leaves salt. The land itself bears witness to the way elements trade places: it is limestone that floated up from the sea, containing within it the delicate, complex forms of small animals from earlier times, snails, plants, creatures that were alive beneath water are still visible beneath the feet. To walk on this earth is to walk on a living past, on the open pages of history and geology.

Now even the dusty road we travel becomes something else as it disappears into the ocean at Celestún. It is a place of endings and of beginnings, full with the power of creation.

Holy Mother Earth, the trees and all nature, are
witnesses of your thoughts and deeds.

WINNEBAGO

For the Maya, time was born and had a name when the sky
                didn't exist and the earth had not yet awakened.
The days set out from the east and started walking.
The first day produced from its entrails the sky and the earth.
The second day made the stairway for the rain to run down.
The cycles of the sea and the land, and the multitude of things,
                were the work of the third day.
The fourth day willed the earth and the sky to tilt so that they
                could meet.
The fifth day decided that everyone had to work.
The first light emanated from the sixth day.
In places where there was nothing, the seventh day put soil;
        the eighth plunged its hands and feet in the soil.
The ninth day created the nether worlds; the tenth
        earmarked for them those who had poison in their souls.
Inside the sun, the eleventh day modeled stone and tree.
It was the twelfth that made the wind. Wind blew, and
        it was called spirit because there was no death in it.
The thirteenth day moistened the earth and kneaded the mud into
        a body like ours.
Thus it is remembered in Yucatán.

EDUARDO GALEANO, *Memory of Fire*

Inside the people who grow out of any land, there is an understanding of it, a remembering all the way back to origins, to when the gods first shaped humans out of clay, back to when animals could speak with people, to when the sky and water were without form and all was shaped by such words as "Let there be."

In nearly all creation accounts, life was called into being through language, thought, dreaming, or singing, acts of interior consciousness. For the Maya, time itself is alive. In the beginning, the day set out walking from the east and brought into being the world and all that inhabited it—jaguar, turtle, deer, trees. It was all sacred.

Then there were the first humans, whose job it was to offer prayer, tell stories, and remember the passage of time. Made of the clay of this earth, the mud people of the first creation did not endure; when it rained, their bodies grew soft and dissolved.

In the next creation, humans were lovingly carved of wood. These prospered and multiplied. But in time, the wooden people forgot to give praise to the gods and to nurture the land. They were hollow and without compassion. They transformed the world to fit their own needs. They did not honor the sacred forms of life on earth and they began to destroy the land, to create their own dead future out of human arrogance and greed. Because of this, the world turned against them. In a world where everything was alive, the forms of life they had wronged took vengeance on them. There was black rain. The animals they harmed attacked them. The ruined waters turned against them and flooded their land.

In the final creation of mankind, the people were created from corn:

And so then they put into words the creation,
The shaping of our first mother
And father.
Only yellow corn
And white corn were their bodies.
Only food were the legs
And arms of man.

Those who were our first fathers
Were the original men.
Only food at the outset
Were their bodies.

QUICHÉ MAYA, POPUL VUH

At first, these care-taking, life-giving people made of corn, the substance of gods, saw what the gods saw. In order to make them more human, less god, some of that vision was taken away so there might be mystery, and the mystery of creation and of death inspired deep respect and awe for all of creation.

In most stories of genesis, unwritten laws of human conduct are taught at creation. For the Maya, too, the story of the hollow people is not only part of a beautiful and complex creation story, but a telling language, one that speaks against human estrangement from land and creation.

Emptiness and estrangement are deep wounds, strongly felt in the present time, as if we are living an incomplete creation. We have been split from what we could nurture, what could fill us. And we have been wounded by a dominating culture that has feared and hated the natural world, has not listened to the voice of the land, has not believed in the inner worlds of human dreaming and intuition, all things that have guided indigenous people since time stood up in the east and walked this world into existence. It is a world of maintained connection between self and land. The best hunters of the far north still find the location of their prey by dreaming. In *Maps and Dreams* by anthropologist Hugh Brody, one informant says, "Maybe you don't think this power is possible. Few people understand. The old-timers who were strong dreamers knew many things that are not easy to understand. . . . The fact that dream-hunting works has been proved many times." Maps of the land are revealed in dreams, and the direction of deer.

Like the wooden people, many of us in this time have lost the inner substance of our lives and have forgotten to give praise and remember the sacredness of all life. But in spite of this forgetting, there is still a part of everyone that is deep and intimate with the

siempre
remos querido
algo más allá de
que quisimos
lo que

world. We remember it by feel. We experience it as a murmur in the
night, a longing and restlessness we can't name, a yearning that tugs
at us. For it is only recently, in earth time, that the severing of the
connections between people and land have taken place. Something in
our human blood is still searching for it, still listening, still remembering. Nicaraguan poet-priest Ernesto Cardenal wrote, "We have
always wanted something beyond what we wanted." I have loved
those words, how they speak to the longing place inside us that seeks
to be whole and connected with the earth. This, too, is a place of
beginning, the source of our living.

So also do we remember our ancestors and their lives deep in
our bodily cells. In part, this deep, unspoken remembering is why I
have come here, searching out my own beginnings, the thread of
connection between old Maya cultures and my Chickasaw one. According to some of our oral traditions, a migration story of our
tribe, we originated in this region, carved dugout canoes, and traveled
to the southeast corner of what is now called Florida, the place of
flowers. It's true, I have always felt a oneness with this Mexican
land, but I know this call to origins is deeper, older, and stronger
than I am, more even than culture and blood origins. Here, there
is a feel for the mystery of our being in all ways, in earth and water.
It is the same mystery that sends scientists in search for the beginning of the universe. We seek our origins as much as we seek our
destinies.

And we desire to see the world intact, to step outside our emptiness and remember the strong currents that pass between humans
and the rest of nature, currents that are the felt voice of land, heard
in the cells of the body.

It is the same magnetic call that, since before human history, has
brought the sea turtles to the beach of Celestún. The slow blood of
the turtles hears it, turtles who have not been here since the original
breaking of the egg that held them, who ran toward an ocean they
did not know, who have lived their lives in the sea, then felt the call
of land in deep memory and return to a place unseen. Forever, it
seems, they have been swimming through blue waters in order to
return, to lay their eggs in sun-warmed sand, and go back to the clear

blue-green waters of their mothers in ancient journeys of creation and rituals of return.

The white shoreline stretches around us, wide and open. It is early for the endangered hawksbills and green turtles to be coming to land. Egg-laying usually begins in late April and early May. Because of the endangered status of the sea turtles, members of an organization called Pronatura will arrive to protect the turtles and the eggs. In this region in 1947, there were so many sea turtles that it was said forty thousand of them appeared on one beach to spawn. Now the hawksbills are the second most endangered species in the world. Today, despite the earliness of the season, there are tracks in the white sand, large tracks that have moved earth as if small tanks had emerged from the water and traveled a short distance up sand. Some of the tracks return, but others vanish, and where they end, there are human footprints.

In the traditional belief systems of native people, the terrestrial call is the voice of God, or of gods, the creative power that lives on earth, inside earth, in turtle, stone, and tree. Knowledge comes from, and is shaped by, observations and knowledge of the natural world and natural cycles.

In fact, the word "god," itself, in the dictionary definition, means to call, to invoke. Like creation, it is an act of language, as if the creator and the creation are one, the primal pull of land is the summoning thing.

It is significant that we explore the contrasts in belief systems. This exploration is meaningful, not only to the survival of the land, but in our terms of living with the land, our agreement with it, the conditions and natural laws set out at creation.

Sometimes beliefs are inventions of the mind. Sometimes they are inventions of the land. But how we interpret and live out our lives has to do with these belief systems, religious foundations, and the spiritual history we have learned.

From the European perspective, land and nature have been changed to fit human concepts, ideas, and abstractions.

The Western belief that God lives apart from earth is one that has taken us toward collective destruction. It is a belief narrow enough to forget the value of matter, the very thing that soul inhabits. It has created a people who are future-sighted only in a limited way, not in terms of taking care of the land for the future generations.

The Lakota knew that man's heart, away from nature, becomes hard; he knew that lack of respect for growing, living things soon led to lack of respect for humans, too.

LUTHER STANDING BEAR

Reflecting on the destruction of the Americas, I can only think that the European invaders were threatened by the vast store of tribal knowledge, and by the land itself, so beautiful and unknown to them in its richness. Though they described it as "heaven" and "paradise," they set about destroying it. For the people described as gentle and generous, the genocide that began in the fifteenth century has been an ongoing process.

Not far from here is where Fray Diego de Landa, in the 1500s, tortured and killed the Maya people and burned their books in the alchemical drive of the Spanish to accumulate wealth, turn life into gold, and convert others to their own beliefs. They set into flames entire peoples, and centuries of remembered and recorded knowledge about the land. It is believed that there were considerable stores of knowledge in these people and in their books, not just history and sacred stories but medical knowledge, a math advanced enough to create the concept of zero, and a highly developed knowledge of astronomy that continues to surprise contemporary astronomers with its intelligence. It is certain that centuries of habitation on this land yielded more knowledge about the earth and its cycles than has been newly understood and recovered in the brief, troubled years that have since followed. And we are left to wonder if that ancient knowledge would help us in this time of threat, if the lost books held a clue to survival.

This burned and broken history is part of the story of the land. It is the narrative of the past we are still living by, a broken order that forgets to acknowledge the terrestrial intelligence at work here.

But the memory of an older way remains, as if in the smallest human corner live the origins of the world, a way that remembers the earth is potent with life and its own divinity. This knowing is stored in the hearts and blood of the people and in the land. Fray de Landa, for one brief moment, acknowledged such life. He said of this land that it is "the country with the least earth that I have ever seen, since all of it is one living rock."

These words could have bridged a different connection, an understanding closer to the way indigenous people see the land, a life-sustaining way of being.

A rib of land separates ocean and barrier beach from the red-colored tidal estuary and wetlands area where the river runs toward larger waters. The river is so full of earth that it is red and shallow. In its marshy places, plants grow from its clay. There are places where freshwater underground rivers surge upward to create conditions that are unique to this place, and exist nowhere else.

There are a salt marsh, a tidal estuary, and mangrove swamps that contain one of the world's largest colonies of flamingos, birds named after flame, as if they belong, in part, to the next element of creation. This red estuary is alive and breathing, moving with embryonic clay and silt.

It is a place crucial not only to the flamingo colonies and water-fowl, but also to migratory birds from as far north as Maine, a connection that closes the miles, another boundary undone.

Traveling into this red water, we are surrounded by the many-rooted mangrove swamps. Mangroves are a part of creation and renewal in this land. Coastal plants, they live in the divide between land and water:

> The tides are always shifting things about among the mangrove roots. . . . Parts of it are neither land nor sea and so everything is moving from one element to another.
>
> LOREN EISELEY, *NIGHT COUNTRY*

They are a network of tangled roots and twisted branches. Both marine and terrestrial, they are boundary-bridgers that have created islands and continents. Consuming their own fallen leaves, they are nurturers in the ongoing formation of the world, makers of earth with a life-force strong enough to alter the visible face of their world, Rachel Carson said, a world "extending back into darkening swamps of its own creation."

The interior of the swamps is dark and filled with the intricate relationships of water with plant, animal, earth, sheltering small lives within them.

Mangroves are plants that reach out to grow, searching for water and mineral with a grasping kind of energy that can be felt. As they send their roots seeking outward, they move forward, leaving behind them the savannah that will become tropical forest. In turn, rainwater, flowing underground, will break through the forest, creating a cenote. No one knows the paths of these rivers; theirs is a vast underground network. It is only known where they rise. And in some of these sinkholes, or cenotes, are species of fish from one river system not found in other cenotes in the region.

The rain clouds have not yet reached us. Light shines through the leaves. A fish jumps. As we move forward, the path of our disturbance is lighter in color, like a vapor trail, behind us. Then it vanishes, unlike the paths we have left behind in other places. There is a dreaminess here where creation continues to happen all around us in time that is alive.

At the far edge of copper-colored water, a white egret steps through the shallows, an eye sharp for fish. On the other side of water's edge stands a solitary blue heron. Herons are fragile birds and it is not unusual for them to die from stress. I think of them when hearing that Hmong men, forced to leave their country and rootless in America, die of no apparent cause while they are sleeping. I understand the loss that leads to despair and to death. It has happened to us, and is happening to the land, the breaking of the heart of creation.

There is a poem that herons fly through. With rigid legs and boomerang wings, they fly beneath rolling clouds through a smoke-blue sky, flying toward dawn, flying without falling from heaven. The poet, Gertrud Kolmar, a woman who loved animals, died in Auschwitz, one of those lost by whatever other failures of the gods have made men hollow and capable of such crimes. But the holocaust began before her time. It began on this continent, with the genocide of tribal people, and with the ongoing war against the natural world. Here is a lesson, that what happens to people and what happens to the land is the same thing.

Shape, I think she meant by boomerang wings, although the boomerang is something more than that: it is something that returns. And there is great hope in return. Not just in returned time or history as the round cycles of the Maya worldview express, but in returned land and species; return is what we are banking on as we attempt to put back what we have disappeared, the songs of wolves in Yellowstone; the pale-edged wings of condors in California sky; the dark, thundering herds of buffalo to Indian country; the flamingos along the River of Hope. This colony, once diminished to five thousand birds in 1955, has increased its numbers to twenty-two thousand, according to Joann Andrews of Pronatura. This, and Ría Lagartos to the north, are the only wintering and nesting areas these flamingos have.

And then we see them, these returned flamingos, in their wintering ground, first as a red line along the darker water, red as volcanic fire breaking open from black rock, revealing its passionate inner light, fire from the center of earth's creative force, lit from within, each individual part of a more complex living whole.

For well over a mile, all along the shore, we see them, like dawn's red path stretched before us. It is almost too much for the eye to see, this great vision, the shimmering light of them. It's a vision so incredible and thick and numinous I know it will open inside my eyes in the moment before death when a lived life draws itself out one last time before closing forever and we are drawn to these birds the way fire pulls air into it. They are proof how far blood will travel to seek its beginning.

❖ ❖ ❖

We sit, floating, and watch these lives with their grace and the black lines of their underwings. They are noisy. The birds at the outermost edges are aware of us. We are careful not to disturb them as they eat; at the end of winter, their mission here is to fill themselves. Already there are mating displays, though true nesting takes place to the north of here in Ría Lagartos, where they build and guard mud nests.

They are restless. One group begins to fly with a running start across water, red clouds rising across the thin red-brown skin of water as if water has come undone from itself, lost something to air where clouds, too, are born of water. Other groups are in water and onshore, long-necked, the rose-colored light coming from the marvelous feathers constructed of centuries of necessity and the love that life has for its many forms and expressions.

They are birds glorious and godly, and like us, are an ancient nation.

The clouds that were out at sea have moved east and now they reach us. Thunder breaks open the sky and it begins to rain a warm afternoon rain. We turn off the engine of the boat and pole into a shadowy corridor of mangroves until we reach a sheltered pool. A faint wind creaks the trees. Above us, in the branches, a termite nest is black and heavy. It is a splendid architecture wedged in the branches of a tree, one come to over time, a creation older than human presence on the earth by millions of years. The nest is a contained intelligence, made up of lives that work together with the mind of a single organism.

The word "termite" was given by Linnaeus and originally meant "end of life." That's how young and new our oldest knowledge is, because these, too, are old participants in creation, in beginnings. They break down wood, forming rich soil in a place that would otherwise be choked.

The overhead canopy of leaves shelters us. We watch the drops meet water, returning to their larger country, becoming it, recreating it out of themselves.

This is one of the places where an underground river has broken through the shelf of limestone and risen to the surface. It is called Ojo de Agua, Eye of Water. Looking into this eye, it seems to gaze back, and in that blue gaze are tiny fish. The water is one of earth's lanterns, the same blue of glacier light and of the earth from out in space. Beneath us, a larger fish eats algae off a fallen tree, long-legged insects move about the unclosed eye of water, the spring of light.

There is a second eye and we decide to crawl through roots and dark mud to find it. Frederico, the guide, is barefoot and barefoot is the only way to move here. As we pass through the tangles and intricacies, he offers me a hand and helps me through. His hand is strong and warm, but in spite of it, my foot slips off the convoluted roots. I think it is all right; I see the blue leaves resting on the water's floor, but it is a false bottom and my leg keeps going until both legs are in to the hip, my foot still slipping down, "To China," Frederico says, as I find a limb to grasp. Here again the boundaries did not hold. What looked like bottom was merely blue leaves and algae held up by a rising current of boundless water.

And here, where the underground river ends, other beginnings are fed, other species and creations. If it were time, instead of space, scholars would call it "Zero Date," that place where, as for the Maya, the end of one world is the beginning of another, the start of this cosmos, a point of this origin. As they interpret the world, time is alive and travels in a circle. There were other creations and worlds before the one we now inhabit; the cosmos has reformed itself.

For those who know only this one universe, to think of its origins is an overwhelming task. It means to think before time, before space, all the way back to the void that existed before creation. And with people of science as with those of religion, the universe in its cosmic birth originated from small and minute beginnings. There was nothing and then life came into existence. Stephen Hawking says, "It was possible for the entire universe to appear out of nothing," the place from which all things grew into a miraculous emergence.

And astronomer-physicist Chet Raymo says, "All beginnings wear their endings like dark shadows." And maybe they do. If endings are foreshadowed by their beginnings, or are in some way the same thing, it is important that we circle around and come back to look at our human myths and stories, not only the creation accounts but stories of the end. Unlike the cyclic nature of time for the Maya, the Western tradition of beliefs within a straight line of history leads to an apocalyptic end. And stories of the end, like those of beginning, tell something about the people who created them. These are prophecies believed to be God-inspired.

In her article "Extinction," Lynda Sexson writes:

We are so accustomed to myths (sacred stories) of extinction, that we are not as practical at imagining that greater gap—continuation. . . . Would the earth or our existence on it be in such peril if we did not harbor a profound desire for extinction? *"They lie down, they cannot rise, they are extinguished, quenched like a wick,"* resonates Isaiah. The crisis of Western culture is ecological. The source of that crisis is in Western culture's own version of reality; the myth of the urge to eradicate: earth and images of earth, body and song.

Without deep reflection, we have taken on the story of endings, assumed the story of extinction, and have believed that it is the certain outcome of our presence here. This belief has brought us to a point of no return, to the near realization of that belief. And from this position, fear, bereavement, and denial keep us in the state of estrangement from our natural connection with the land.

Maybe we need new stories, new terms and conditions that are relevant to the love of land, a new narrative that would imagine another way, to learn the infinite mystery and movement at work in the world. And it would mean we become the corn people who are givers of praise and nurturers of creation, lovers of life. There must be nothing that gives us permission to let some lives pass from sight and disappear forever, no acceptance of an end, and we must remember that all places are places of creation.

Indian people cannot be the only ones who remember the agreement with the land, the sacred pact to honor and care for the life that, in turn, provides for us. We need to reach a hand back through time and a hand forward, stand at the zero point of creation to be certain that we do not create the absence of life, of any species, no matter how inconsequential they might appear to be.

Belief, it is good to remember, is built on old beliefs, overturned, in science and philosophy as well as in religion. We have held too tightly to what we think, believe. The act of belief itself is nothing. And has mighty consequences in the world around us.

It is a mistaken vision that has seen earth dead or lifeless, without intelligence. Everything tells us this. The divine is on earth, is earth itself. We need to expand our knowing, our understanding, and our vision. And in this, we need to consider the scale of human suffering, as well. The hunger and loss of humans, too, are crimes against creation.

At the beginning, there was nothing and then there was something and, except in theory, in mathematical terms, we have not been able to map it. Like the rivers, we only see where it surfaces with the same mystery of swimming turtles, early morning's new light, the limestone floor of sea that rose up to become land. Every piece fits and has its place, we learned from Darwin. And that fitting has grown infinitely more complex and intricate as our knowledge has increased. There is an integrity, a terrestrial intelligence at work. It's an intelligence far-reaching and beyond our comprehension. As Alan Lightman says: "Creation lies outside of physics."

The immeasurable *quality* of this world has depth and breadth we can't measure. Yet we know it's there, and we believe in it, the whole of it, to the outermost strands of infinity. Slowly, a piece at a time, it is revealed to us. Cosmologists now surmise there are other universes. So for us, creation is still growing, and as the story becomes larger, we become smaller. Perhaps that is why we shape belief around mystery.

And those of us who love the land are searching for a language to say it because sometimes words are the only bridge between us and all the rest, as in prayer and ceremony, as in the creation of the world.

We come from the land, the sky, from love and the body. From matter and creation. We are, life is, an equation we cannot form or shape, a mystery we can't trace in spite of our attempts to follow it back to its origin, to find out when life began, even in all our stories of when the universe came into being, how the first people emerged. It is a failure of human intelligence and compassion that doesn't wonder about, and love, the mystery of our lives and all the rest.

As Cardenal knew by those words about the want behind our wanting, we do not even have a language to speak words deep enough, strong enough to articulate what it is we truly desire. And this is just one hint of our limitations. The real alchemy of our being here is the finest of transformations and we do not know it. We are atoms that were other patterns and arrangements of form.

We do not know the secrets of stars. We do not know the true history of water. We do not know ourselves. We have forgotten that this land and every life form is a piece of God. It's a divine community, with the same forces of creation in the plants as in the people. All the lives around us are lives of gods. The sometimes long history of creation that shaped plankton, shaped horseshoe crabs. Everything is Maker; mangroves, termites, all are sources of one creation or another. Without respect and reverence for it, there is an absence of holiness, of any God.

> *All over the earth, faces of all living things are*
> *alike. Mother Earth has turned these faces out of the*
> *earth with tenderness.*
>
> LUTHER STANDING BEAR

Men talk much of matter and energy, of the struggle for existence that molds the shape of life. These things exist, it is true; but more delicate, elusive, quicker than fins in water, is that mysterious principle known as organization, which leaves all other mysteries concerned with life stale and insignificant by comparison. . . . Like some dark and passing shadow within matter, it cups out the eyes' small windows or spaces the notes of a meadowlark's song in the interior of a mottled egg. That principle—I am beginning to suspect—was there before the living in the deeps of water. . . .

If "dead" water has reared up this curious landscape . . . it must be plain even to the most devoted materialist that the matter of which it speaks contains amazing, if not dreadful powers, and may not impossibly be, as Hardy has suggested, "but one mask of many worn by the Great Face behind."

LOREN EISELEY, *NIGHT COUNTRY*

The face of the land is our face, and that of all its creatures. To see whole is to see all the parts of the puzzle, some of which have not even been found, as there are still numerous animals and plants who have not been identified. Even here at Celestún there are faces still unseen. What grows here and what grows within us is the same.

We are at the end of a way of knowing, being, and believing, and many of us are searching for a deeper insight into earth as a living organism, a return to the old beliefs, now called new. Or we are at a beginning, an old understanding of the world, newly brought to mind. It's a new and ancient spirituality and this knowing is stored in the hearts and blood of the people and in the living rock.

Later, swimming, I see a silver circle of fish, swimming in a cluster. In this place are spectacular fish, deep blue ones, green and yellow, but I see these small fish, silver and swimming in their circle, and they are fascinating. All of them turn at one time and they still hold the circle together. They avoid me, moving away, and they are still round, their circle holds. They share a mind, the way termites do, share a common mission of survival, like all the faces turned out of the earth, all part of one face, the one mask of many worn by the Great Face behind.

> The lands around my dwelling
> Are more beautiful
> From the day
> When it is given me to see
> Faces I have never seen before.
> All is more beautiful,
> All is more beautiful.
> And life is thankfulness.
> These guests of mine
> Make my house grand.
> ESKIMO SONG

What does God look like? These fish, this water, this land.

Linda Hogan is a Chickasaw poet, novelist, and essayist. She is the author of *Mean Spirit*, several books of poetry, and a collection of short fiction. She is an associate professor at the University of Colorado.

Playing God on the Lawns of the Lord

❖❖❖

There are a thousand of us and three hundred of them. We are *Homo sapiens* and they are *Bison bison bison*. We have come to this spot in the Flint Hills of northern Oklahoma to watch them released onto five thousand acres of native tallgrass prairie. The prairie and the bison evolved together over thousands of years. They have been separated for well over a century. They are coming together now, some order is being restored, and we are in a celebratory mood.

Each of us feels honored to be here. This is an invitational event, open to members of the Osage Tribe, which owns the vast oil reserves under this ground but not the ground itself; to members and friends of The Nature Conservancy, which now owns the ground; to General Norman H. Schwarzkopf, Retired, of the U.S. Army, who has just a few hours before, at dawn, received his Osage name of Tzizho Kihekah, or Eagle Chief; and to a swarm of schoolchildren, who sit restlessly on the grass waiting for the bison to appear.

No one denies that we are part of a spectacle. CBS is here. NBC is here. CNN is here. The *New York Times* is here. They have the best seats in the house, on the elevated platform near the gate through which the bison will run. Excitement fills the air, something akin to what one feels at a homecoming game, and we all have our cameras in our hands. Now we see the bison in the distance, a bounding line of darkness above the tallgrass, heading the wrong way at a dead run.

The cowboys do not ride horseback, but in pickups and on four-wheel all-terrain vehicles. They turn the bison toward the gate; the animals turn back the other way. The cowboys turn the bison again; once more, they refuse. The cowboys try a third time, and this time the great shaggy beasts come through the gate on the run, three hundred head, a diversified herd, ranging from calves born only a few months earlier, in the spring, to massive bulls a dozen years old that weigh nearly a ton.

We have grown quiet, as we've been instructed to do in order not to startle the animals, and our silence turns quickly to awe. So it's true, what we have read in books and seen in movies. The sound of bison on the run really does travel over a long distance. This is a quintessential American sound, something we must carry in our genes, bred into Native Americans by thousands of years hunting and eating and living side by side with the beasts; bred into Euro-Americans as a haunting legacy of what our ancestors annihilated in a few short years only slightly more than a century ago. This is the sound of history and valor and triumph and squalor and sorrow, and it really does sound like thunder. But thunder would be borne by the air. We would feel it in our chests, our diaphragms. This sound comes up from the ground, through the soles of our feet. The sensation increases as the bison near, and they move like a dark roiling sea, swift and high bounding, closely packed. The damp overcast of the sky brings out the full spectrum of gold in their shaggy roughs and darkens the burnt sienna of their atavistic forms. They pass and we are no longer members of a crowd of spectators. Each one of us is alone, watching as if from great distance something primal and real. And most of us are weeping.

A few days before the official release, the bison had been trucked to a holding pen on the Tallgrass Prairie Preserve so they could acclimatize before being set free. Minutes after being unloaded, several of them found old wallows, depressions in the ground hollowed out by their ancestors when they had rolled to rub off flies or shed their winter coats. No creatures had used the wallows for at least a hundred and fifty years, but the newcomers, fresh off the truck, instinctively made for the depressions and started rolling. It was as if both the animals and the land remembered.

It is easy to romanticize such a thing, and yet the bison and the prairie had evolved together since the last ice age, or for what would be, in Oklahoma, somewhere in the neighborhood of twelve thousand years. The prairie ecosystem is "disturbance dependent," driven by the interaction of climate, fire, and the grazing of vast nomadic herds. Before white settlement, it was one of the most far-reaching ecosystems in what is now America, with bison numbering between 30 and 60 million and prairie grasses—tall, short, and mixed—covering well over a million square miles.

It worked like this: as herds of bison, elk, and other grazers ate their way back and forth across the country, their hooves tilled the soil and their dung fertilized it. Parts of the prairie went ungrazed and those grasses aged and dried, becoming less palatable and more susceptible to fire as fuel loads increased. Fire occurred naturally from lightning strikes and was also set by the native tribes that used flame to help with hunting, defense, and ceremony. Millions of acres burned every year; fire could move so fast and devour so much territory that some Plains tribes called it the Red Buffalo. Fire removed old growth and returned minerals to the ground; once an area had burned, it greened up almost immediately. New, tender shoots attracted herds which were then more likely to ignore areas that hadn't been so recently burned—often those that had been grazed a year or two earlier. These areas would then accumulate plant material that would make them more susceptible to fire and the cycle would start all over again in the miraculous combination of leapfrog, synergy, and chance that we call nature.

Tall grasses covered the more humid, eastern parts of the prairie, some 200,000 square miles of Texas, Oklahoma, Arkansas, Missouri, Kansas, Nebraska, Iowa, Illinois, Minnesota, the Dakotas, and southern Manitoba. There, this constantly shifting balance of elements provided habitat for a staggering variety of plants, birds, and animals. But westward expansion eliminated the bison, suppressed fire, and plowed up the land. Today, the tallgrass prairie exists only in small and isolated patches.

The largest expanse survives in the Flint Hills of Oklahoma and Kansas where the soil is rocky and thin, and the land, for the most part, has never been plowed. Unfit for farming, the grasses have continued to be grazed, by cattle rather than bison. The cattle have been managed well, and responsible ranching has kept much tallgrass prairie in the Flint Hills in good shape. The Barnard Ranch that forms the core of The Nature Conservancy's 36,600-acre preserve is an exemplary case. According to Bob Hamilton, director of Science and Stewardship, all of the grasses and other plants in the original tallgrass prairie are present on the preserve, at least so far as range experts have been able to determine. The prairie *ecosystem*, however, that living give-and-take of nature, is essentially extinct. The suppression of fire and the somewhat different grazing habits of cattle from bison have changed the proportions of things; woody plants, once kept at bay by fire, have in some places invaded; seeds that need fire to germinate have laid dormant in the ground; broad-leafed plants that are more appealing to cows than to bison have been grazed back, and other, less tasty ones have come in. Whatever natural evolution and progression was in place before whites came has been interrupted; as naturalist John Madson has pointed out, this may look like a prairie, but without fire or bison, it can't act like one.

The hope on the preserve is to restore the functioning ecosystem. Fire has been reintroduced and about one-fifth of the bison unit goes up in flames each year in a number of small, controlled burns designed to mimic the original frequency of fires—several large burns in the dormant fall and spring, which historically would have been set most often by Native Americans; more frequent but smaller fires in the more humid midsummer lightning season when the prairie is actively growing. Burn-unit locations are designed not on the basis of a predetermined formula, but by the buildup of fuel. "The prairie," Hamilton says, "tells us what to do."

The newly introduced herd of bison will increase, over the next few years, to eighteen hundred head; the management team will cull them to simulate what predators once achieved. And, as their numbers increase, the bison will eventually range over the full preserve, in areas that are now being grazed by cattle managed to imitate the habits of bison.

There is irony that we need so much management to re-create what nature once did by herself. Once the ecosystem operated within boundaries defined by climate and geography; today, in an area populated by both Native Americans and Anglos, dotted by ranchsteads and towns, and crisscrossed by highways, it must operate within boundaries defined by man. These boundaries are too narrow to allow nature to follow its own course; untended fire, for instance, could wipe out neighboring homes or cause havoc with Osage oil reserves. When asked what the Conservancy will do about lightning strikes or accidental fires, Harvey Payne, the preserve's director, answers without hesitation: "Any fires we don't set, we will extinguish immediately." Payne comes from a family that has ranched in the Flint Hills for five generations, and he knows the importance of being a good neighbor. He also knows that the natural ecosystem had room for the law of averages to play out; here, an unplanned fire could upset the balance the preserve is trying to attain. Man has always played a part in this ecosystem; now the only hope to save it is to control it totally. Payne is pragmatic. "On this preserve," he says with sadness rather than hubris, "we play God."

Some hours after the bison were released, after the barbecue had ended, the band had left and the hundreds of guests had gone back to Pawhuska, Bartlesville, Tulsa, and points beyond, I took a long walk. The bison had settled down and were contentedly grazing; one old bull had wandered off by himself. I enjoyed my own solitude, walking in grass that towered over my head.

After the bustle of the day, the sounds of the prairie were soothing: the buzz of cicadas and crickets, the dee-dee-dee of a black-capped chickadee, the rustle of a rabbit I couldn't quite see, my own steps swishing through the grass.

John Madson once described the tallgrass prairie as the lawns of God, and it was easy to hear a prayer in the whispers around me. I topped a ridge and looked out over thousands of acres of gently rolling hills, a sea of grass turned auburn with autumn, interrupted here and there, along creeks and on rims of limestone, with dark lines of oak. The grasses seemed to stretch forever and yet there were variations—sagey green in wallows, brighter green on burns, darker greens and grays in gullies. The clouds broke for a moment and the grasses waved iridescent gold, eighteen karat; the sky closed back down and they turned smoky blue. I rubbed my eyes and everything was so rose-colored I couldn't imagine anything could ever be wrong.

The lawns of the Lord are different than the lawns we mortals have created, those greenswards of infinite sameness. When I sank down on my haunches, I could number a dozen plants within a single arm's reach, from the big bluestem that soared over eight feet tall to the low-growing violet wood sorrel. Biologists have counted over five hundred different plants on the acres around me and the names form a prayer of their own: jack-in-the-pulpit and fire-on-the-mountain, wild white indigo and soft golden aster, witchgrass and weeping love grass, switchgrass and twisted ladies' tresses, shepherd's purse and button blazing star. And that doesn't begin to name the more than three hundred birds and eighty mammals that thrive here as well. Surrounded by such riches and hidden from view, I could forget for a moment the power lines and roads and fences that delimit this prairie world. It was a pleasing fantasy, but passing. We live within such boundaries. The question is where we go from here.

"When we have something valuable in our hands, and deal with it without hindrance," wrote Pedro de Castañeda de Najera over 450 years ago, "we do not value or prize it as highly as if we understood how much we would miss it after we had lost it." A member of Coronado's expedition north from Mexico in search of the mythical Seven Cities of Cíbola, Castañeda was among the first Europeans to set foot on the western prairies, and he presaged a sadness that many of us feel today. "The longer we continue to have it the less we value it," he wrote, "but after we have lost it and miss the advantages of it, we have a great pain in the heart, and we are all the time imagining and trying to find ways and means by which to get it back again."

Sometimes we notice in time, and we can go some lengths toward repair. There would be no bison at all without the work of conservationists nearly a century ago. When a census turned up fewer than 550 of the animals, Theodore Roosevelt, ammunition king William Hornaday, and Molly Goodnight, wife of Texas cattleman Charlie Goodnight, joined others to establish the American Bison Society and preserve a small herd through the New York Zoological Society. The bison that now roam the tallgrass in Oklahoma are direct descendants of those that once lived in the Bronx. With luck, the prairie ecosystem itself will enjoy a similar salvation.

The Indian tribes that Castañeda encountered lived within the arms of God. They gave thanks for the life of each bison that fed them. Modern agriculture, on the other hand, has given us the sense that we *are* God. Developed over thousands of years, it has been the enthusiasm and genius of many of the world's peoples, and it has led us to believe that the earth should bend to our will. Science made us arrogant; now, as we begin to understand the ways in which we have damaged the systems that sustain us, it is making us humble. Perhaps, just perhaps, it can pave the path of our redemption. We have tried to tell the earth what to do; maybe now we can learn how to listen.

Teresa Jordan is the author of *Riding the White Horse Home* and *Cowgirls: Women of the American West* and writes frequently about the West and rural culture. Her fiction, nonfiction, and poetry have appeared in *Ms., Lears*, and the *Washington Post*.

WILLIAM KITTREDGE

Warner Valley, Oregon

Reimagining Warner

❖❖❖

A scab-handed wandering child who rode off on old horses named Snip and Moon, I grew up with the constant thronging presence of animals. Herds of feral hogs inhabited the swampland tule beds where the water birds nested. Those hogs would eat the downy young of the Canada geese if they could, but never caught them so far as I knew.

Sandhill cranes danced their courtship dances in our meadows. The haying and feeding and the cowherding work couldn't have been done without the help of horses. We could only live the life we had with the help of horses.

All day Sunday sometimes in the summer my family would spread blankets by Deep Creek or Twenty-mile Creek and even us kids would catch all the rainbow trout we could stand.

Warner Valley was a hidden world, tucked against an enormous reach of Great Basin sagebrush and lava-rock desert in southeastern Oregon and northern Nevada. The landlocked waters flow down from the snowy mountains to the west but don't find a way out to the sea. They accumulate and evaporate in shallow lakes named Pelican, Crump, Hart, Stone Corral, and Bluejoint.

The late 1930s, when I was a child in that valley, were like the last years of the nineteenth century. What I want to get at is our isolation. We were thirty-six gravel-road miles over the Warner Mountains from the little lumbering and rancher town of Lakeview (maybe twenty-five hundred souls). Warner Valley was not on the route to anywhere.

The way in was the way out. The deserts to the east were traced with wagon-track roads over the salt-grass playas and around rimrocks from spring to spring, water hole to water hole, but nobody ever headed in that direction with the idea of going toward the future.

To the east lay deserts and more deserts. From a ridge above our buckaroo camp beside the desert spring at South Corral, we could see the long notched snowy ridge of Steens Mountain off in the eastern distances, high country where whores from Burns went in summer to camp with the sheepherders amid aspen trees at a place called Whorehouse Meadows, where nobody but wandering men ever went, men who would never be around when you needed them. And beyond, toward Idaho, there was more desert.

By the end of the Second World War my grandfather had got control of huge acreages in Warner, and my father was making serious progress at draining the swamplands. The spring of 1946 my grandfather traded off close to two hundred or so work teams for chicken feed. He replaced those horses with a fleet of John Deere tractors. Harness rotted in the barns until the barns were torn down.

I wonder if my father and his friends understood how irrevocably they were giving up what they seemed to care about more than anything when they talked of happiness, their lives in conjunction to the animals they worked with and hunted. I wonder why they acted like they didn't care.

Maybe they thought the animals were immortal. I recall those great teams of workhorses running the hayfields in summer before daybreak, their hooves echoing on the sod as we herded them toward the willow corral at some haycamp, the morning mists and how the boy I was knew at least enough to know he loved them and that this love was enough reason to revere everything in sight for another morning.

Those massive horses were like mirrors in which I could see my emotions reflected. If they loved this world, and they seemed to, with such satisfaction, on those mornings when our breaths fogged before us, so did I.

Soon after World War II electricity from Bonneville Power came to Warner, and telephones that sort of worked. The road over the mountains and down along Deep Creek was paved. Our work in the fields had in so many ways gone mechanical. Eventually we had television. Our isolation was dissolving.

About the time I watched the first Beatles telecast in the early 1960s, Chamber of Commerce gentlemen in Winnemucca got together with like-minded gentlemen from Lakeview, and decided it made great economic sense to punch a highway across the deserts between those two little cities. Think of the tourists.

The two-lane asphalt ran north from Winnemucca to Denio, then turned west to cross the million or so acres of rangeland we leased from the Bureau of Land Management, or BLM (we saw those acreages as ours, like we owned them: in those days we virtually did), over the escarpment called the Dougherty Slide, across Guano Valley and down Greaser Canyon, and directly through our meadowlands in Warner Valley.

I recall going out to watch the highway-building as it proceeded, the self-important recklessness of those men at their work, the roaring of the D-8 Caterpillars and the clouds of dust rising behind the huge careening of the self-propelled scrapers, and being excited, sort of full up with pride because the great world was at last coming to us in Warner Valley. Not that it ever did. The flow of tourism across those deserts never amounted to much. But maybe it will, one of these days.

Enormous changes were sweeping the world. We didn't want to encounter hippies or free love or revolutionaries on the streets in Lakeview. Or so we said. But like anybody, we yearned to be in on the action.

We were delighted, one Fourth of July, to hear that the Hell's

Angels motorcycle gang from Oakland had headed across the deserts north to Winnemucca on their way to a weekend of kicking ass in Lakeview, and that they had been turned back by a single deputy sheriff.

There had been the long string of lowriders coming on the two-lane blacktop across one of the great desert swales, and the deputy, all by himself, standing there by his Chevrolet. The deputy, a slight, balding man, had flagged down the leaders and they'd had a talk. "Nothing I can do about it," the deputy said, "but they're sighting in their deer rifles. These boys, they just mean to sit back there three hundred yards and just shoot you off them motorcycles. They won't apologize or anything. You fellows are way too far out in the country."

According to legend, the leaders of the Hell's Angels decided the deputy was right: they knew they were way too far out in the country, and they turned back. I never talked to anybody who knew if that story was true, but we loved it.

It was a story that told us we were not incapable of defending ourselves, or powerless in a nation we understood to be going on without us. We never doubted some of our southeastern Oregon boys would have shot those Hell's Angels off their bikes. Some places were still big and open enough to be safe.

During the great flood in December of 1964, when the Winnemucca-to-the-Sea highway acted like a dam across the valley, backing up water over four or five thousand acres, my brother Pat walked a D-7 out along the asphalt and cut the highway three or four times, deep cuts so the floodwaters could pour through and drain away north. What he liked best, Pat said, was socking that bulldozer blade down and ripping up that asphalt with the yellow lines painted on it. We were still our own people.

But even as huge and open to anything as southeastern Oregon may have seemed in those old days, it was also inhabited by spooks. In autumn of the same year the Winnemucca-to-the-Sea highway came across our meadowlands, I had our heavy equipment, our Carry-All scrapers and D-7 Caterpillars, at work on a great diversion canal we were cutting through three hundred yards of sage-covered sandhills at the south end of Warner, rerouting Twenty-mile Creek.

Soon we were turning up bone—human bones, lots of them. I recall a clear October afternoon and all those white bones scattered in the gravel, and my catskinners standing there beside their great idling machines, perplexed and unwilling to continue. Ah, hell, never mind, I said. Crank 'em up.

There was nothing to do but keep rolling. Maybe bones from an ancient Indian burial ground were sacred, but so was our work, more so, as I saw it. My catskinners threatened to quit. I told them I'd give them a ride to town, where I'd find plenty of men who would welcome the work. My catskinners didn't quit. I ducked my head so I couldn't see, and drove away.

If you are going to bake a cake, you must break some eggs. That was a theory we knew about. We thought we were doing God's work. We were cultivating, creating order, and what we liked to think of as a version of Paradise.

What a pleasure that work was, like art, always there, always in need of improving, doing. It's reassuring, so long as the work is not boring, to wake up and find your tools are still in the tunnel. You can lose a life in the work. People do. Oftentimes they are taken to be the best people, the real workers.

But we left, we quit, in a run of family trouble. I have been gone from farming and Warner for twenty-five years. People ask if I don't feel a great sense of loss, cut off from the valley and methods of my childhood. The answer is no.

Nothing much looks to have changed when I go back. The rimrock above the west side of the valley lies as black against the sunset light as it did when I was a child. The topography of my dreams, I like to think, is still intact.

But that's nonsense. We did great damage to the valley as we pursued our sweet impulse to create an agribusiness paradise. The rich peat ground began to go saline, the top layer just blew away. We drilled chemical fertilizers along with our barley seed, and sprayed with 24D Ethyl and Parathion (which killed even the songbirds). Where did the water birds go?

But the water birds can be thought of as part of the *charismatic megafauna.* Everybody worries about the water birds. Forms of life we didn't even know about were equally threatened.

Catostomus warnerensis, the Warner sucker, is endangered. So are eight other fish species in the region, seven plant species, and seven plant communities such as *Poptri/corsto-salix,* a riparian plant community centered on black cottonwood, red osier dogwood, and willow.

As a child I loved to duck down and wander animal trails through dense brush by the creeksides, where ring-necked Manchurian pheasants and egg-eating raccoons and stalking lynx cats traveled. I wonder about colonies of red osier dogwood and black cottonwood. I was maybe often among them, curled in the dry grass and sleeping in the sun as I shared in their defenselessness and didn't know it.

The way we built canals in our efforts to contain the wildness of the valley and regulate the ways of water to our own uses must have been close to absolutely destructive to the Warner sucker, a creature we would not have valued at all, slippery and useless, thus valueless. It's likely I sent my gang of four D-7 Caterpillar bulldozers to clean out the brush along stretches of creekside thick with red osier dogwood and black cottonwood.

Let in some light, let the grass grow, feed for the livestock, that was the theory. Maybe we didn't abandon those creatures in that valley, maybe we mostly destroyed them before we left. We did enormous damage to that valley in the thirty-some years that we were there. Countrysides like the Dordogne and Umbria and Tuscany, which have been farmed thousands of years, look to be less damaged. But maybe that's because the serious kill-off took place so long ago.

I love Warner as a child loves his homeland, and some sense of responsibility for what's there stays with me. Or maybe I'm just trying to feel good about myself.

But that's what we all want to do, isn't it? It's my theory that everyone yearns, as we did in Warner, plowing those swamps, with all that bulldozing, to make a positive effect in the world. But how?

How to keep from doing harm? Sometimes that seems to be the only question. But we have to act. To do so responsibly we must first examine our desires. What do we really want?

A few years ago I went to Warner with a couple of filmmakers from NBC. Some footage ran on the "Today" show. Sitting in an antique GMC pickup truck alongside a great reef of chemically contaminated cowshit which had been piled up outside the feedlot pens where our fattening cattle had existed like creatures in a machine, I found it in myself to say the valley should be given back to the birds, and turned into a wildlife refuge.

It was a way of saying good-bye. I was saying the biological health of the valley was more important to me than the well-being of the community of ranchers who lived there. I had gone to grade school with some of them. It was an act people living in Warner mostly understood as betrayal.

Some eggs were broken, but I had at last gotten myself to say what I believed. Around 1990, when I heard that our ranch in Warner, along with two others out in the deserts to the east, were for sale, and that The Nature Conservancy was interested, I was surprised by the degree to which I was moved and excited.

A huge expanse of territory, adjacent to and including our ranch, would be affected. The total area comprised 1,111,587 deeded and permitted acres in an intricate run of private, BLM, and state lands. This included:

(1) the wetlands we farmed in south Warner (more than 20,000 irrigated acres belonging to the MC Ranch and close to 10,000 acres of floodplain in the valley leased from the state of Oregon—which could possibly be drained and farmed);

(2) the wetlands of the Malheur National Wildlife Refuge (some 380,000 ducks, 19,000 geese, and 6,000 lesser sandhill cranes migrate through Warner and the Malheur);

(3) Catlow Valley with its wetlands;

(4)   Guano Valley;

(5)   the Beatty Buttes;

(6)   Hart Mountain Wildlife Refuge (where a new management plan banning grazing for the next fifteen years has just been announced);

(7)   a 78,000-acre grazing allotment held by the MC Ranch on the Sheldon National Wildlife Refuge in northern Nevada;

(8)   alpine habitats on Steens Mountain, the largest fault-block mountain in North America, with alpine aspen groves and great glacial cirques 3,000 feet deep and 20 miles in length (an area often mentioned as a possible national park);

(9)   the alkaline playas, sand dunes, and desert saltbrush expanses of the Alvord Desert.

Maybe, I thought, this would be a second chance at paradise in my true heartland, an actual shot at reimagining desire.

What did I really want? A process, I think, everybody involved —ranchers and townspeople, conservationists—all taking part in that reimagining. I wanted them to each try defining the so-called land of their heart's desiring, the way they would have things if they were running the world. I wanted them to compare their versions of paradise, and notice again the ways we all want so many of the same things—like companionship in a community of people we respect and meaningful work.

Then I wanted them to get started on the painstaking work of developing a practical plan for making their visions of the right life come actual, a plan for using, restoring, and preserving the world in which I grew up. I liked to imagine some of the pumps and dikes and headgates would be torn out in Warner, and that some of the swamps would go back to tules. That's part of my idea of progress —re-create habitat for the water birds, and the tiny, less charismatic creatures. But nothing like that has happened.

Although they still maintain a strong presence in the high desert country of southeastern Oregon (a full-time staff person is assigned to the region, and they are negotiating on important parcels in Warner), The Nature Conservancy did not end up buying the MC Ranch, our old property in Warner Valley. Instead, the ranch was stripped of livestock and machinery, and sold to what I understand to be a consortium of local ranchers. I have no idea of their plans—they don't confide in me, the turncoat.

But the world is inevitably coming to Warner Valley. The BLM recently purchased several thousands of acres of prime hayland in north Warner, and included it in a special management unit in which no grazing is allowed. The idea of the federal government buying land and taking it out of production (out of the tax base) was unthinkable when I lived in Warner.

Other unthinkable ideas are blowing in the wind. In May 1991, a consortium of environmental groups led by the Oregon Natural Resources Council announced their plan for southeastern Oregon. It included the national park on Steens Mountain; three new national monuments; forty-seven wilderness areas totaling more than 5 million acres; expanding the Hart Mountain Refuge to include the wetlands in Warner Valley; a new national wildlife refuge at Lake Abert; wild and scenic river status for fifty-four streams totaling 835 miles, mostly creeks in the glacial cirques in the Steens and Pueblo mountains; and phasing out, over a ten-year period, all livestock grazing on federal lands designated as national park, preserve, wildlife refuge, wilderness, or wild and scenic river (about 5.9 million acres).

There's no use sighting in the scopes on deer rifles, not anymore. This invasion will not be frightened away. There is not a thing for the people in my old homeland to do but work out some accommodation with the thronging, invading world.

So many of our people, in the old days of the American West, came seeking a fold in time and actuality, a hideaway place where they and generations after them could be at home. Think of *familia*, place and hearth and home fire, the fishing creek where it falls out of the mountains, into the valley, and the Lombardy poplar beside the white house, and the orchard where the children ran in deep sweet clover under the blossoming apple trees. But that's my paradise, not yours.

We have taken the West for about all it has to give. We have lived like children, taking and taking for generations, and now that childhood is over.

It's time to give something back to the natural systems of order which have supported us, some care and tenderness, which is the most operative notion I think—tenderness. Our isolations are gone, in the West and everywhere. We need to give some time to the arts of cherishing the things we adore, before they simply vanish. Maybe it will be like learning a skill: how to live in paradise.

William Kittredge teaches creative writing at the University of Montana, and is the author of the books *We Are Not in This Together*, *Owning It All*, and *Hole in the Sky*.

JAMES WELCH

Northern Continental Divide, Montana

The Far North People

❖❖❖

There is a story told by the Blackfeet which is true. It concerns origins. According to the story, Old Man came from the south and began to make things. He made the mountains, rivers, prairies, timber, and brush. He made grass and roots and berries. Then he put animals on the ground—the bighorn, the antelope, the buffalo, the wolf, and all the other four-leggeds. He made the flyer for the air and the swimmer for the waters.

Then one day he looked out over his creations and determined that he needed some two-leggeds. So he took a lump of clay from a riverbank and formed it into two shapes—a woman and a child. He covered up the lumps and went away. On the fourth day he came back and took the brush away and told the two shapes to rise and walk, and they did so. He told them his name was Napi, Old Man.

According to the story, the woman said, "How is it? Will we always live, will there be no end to it?" And Napi acknowledged that he hadn't thought of that. So he picked up a buffalo chip and he told the woman, "I will take this buffalo chip and throw it into the river. If it floats, when the people die, in four days they will become alive again; they will die for only four days. But if it sinks, there will be an

end to them." So saying, he flung the buffalo chip into the river—
and it floated. But the woman picked up a stone and said, "No, I
will throw this stone in the river; if it floats we will always live; if it
sinks people must die, that they may always be sorry for each other."
The woman threw the stone into the river and it disappeared.
"There," said Napi, "you have chosen. There will be an end to them."

People come and people go, but the country that Napi created
remains nearly the same as it was in the beginning. Napi retired into
the Backbone of the World, the Rocky Mountains, just about where
Glacier National Park is today.

This is the country I am from. I was born on the Blackfeet reservation and am a member of that tribe. My great-grandmother, Red
Paint Woman, lived in the time when there were still herds of buffalo
around. I never met her but she told my father stories when he was
a kid that he passed on to me. Most of the stories were happy ones
of a happier time—the summers she picked berries along the Two
Medicine River; the time her husband brought back many Crow
horses; the day she had her first child, my grandmother. But one of
these stories tells of the conflict that occurred when the whites began
to come into this country in great numbers, pushing the Blackfeet
from the plains onto the eastern edge of the mountains. The story
tells of a massacre in which 173 Blackfeet men, women, and children
were murdered by United States soldiers. It happened on January 23,
1870, at dawn, on the Marias River. The soldiers were sent to punish
the Blackfeet for treaty violations committed by young men who
wanted still to be warriors. They raided settlements, ranches, even
ranging down to the gold fields around Virginia City. White people
were killed, horses and mules were stolen, gold dust was taken.

On January 1, 1870, a General Sully met with tribal chiefs and
told them that the raids must stop, all the stolen items must be returned, and the guilty parties turned over to the military. He read
them a list of demands. But he apparently did not know that chiefs
have little control over young men who are out to gain honor, make
a name for themselves, and acquire wealth. Chiefs led their people
through wisdom, charisma, and paternalism. But they could not
influence those who had agendas counter to the tribal good. And so,
even as they agreed to Sully's demands, these chiefs knew that it

would be impossible to satisfy them. One of the chiefs was a man named Heavy Runner, who had earned a reputation as being agreeable to the whites, even to the point of appeasing them to the detriment of the tribe. My great-grandmother was a member of his band.

The band that the soldiers wanted to punish was the Many Chiefs, led by Mountain Chief. The young man most hostile to the whites, Owl Child, was a member of that band. Owl Child led many expeditions against the whites, mostly the people who had settled on Blackfeet land in violation of several treaties; in fact the Blackfeet territory had been reduced at least four times because of these illegal settlements. Owl Child considered the whites hostiles on his land and his own chiefs traitors.

The soldiers, led by Colonel Eugene Baker, left Fort Shaw on the Sun River and rode north into the teeth of a Montana winter that was especially cruel. The temperature was nearly 30 degrees below zero. The men rode for four days until they found themselves in the darkness before dawn on a ridge, looking down at the sleeping camp of Heavy Runner on the Marias River. Heavy Runner, in the meeting with General Sully, had obtained a piece of paper that said that he was a friend of the whites. It is said that when the shooting started, the old chief ran out of his lodge, waving the paper. He was among the first to fall. Most of the rest were killed in their lodges, many while they slept. The soldiers fired thousands of rounds of ammunition, turning the dawn air blue with smoke. Then they went into camp, cut the lodge bindings, and burned the lodges with most of the dead people still inside them.

My great-grandmother was one of a small group of women and children who managed to slip away toward the river, where they made their way upstream under cover of cutbanks. Although she was little more than a child herself, she attracted the attention of one of the marksmen on the ridgetop. She was shot through the leg, but with the aid of her friends, she got away. My father says she walked with a limp all her life. I never met her but I wish I had. She refused to speak English, even though she lived to see her culture almost destroyed by the conquering whites who forbade the Blackfeet to speak their own language and to practice the old ceremonies.

The Northern Continental Divide ecosystem is, or was, Blackfeet country. Blackfeet territory extended from the Rocky Mountains to the Bears Paw Mountains, from the northern reaches of Canada almost to the Yellowstone country in the south of Montana. Their only real rivals were the Crows and Shoshones to the south, and the Assiniboines and Gros Ventres to the east. The Salish Indians lived on the other side of the mountains to the west.

The Blackfeet were a much-feared tribe. They warred constantly with their neighbors. Captain Meriwether Lewis (of Lewis and Clark fame) said the Blackfeet were the only tribe they used arms against. Even the Sioux were more friendly.

The Blackfeet were also greatly admired. Artist and author George Catlin, in 1832, wrote: "In my travels I have more than realised my former predictions that those [plains] Indians, who could be found almost entirely in a state of nature, with the least knowledge of civilised society, would be found the most cleanly in their persons, elegant in their dress and manners, and enjoying life to the greatest perfection. Of such tribes perhaps the Crows and Blackfeet stand first; and no one would be able to appreciate the richness and elegance with which some of these people dress without seeing them in their own country."

Ironically, one of the most impressive features of this Blackfeet country is a man-made intrusion—the Old North Trail. This trail runs along the eastern slope of the Rocky Mountains from Canada down to Mexico. It is said that this trail dates back to the time that the original people crossed the land bridge from Asia to Alaska and traveled south to warmer climates. It dates back to the last ice age. And it was used constantly until recent times, say the mid-nineteenth century. Indians traded along this route. In some parts of Montana, between Augusta and Browning, the trail is still visible. That is how fragile the land along the Rocky Mountain Front is.

To give an idea of how extensive the travel and trade was in the old days, I will relate an incident that occurred almost sixty years ago. A Métis family who lived along the Old North Trail just outside the canyon of the South Fork of the Teton, near the Circle 8 Ranch, found a gold coin on their property. On the advice of the noted journalist and historian, Joseph Kinsey Howard, they had the coin sent to the Smithsonian Museum. Several weeks later, the coin came back with a note of verification: it dated back to the time of the Roman Emperor Hadrian, who reigned from A.D. 117 to 138. It was conjectured that perhaps a Spanish explorer in Mexico had once possessed it, lost it somehow, and it made its way through trading all the way to Montana. The Métis, a man named Bruno, who found it, kept it as his lucky coin. Perhaps the Spaniard had done the same. The coin had been fourteen hundred years old when it arrived on this continent—not a common currency.

In spite of the Old North Trail, the land, from a distance, looks relatively intact. The high mountains are protected by the Bob Marshall Wilderness, the Scapegoat Wilderness, and Glacier National Park. The plains that lead out to the east of the foothills show signs of traditional activity—ranching and farming. Most of the ranches have been passed on for generations, since the first settlers took the land from the Indians. Many of them are quite large and prosperous. Many of the farms are thriving, too, but many are not. One can see the remains of a very large wheat farm near the foothills west of Choteau. The rolling strips of overturned earth and stubble remind one of abandoned homesteads, with their fields and barbed wire and buildings. But this attempt at farming occurred not long ago. It is clear that the wheat fields failed because the soil near the foothills will not nourish anything but native grasses. It is also sadly clear that those strips will still be visible a hundred years from now.

The ranchers along the Front are an independent lot who feel it is their God-given right to dominate their particular landscapes. This has led to problems with grizzly bears and Fish and Game people and environmentalists. Grizzlies like to come down out of the mountains once in a while for a change in their diet, which normally consists of berries, shoots, and insects. Unfortunately, they sometimes head for the nearest cattle herd, where they might take a calf or a sick cow, but more often the carcass of an animal which has died and which the rancher has not disposed of. Bears find dead animals particularly tasty. At any rate, ranchers do not like grizzlies prowling around their herds. They want to kill them. In fact, most ranchers consider the grizzly the lowest form of life on the landscape, evil incarnate, and would be very happy if this endangered species were removed from the list permanently. They talk about extinction.

The late A. B. Guthrie, Jr., the distinguished author of *The Big Sky*, who lived on the Front under Ear Mountain, was an outspoken advocate of the grizzly bear. He believed the grizzly had a God-given right to roam freely on the plains as well as in the mountains. He liked to remind folks that, in fact, it was the white settlers who chased the grizzly off the plains in the first place. It goes without saying that Guthrie's views were not popular with his ranching neighbors.

There is one spot on the plains where the grizzly is most welcome. This is the Pine Butte Swamp Preserve, a stunningly unique mini-ecosystem five or six miles out from the Front. The preserve is truly a fen, surrounded by the rolling dry hills of that part of Montana. There are several types of vegetation here, from water plants to reeds, grasses, berry bushes, willows, and evergreen and deciduous trees. The preserve contains waterfowl, songbirds, raptors, grouse, fish, amphibians, beaver, muskrat, the rare otter, deer, badgers—and the grizzly bear. The grizzlies come down from the mountains in the fall and spring to gorge themselves on food not found in the higher elevations. They feel safe here and nearly everything is good to eat. To a grizzly bear, whose range can be one hundred square miles, Pine Butte is the last best place.

Of course, there are threats to the Rocky Mountain Front. Such remote country invites certain types of activities designed to destroy its semi-pristine beauty. One of these threats comes from the oil and gas industry. The eastern slope of the Rockies is pocked by seismic test holes, drilled and blasted into the earth to see if there is oil or gas potential. These holes occur in the most unlikely places. Once a couple of friends and I were walking over a ridgetop above where the North and South Fork of the Teton meet. Since all three of us were poets, we were talking about poetry—I think we were discussing Walt Whitman's *Leaves of Grass*—when I happened to look down and see a seismic hole and managed to jerk my friend away just before a disastrous next step. We kept our eyes fixed on the ground in front of us, rather than on the stunning mountain peaks, after that. I have seen fires in the night sky above the North Fork where a drilling company was burning off gas. I have heard the thundering noise of large helicopters as they transport drilling equipment into these otherwise inaccessible sites.

But perhaps the biggest current threat to the Front is occurring right now in the Badger–Two Medicine area of Blackfeet country. An oil company, backed up by the oil and gas industry and a government agency, insists it has the right to drill there. Although they have already made an incursion into the area, they have been stopped from drilling by the Blackfeet tribe and allied environmental groups. The Badger–Two Medicine is sacred country to the Blackfeet. Many young warriors in the past went into this area to pursue their vision quests. Many long-ago people are buried there. Ceremonies are still performed there. And this is the country into which Napi disappeared after he made all things. He still lives there.

In the beginning of this proposed development, the tribe was divided as to where it stood. Some of the more progressive members said the tribe needed the money that the oil company would pay for permission to drill. Many of the traditionalists said that if the drilling were allowed it would destroy the sanctity of the area. Both sides were right—the tribe desperately needs the money but drilling will defile an important sacred site. Now it appears that the traditionalists have carried the day. The tribe is on record as opposing the drilling. But the matter is still far from resolved and will likely end up in the courts.

Another threat to the Northern Divide country comes from land developers and agents who are selling traditional ranch and farm lands for subdivisions. Movie stars and just plain rich people are buying up large ranches in the most beautiful parts of Montana for their personal enjoyment. The Flathead Valley, the Bitterroot Valley, the Gallatin Valley, the Paradise Valley, and the Boulder River Valley are becoming playgrounds for the rich and famous. This does not sit well with local folks, who see their property taxes soaring, who find themselves locked out of traditional hunting and fishing areas, who see these wealthy out-of-staters as a threat to their way of life. Letters-to-the-editor columns in newspapers across the state are filled with letters which begin with "I'm a Native Montanan" and go on to tell these interlopers to go back to California or wherever they came from. Often the language just barely passes the standards of decency. Not many of the letters acknowledge that these "natives" descended from immigrants who came here and took the land from the natives. Most of the letters are stupid. But it is true that the outrage is real, and so is the threat. Land development and sales will have to have more stringent controls. Good luck to the legislators.

One could go on about the problems confronting the Northern Continental Divide. The struggle between economic interests and environmental interests must be resolved equitably. The timber industry is reeling, farming and ranching not much better off. These people who make a living off the land feel that too much land is being locked up by environmentalists. My own family farmed and ranched in Montana. I sympathize with those who would like to maintain this way of life. On the other hand, this is a new day. People who are concerned about the environment will not permit old practices that led to clear-cuts and silting up of spawning streams, to fragile land broken out by farmers and abandoned, to large herds of cattle grazing down mountain sides and fouling creeks. Recreationists, on the other hand, oppose any new wilderness area designations. They want to drive their four-wheelers and snowmobiles anywhere they want. These are the same native Montanans who say the grizzly bear is an evil presence and should be exterminated.

With all of the foregoing said, the northern Rockies and the land surrounding them remain uncommonly attractive. This country is becoming something of a mythical place to those easterners who live in industrial cities, to those Californians who drive the freeways all day, to those Americans who dream of a country of fishing and hiking, clean air and quiet, stunning mountains and valleys, and rivers that always run clear. Those of us who live here know the reality of it—brutal winters, congestion and smog in our mountain valley towns, rivers and creeks seemingly elbow to elbow with Orvis-fitted anglers. Some of us gripe about the way things have changed in the past ten or fifteen years. But when we pass through the airports of Chicago, New York, Atlanta, and Los Angeles on our way home, we become sickeningly happy. Like the Blackfeet, and yes, the

native Montanans, we know that somewhere along the line we were
blessed.

James Welch is the author of *The Indian Lawyer*, *Fools Crow*, and other
novels. A Native American, he has received an American Book Award
and the *Los Angeles Times* Book Prize.

Gray Ranch, New Mexico

The Beginner's Mind

❖❖❖

At the onset it has occurred to me as a novelist and poet that I could not write a legitimate natural history essay at gunpoint. As indicated earlier in my life by my grades in high school or college in the life sciences and geology, my mind was either elsewhere or nowhere in particular. I was apt at metaphor but a zygote resembled a question mark without a question. After setting a new record for a low grade in the one-hundred-rock identification test in the Natural Sciences Department at Michigan State University the professor gazed at me with the intense curiosity owned by the man who discovered the duckbill platypus. At the time, nineteen, my mind had been diverted by Rimbaud and Dostoyevsky, Mozart and Stravinsky, and if Rilke had said in his "Letters to a Young Poet" to study invertebrate zoology I would have done so, only he never broached the subject.

Curiously, I'm still trying. There's an old wood Burgundy carton in my four-wheel drive that contains a dozen or so natural history guidebooks that I use frequently. Once in the sandhills of Nebraska I sat on a knoll on a June afternoon and identified all the weeds and grasses around me using Van Bruggen's *Wildflowers, Grasses and Other Plants of the Northern Plains and Black Hills*. I also fell asleep and saw

Crazy Horse, who helped me dream up the heroine for my then unwritten novel, *Dalva*. On waking, it dawned on me as it had dozens of times before that everything goes together or we're in real trouble. Mozart and the loon belong to the same nature, as does the mind of Lorca and the gray hawk I'm lucky to have nesting near our adobe in Patagonia, Arizona. The coyote's voice and the petroglyph of the lizard king near Baboquivari marry in a purer voice than any of our current machineries of joy. The elf owls that flocked into the black oak above our campfire on the Gray Ranch made me feel more at home on earth than my farmhouse of twenty-five years. That many elf owls in one tree lifts your skull so you may see them with another eye that more closely resembles their own. William Blake's line is appropriate, "How do we know but that every bird that cuts the airy way is an immense world of delight closed to our senses five?" This is the opposite of the anthropomorphism so properly scorned in literary types of scientists. I simply agree with the visionary notion of Neil Claremon that reality is the aggregate of the perceptions of all creatures.

But back to the not-so-ordinary earth and the Gray Ranch. On my first trip there a few years ago I realized it takes a golden eagle or a bush pilot to make a quick read of five hundred square miles. I was thrown directly back into the dozens of Zane Grey novels I had read in my youth, which was not a bad place to be considering the direction of current events toward chaos and fungoid tribalism. There was an urge to yodel "purple mountain's majesty," or reconcoct that Rousseauian fantasy that far up some distant arroyo in the Animas, now shrouded in January shadows, all the local creatures were drinking milk from the same golden bowl. It was, and is, that kind of place. Of course I wondered why Dad didn't own this rather than the three-acre Michigan swamp which, nonetheless, was good birding. My science aversion did not include the birds that were introduced in the third grade by Audubon cards which had a specific leg up on baseball cards.

The fact is the Gray Ranch is breathtaking, that is, you forget to breathe, the vision before when you come over the back road from Douglas is vertiginous, surreal, the vast expanse of valley before you not quite convincingly real. Frankly, the only thing that could improve on it would be an Apache village, but that one has been kissed permanently good-bye. I have never quite understood why much of our Bureau of Land Management and Forest Service land could not be returned to its original owners. There is firm evidence that they would do a better job of managing it.

From painful experience I mentally rattled off a number of cautionary notes. There is a wonderful quote in Huanchu Daoren's reflections on the Tao, *Back to Beginnings*. "Mountain forests are beautiful places, but once you become attached to them, they become cities." What is meant by *attached* here is a desperate clinging, an obsessiveness that finally blinds you to the wilderness before you, at which point you may as well be in Times Square or touring the Pentagon. More importantly, in this state of mind you cannot competently defend the wilderness you presume to love.

On the first trip my camping partner, Doug Peacock of grizzly bear renown, was intent on sleeping out in the really high lonesome despite the warnings at ranch headquarters that it was going to be "mighty cool" in the high country. This turned out to be a cowboy euphemism for a temperature of 15 degrees. The tip-off about the cold front had actually come the day before when we were looking for water birds out on the Wilcox playa in a snowstorm. The bedrooms at ranch headquarters looked rather attractive and so did the idea of central heating, but then I had just come down from northern Michigan where it is truly frigid in January and it was unseemly for me to hedge. That night when the temperature plummeted it occurred to me I hadn't slept outside in Michigan during the winter since I won my Polar Bear merit badge in the boy scouts, after which I was booted out as a malcontent.

Peacock, however, is the ultimate camper, in some years spending over half his nights under the stars. We simply used two sleeping bags apiece, one stuffed in another, and wore stocking caps. I had been having the most intense of Hollywood screenplay problems but they drifted away in the face of stars that glittered barely above the treetops and sycamores so burnished by the moonglow they kept rearranging themselves as if their roots were underground legs. Our only real problem was the olive oil congealed around the edges of the frying pan and the Bordeaux was overchilled in our gloved hands. There was a mighty chorus from a nearby bobcat who was treating the new odors of garlic and Italian sausage with noisy surprise. The most recurrent thought during those two days was wishing for a seven-year vacation so I could adequately walk out the ranch, slowly identifying everything that wasn't underground. I might even memorize the clouds.

Two years later on the eve of our return there is a specific freight of confusion about the Gray Ranch. In the interim I had been assured in both Montana and Michigan that the ranch had been sold to Ted Turner. Since I'm quite a fibber myself, what with being a novelist, I tend to believe other fibbers whole cloth. I fully understood that The Nature Conservancy might not wish to keep that much capital in one basket, the mildest of understatements, and though Turner is indeed an environmentalist, I feared his interest in buffalo that do not belong in the area.

Another, rather astounding, rumor arose that Drum Hadley was buying the ranch through his Animas Foundation, with the Conservancy retaining large easements in the higher altitudes. As an option to sitting around in a dither, I checked the rumor out and found it was true. "Astounding" is not too strong a word, as I knew of Hadley only through his poetry which had been recommended to me by Charles Olson one sunny spring afternoon in Gloucester, Massachusetts, long ago, and later by Gary Snyder. In the religious world this would be similar to being lauded by Pope John XXIII and Gandhi. I had always thought of Hadley as a Black Mountain populist who had holed up on a ranch in a canyon near Douglas, Arizona, and certainly hadn't guessed that he could muster the wherewithal to buy a ranch of this awesome proportion.

I recalled a quote from Hadley's mentor, Olson, in his book on Melville, *Call Me Ishmael*, "I take space to be the central fact to man born in America, from Folsom cave to now." This, whether illusion or reality, is a whopper of a statement, but it was more true when Olson wrote the book forty years ago, and certainly purer truth in Melville's time.

Why, then, should I be such an ardent claustrophobe, despite the fact that I spend nine months of the year in Michigan's Upper Peninsula and Patagonia, Arizona, the coenvirons of bear, mountain lion, all sorts of creatures, and in each place, the stray wolf still passes by? It wasn't just the hearing of the dark wings of the madness of overpopulation in the future. More real is the prospect that developers buy wild regions and dice them into parcels for us who love the outdoors and have the cash to buy them. The Forbes ranch in northern New Mexico was a dire portent, and one could, properly informed, add a thousand other places this was happening. There is a nearly spiritual truth in Edward Abbey's comment, "It's not the beer cans I mind, it's the roads." With Hadley's purchase and the Conservancy's easements, this immense ranch would remain intact, and I could stop mentally turning it into a city.

Late on an April afternoon we set up camp with Peacock in a hurry to take a walk for another look at some petroglyphs he had noted two years before. What he thinks of as a stroll is an aerobic nightmare for the less hardy. Ten miles is not improbable for this geezer in the Michigan woods, but in the rumpled West I go my own slower way when camping with my partner who is thought by many to be the world's largest billy goat. I also fall with some frequency, my feet refusing to acknowledge a terrain where you have to watch where your feet are stepping. The tendinitis in my bursae was throbbing, the result of doing the splits in a fifty-yard skid down an arroyo near Patagonia, so I made my way slowly up a creek bed that owned an aura of mystery. The notion arose that I was a flatlander down to my very zygotes, my feet requiring moss, ferns, deadfalls, tamarack bogs, and osier-choked gullies.

❖ ❖ ❖

Not so long ago, only a few minutes in geologic time, we attacked the wilds with implements of greed and domination. Now, or so it appears, we are having run at it with sporting equipment, none of it as friendly to the earth as the human foot or the hooves of horses. Walking makes the world its own size and a scant hour in a forty-acre woodlot is liable to dissipate the worst case of claustrophobia. The same hour in the high country of the Gray Ranch and you're ready to levitate. I remind myself again not to burden the air with requests from the wild but to see what I can see with the attentiveness of the creature world. I scout the creek canyon just far enough to see an enormous opening which I'll save for the morning.

We had our customary first-night camping dinner of thick rare Delmonicos wrapped in tortillas, accompanied by Bordeaux, which increases goodwill as proven by the French, those kindly souls. It was that first night that the curious elf owls gathered in the black oak branches above us. Doug had only seen them grouped this way once before down in the remotest Pinacates. Such splendor is humbling and properly so. It was the equivalent of wandering the Upper Peninsula for twenty years hoping to see a wolf and then seeing one a scant hundred yards from my cabin. When the owls left there were the nightjars, a song closet to the loon for the resonance of the memories it evokes. We were camped in the same place that we had been the cold night two years before, but now the dark was soft and dulcet and I watched the entire arc of the moon until it burst against Animas Peak, the last golden light shedding down the talus.

At dawn, for eccentric reasons, I scoured my guidebooks for something odd to look for on my walk, deciding on the rare night-blooming cereus. My hip pain was a torment, so every hundred yards or so I'd go blank and lay down like a tired deer. There was a wan hope to see the enormous male mountain lion that was said to live in the area. He kept himself as hidden as the night-blooming cereus though at one point I had the feeling I was being observed. Since I'm a somewhat goofy poet, I do not feel obligated like the scientist to regard these intuitions as nonsense. It is easy to forget that we are, above all else, mammals. An anthropology text has curled the hair of many an aesthete.

I mostly crawled up a steep hill that would have been regarded as Michigan's only mountain. It was rocky but in the crevices wild flowers bloomed and far above was a bona fide golden eagle. Two years before we had seen several at once in the area called the "flats," which is a single seventy-square-mile pasture, sort of an Ur-pasture still in the condition that pioneers had found it, along with the Apache. I'm not cattle shy as most amateur environmentalists, but my father was an agronomist and soil conservationist and I know overgrazing when I see it. You don't look sideways at grass, you look down. Cattle exposure that precipitates erosion is a good start.

Any sort of contentiousness was far from my mind, though, when I reached the mountaintop. One boulder was smooth and I imagined it was a habitual sitting spot for those of the Casas Grandes culture who had preceded me there by more than a thousand years. The area is visited by violent thunderstorms and I could see lightning had struck the place numerous times, shattering boulders into small chunks of crystal. The place would be a New Ager fantasy but then I was not in the mood to dislike anyone. Back home the anishinabe (Chippewa Indians) favor lightning trees and this place had endured godly punishment way beyond trees which burn and half-explode. It would be a good place, finally, to die, and we don't find many such locations in a lifetime. This is an utterly normal thought rather than a sad one. I'm unaware of anyone who has gotten off this beauteous earth alive save the Lord, and that is disputed by many.

The natural world had so grasped me that morning that I forgot lunch, but far up the draw I could smell it on my way back with an ursine wag to my head and a crinkled nose. I share with Peacock a love for all the simple pleasures, not just a few of them, and that dawn we had put together lamb shanks, a few heads of garlic, cascabels, and a pound of white tepary beans got from Gary Nabhan's Native Seed Search. Trail mix and freeze-dried offal doesn't soothe the imagination. We had heaped coals around the Dutch oven, and I judged by the odor a quarter-mile distant that it was ready. This kind of lunch is necessary if you are to take a nap, and if you don't take a nap you are not fresh for the day's second half. You become a conniving eco–ward heeler with fatigued ideas how you would run the West if you were king of the cordillera. By taking a nap I stay put as plain old Jim, who occasionally has something fit for the collective suggestion box. A nap can give you an hour's break from needing to be right all the time, an affliction leading to blindness to the natural world, not to speak of your wife and children.

Late that afternoon, after studying petroglyphs and flycatchers, we had a long jouncing drive to ranch headquarters to meet Mr. Hadley for dinner. I had prepared a list of questions about everything from the BLM, the Savory grazing methods, Wes Jackson, Bruce Babbitt (hooray, at last), the Gray Ranch's carrying capacity, methane, the flavor of local beef (excellent), none of which I asked because we started talking about twentieth-century poetry. All tolled, your putative reporter did not put forward a single germane question about the ranch, somewhat in the manner of my beloved Omaha Indians to whom it is impolite to ask questions of anyone about anything, so they don't. There is also a specific ranch etiquette I learned in the sandhills, certainly the best managed grazing area in the United States, where information is volunteered rather than extracted.

After dinner we took a walk down a moonlit road and Hadley quoted the third of Rilke's *Duino Elegies* in its entirety in German, the sort of act that raised his credibility in my belief system up there with Thomas Jefferson, whether he likes the comparison or not. Though I was modestly groggy at the time, it seemed reasonable that a poet could run a huge ranch better than anyone else, especially as in Hadley's case, he had thirty years of experience.

On the slow ride back, which was much shortened by Peacock's braying of every blues tune in his head, the moon lit up Animas Peak so it looked a short trot away, and as we gained altitude the wind stiffened. The sand and grit in the air yellowed the moon and the landscape. I guessed the wind by my Great Lakes standards to be about forty knots and we secured our campsite with difficulty. I turned my sleeping bag so that it would stop billowing like a wind sock, and looked out from our grassy bench at the landscape, which now was shimmering and haunted. Spirits were afoot. First came the

Natives, then the turn-of-the-century cowboys, the night and day laborers of the cattle empires. A hundred years ago, or thereabouts, 400,000 cattle had perished to starvation in this two-hundred-mile-wide neighborhood between Cloverdale (population none) and Nogales on the Mexican border of Arizona. Despite the legion of naysayers, we're doing much better now. In fact, I was sleeping on a heretofore improbable experiment whether the natural and the man-organized communities could not only coexist but thrive to the mutual benefit of both. This was the teeter-totter that needed to be balanced between radical environmentalists and the stock associations, neither of which was going to go away. I was pretty much in the camp of the former and retained the right to shoot off my mouth about public grazing, but it was a splendid tonic that night to see what the private initiative that surrounded me with sure and certain hope had accomplished. The Gray Ranch was still here, big as all outdoors.

Jim Harrison is a poet and novelist living in northern Michigan.

Northern Tallgrass Prairie, North Dakota

Big Grass

❖❖❖

My father loves the small and receding wild places in the agribusiness moonscape of North Dakota cropland, and so do I. Throughout my childhood, we hunted and gathered in the sloughs, the sandhills, the brushy shelterbelts and unmowed ditches, on the oxbows and along the banks of mudded rivers of the Red River valley. On the west road that now leads to the new Carmelite monastery just outside of Wahpeton, we picked prairie rosehips in fall and dried them for vitamin C–rich teas in the winter. There was always, in the margins of the cornfield just beyond our yard, in the brushy scraps of abandoned pasture, right-of-ways along the railroad tracks, along the river itself, and in the corners and unseeded lots of the town, a lowly assertion of grass.

It was big grass. Original prairie grass—bluestem and Indian grass, side oats grama. The green fringe gave me the comforting assurance that all else planted and tended and set down by humans was somehow temporary. Only grass is eternal. Grass is always waiting in the wings.

Before high-powered rifles and a general dumbing down of hunting attitudes, back when hunters were less well armed, and anxious more than anything to put meat on their tables, my father wore dull green and never blaze orange. He carried a green fiberglass bow with a waxed string, and strapped to his back a quiver of razor-tipped arrows. Predawn on a Saturday in fall he'd take a child or two into the woods near Hankinson, Stack Slough, or the cornfields and box elder and cottonwood scruff along the Wild Rice or Bois de Sioux rivers. Once, on a slim path surrounded by heavy scrub, my father and I heard a distant crack of a rifle shot and soon, crashing toward us, two does and a great gray buck floated. Their bounds carried them so swiftly that they nearly ran us over.

The deer huffed and changed direction midair. They were so close I felt the tang of their panic. My father didn't shoot—perhaps he fumbled for his bow but there wasn't time to aim—more likely, he decided not to kill an animal in front of me. Hunting was an excuse to become intimate with the woods and fields, and on that day, as on most, we came home with bags of wild plums, elmcap mushrooms, more rosehips.

Since my father began visiting the wild places in the Red River valley, he has seen many of them destroyed. Tree cover of the margins of rivers, essential to slow spring runoff and the erosion of topsoil—cut and leveled for planting. Wetlands—drained for planting. Unplowed prairie (five thousand acres in a neighboring Minnesota county)—plowed and planted. From the air, the Great Plains is now a vast earth-toned Mondrian painting, all strict right angles of fields bounded by thin and careful shelterbelts. Only tiny remnants of the tallgrass remain. These pieces in odd cuts and lengths are like the hems of long and sweeping old-fashioned skirts. Taken up, the fabric is torn away, forgotten. And yet, when you come across the original cloth of grass, it is an unfaded and startling experience. Here is a reminder that before this land was a measured product tended by Steiger tractors with air-cooled cabs and hot-red combines, before this valley was wheat and sugar-beet and sunflower country, before the drill seeders and the windbreaks, the section measures and the homesteads, this was the northern tallgrass prairie.

It was a region mysterious for its apparent simplicity.

Grass and sky were two canvases into which rich details painted and destroyed themselves with joyous intensity. As sunlight erases cloud, so fire ate grass and restored grass in a cycle of unrelenting power. A prairie burned over one year blazes out, redeemed in the absolving mist of green the next. On a warm late-winter day, snow slipping down the sides of soft prairie rises, I can feel the grass underfoot collecting its bashful energy. Big bluestem, female and green sage, snakeweed, blue grama, ground cherry, Indian grass, wild onion, purple coneflower, and purple aster all spring to life on a prairie burned the previous year.

To appreciate grass, you must lie down in grass. It's not much from a distance and it doesn't translate well into most photographs or even paint, unless you count Albrecht Dürer's *Grosses Rasenstuck*, 1503. He painted grass while lying on his stomach, with a wondering eye trained into the seed tassles. Just after the snow has melted each spring, it is good to throw oneself on grass. The stems have packed down all winter, in swirls like a sleeper's hair. The grass sighs and crackles faintly, a weighted mat, releasing fine winter dust.

It is that smell of winter dust I love best, rising from the cracked stalk. Tenacious in its cycle, stubborn in its modest refusal to die, the grass embodies the philosopher's myth of eternal return. *All flesh is grass* is not a depressing conceit to me. To see ourselves within our span as creatures capable of quiet and continual renewal gets me through those times when the writing stinks, I've lost my temper, overloaded on wine chocolates, or am simply lost to myself. Snow melts. Grass springs back. Here we are on a quiet rise, finding the first uncanny shoots of green.

My daughters' hair has a scent as undefinable as grass—made up of mood and weather, of curiosity and water. They part the stiff waves of grass, gaze into the sheltered universe. Just to be, just to exist— that is the talent of grass. Fire will pass over. The growth tips are safe underground. The bluestem's still the scorched bronze of late-summer deer pelts. Formaldehyde ants swarm from a warmed nest of black dirt. The ants seem electrified, driven, ridiculous in tiny self-importance. Watching the ants, we can delight in our lucky indolence. They'll follow one another and climb a stem of grass threaded into their nest to the end, until their weight bows it to the earth. There's a clump of crested wheatgrass, a foreigner, invading. The breast feather of a grouse. A low hunker of dried ground cherries. Sage. Still silver, its leaves specks and spindrels, sage is a generous plant, releasing its penetrating scent of freedom long after it is dried and dead. And here, the first green of the year rises in the female sage, showing at the base in the tiny budded lips.

Horned larks spring across the breeze and there, off the rent ice, the first returning flock of Canada geese search out the open water of a local power plant on the Missouri River. In order to re-create as closely as possible the mixture of forces that groomed the subtle prairie, buffalo are included, at Cross Ranch Preserve, for grazing purposes. Along with fire, buffalo were the keepers of the grass and they are coming back now, perhaps because they always made sense. They are easier to raise than cattle, they calve on their own, and find winter shelter in brush and buffalo-berry gullies.

From my own experience of buffalo—a tiny herd lives in Wahpeton and I saw them growing up and still visit them now—I know that they'll eat most anything that grows on the ground. In captivity, though, they relish the rinds of watermelon. The buffalo waited for and seemed to know my parents, who came by every few days in summer with bicycle baskets full of watermelon rinds. The tongue of a buffalo is long, gray, and muscular, a passionate scoop. While they eat watermelon, the buffalo will consent to have their great boulder foreheads scratched but will occasionally, over nothing at all, or perhaps everything, ram themselves into their wire fences. I have been on the other side of a fence charged by a buffalo and I was stunned to a sudden blank-out at the violence.

One winter, in the middle of a great snow, the buffalo walked up and over their fence and wandered from their pen by the river. They took a route through the town. There were reports of people stepping from their trailers into the presence of shaggy monoliths. The buffalo walked through backyards, around garages, took the main thoroughfares at last into the swept-bare scrim of stubble in the vast fields—into their old range, after all.

Grass sings, grass whispers. Ashes to ashes, dust to grass. But real grass, not the stuff that we trim and poison to an acid green mat, not clipped grass never allowed to go to seed, not this humanly engineered lawn substance as synthetic as a carpet. Every city should have a grass park, devoted to grass, long grass, for city children haven't the sense of grass as anything but scarp on a boulevard. To come into the house with needlegrass sewing new seams in your clothes, the awns sharp and clever, is to understand botanical intelligence. Weaving through the toughest boots, through the densest coat, into skin of sheep, needlegrass will seed itself deep in the eardrums of dogs and badgers. And there are other seeds, sharp and eager, diving through my socks, shorter barbs sewn forever into the laces and tongues of my walking boots.

Grass streams out in August, full grown to a hypnotizing silk. The ground begins to run beside the road in waves of green water. A motorist, distracted, pulls over and begins to weep. Grass is emotional, its message a visual music with rills and pauses so profound it is almost dangerous to watch. Tallgrass in motion is a world of legato. Returning from a powwow my daughter and I are slowed and then stopped by the spectacle and we drive side roads, walk old pasture, until we find real grass turned back silver, moving, running before the wind. Our eyes fill with it and on a swale of grass we sink down, chewing the ends of juicy stems.

Soon, so soon.

Your arms reach, dropping across the strings of an air harp. Before long, you want your lover's body in your hands. You don't mind dying quite so much. You don't fear turning into grass. You almost believe that you could continue, from below, to express in its motion your own mesmeric yearning, and yet find cheerful comfort. For grass is a plant of homey endurance, pure fodder after all.

I would be converted to a religion of grass. *Sleep the winter away and rise headlong each spring. Sink deep roots. Conserve water. Respect and nourish your neighbors and never let trees gain the upper hand.* Such are the tenets and dogmas. As for the practice—*grow lush in order to be devoured or caressed, stiffen in sweet elegance, invent startling seeds*—those also make sense. *Bow beneath the arm of fire. Connect underground. Provide. Provide. Be lovely and do no harm.*

Louise Erdrich is the author of the novels *The Bingo Palace, The Beet Queen, Love Medicine,* and *Tracks,* and a volume of poems entitled *Jacklight.* She is a winner of the National Book Critics Circle Award for fiction. She grew up in North Dakota and is of German-American and Turtle Mountain Ojibwa descent.

ANN ZWINGER

Big Darby Creek, Ohio

Back Home Again

❖❖❖

When I settle into the canoe, curve my hand around the paddle shaft, and push off into the energetic spring flow of Big Darby Creek, I feel as if I've magically gone home again. Never mind that I grew up in Indiana, not Ohio, on the White River, not Big Darby Creek. What surrounds me is the imprinted landscape of my childhood where the air lies gentle as a feather cloak. Outlines and colors match, scents and sounds mesh, and the memories rush back of fireflies rising on a summer evening, the fair moonlight, the cloudscape that spawned Zeusian thunderstorms, picnics on the Fourth of July, and a small brown river at our doorstep, spinning purposefully downhill.

It is early Monday morning, the first day of summer. A storm blew through at dawn and vaporous clouds mist the sun, leaving soft-edged shadows. Witchity witchity witchity, carols a northern yellow-throat, a warbler that prefers these thicketed water edges. I catch a glimpse of a yellow cravat and a rakish mask. He repeats his song, lecturing the interlopers, descanting upon insect availability and the virtues of green leaves.

The canoe floats out into a soft, silvery-green English watercolor-landscape where light glosses a whole vocabulary of leaf shapes—

ferny, feathery, and filmy, lobed, oval and lanceolate, palmate and notched, ruffled and toothed. The leaves cluster in bountiful bundles, overlaid layer on layer, all the kinds of greens Winsor & Newton manufactured for English watercolorists. Despite this halcyon aspect of a stream miles away from anywhere, Big Darby Creek runs through a well-settled area only twenty miles west of the state capital.

Big Darby Creek, only 78 miles in length, is a modest stream that wends southeast across southeastern Ohio. It meanders across fairly flat, glaciated land, draining 560 square miles, 80 percent of which is farmland. Its name comes from a Wyandot Indian chief with the unlikely name of Darby who lived on the creek when government surveyors came through in the eighteenth century.

Big Darby cossets its treasures: small clockwork creatures that wend their way through its bottom pebbles, freshwater mollusks that siphon and filter hidden within its gravels, small fish that dart like jewels among the stems of its waterweeds—beneath its quiet surface is one of the most valuable and healthy warm-water streams in the Midwest. It has little of the urban pollution that besets so many waterways and is unique in being relatively undammed. Big Darby has been spared a great deal of what has happened to many other midwestern streams even though it retains only 10 percent of its original forests. Hydrographic communities in Ohio generally alternate between flood and dry, boom or bust, a regimen hard on fish because it strands them in small pools. Most streams have dams, and trees cut along the edges allow heavy siltation. Big Darby's substrate has remained relatively sandy and clean.

Big trees lean out over the water, address their reflections, replicate their colors. The leaf-fall litter from these trees is the base of the stream community's food chain. Vortices spin off the paddle stroke, gurgling miniature tornadoes into the slithering surface. When the breeze blows, red maple leaves flash silver as the underside of their leaves flips over, as quickly as a school of minnows turning. The wooded riparian corridor is critical, for the detritus that falls into the stream provides the food base for the dragonfly and caddis fly larvae that supply the food for the darter that provides the food for the gar.

After the glaciers withdrew 16,800 years ago, even though the ice had disappeared, the climate remained harsh and the ground wet, forming an Arctic tundra. Threads of meltwater trickled out from the retreating ice sheet, braided together, nibbled out a streambed, worried a channel through the glacial till and sometimes into the underlying limestone country rock. As the climate warmed and dried, spruce and fir filtered in. By 11,000 years ago pine trees invaded. Eight thousand years ago the climate had warmed enough to replace the trees with "peninsulas" of prairie vegetation. By 4,000 years ago a cooler, more humid climate again allowed trees to come in, and mixed forests darkened the Darby Plains that flanked Big Darby Creek.

The Darby Plains provided good hunting and shelter for Native Americans. In February 1751, Christopher Gist described the area as "full of beautiful natural meadows" rich with "turkeys, deer, elks and most sorts of game, particularly buffalos." Jonathan Alder, who was captured and raised as a Native American, thought it the "greatest and best hunting ground of the whole Indian territory." Indian trails webbed the landscape. European settlers moved in after the Treaty of Greenville in 1795, forcing out Native Americans by 1820. The settlers drained the meadows and changed the prairies to bluegrass pasture or plowed it under, land today productive with corn and soybeans.

Virtually all the land in Big Darby watershed is as domesticated as the family dog. Such a large drainage is owned by so many people and managed by so many agencies, it is impossible to sequester it as a unit under single management. The solution to preserving Big Darby Creek and its watershed is not in managing acreage per se (as often happens in the West where I live), but managing the watershed. Big Darby is in good health because twenty-five different agencies, under the leadership of The Nature Conservancy, have formed a complex partnership to keep it so.

This pleases me inordinately, because where I grew up the White River was rust-colored due to a wire mill upstream polluting the river. Nobody ever caught anything but carp. People accepted it. No one objected. Big Darby is healthy because people *did* object to misuse and cared enough to make changes to preserve its health.

Leaning over the gunwale to check what's going on in the shallows I find myself watching some minute riffle beetles, hard to see because they're so small. Their extra-long claws enable them to anchor onto stones in riffles where the water is well aerated. They don't frequent streams with heavy sediment load, low oxygen content, or muddy bottoms, so their presence indicates good water conditions.

The salubriousness of Big Darby Creek is measured by the invertebrates that crawl and slither, burrow and hide, in the creek's glacial gravels and pebbles, a heritage that allows a multitude of interstices for these small feeders and snorkelers. Rather than using pure chemical analyses as a yardstick for measuring a stream's conditions, biologists now use the stream's inhabitants.

Scarves and sprinkles of foam vein the serene surface. The creek, flowing one to two miles per hour, is fast enough to oxygenate water for the rich assortment of mollusks that live here. Big Darby, with its forty species, has, for its size, by far the richest mollusk fauna in the Midwest. Freshwater bivalves developed in the New World, probably in the Mississippi drainage basin, for the best diversity of species occurs here. As often happens when a creature is sought and used over many generations, it garners colorful names, some of the printable ones being pig toe, washboard, elephant's ear, slop bucket, and spectacle case. These long-lived freshwater bivalves are neither mussels nor clams, although commonly called so because they resemble the familiar saltwater ones, but are "unionids," a separate family of bivalves restricted to fresh water. When I hold one of these unionids in my hand, it fills my palm, its paired shells heavy. Like clams, they have two shells hinged together, siphons, and a foot that anchors them in the substrate. They require good water, for heavy siltation clogs their breathing tubes. One species, the fat mucket, tolerates contamination, and when these occur in numbers, they indicate poor water. Big Darby's two endangered species, the northern club shell and northern riffle shell, are those that require the cleanest water.

The young of unionids, called glochidia, are parasitic and encyst upon fish gills or fins. By hitching a ride on wide-ranging fish, unionids eventually occupy a whole drainage. Dams that confine fish passage also localize unionids. Glocidia do not appreciably damage the fish, who build up an immunity toward the mollusks through time and as adults rarely carry the encysted freeloaders.

Unfortunately there's a large market for the shells and poaching is prevalent. The shells are heavily in demand for buttons and ground up as pearl-starters—bits of shell rounded and inserted in a freshwater oyster shell to produce the irritation for pearl formation.

Drifting quietly downstream, I watch for a longnose gar, a primitive-looking fish with vertebrae that extend out into the tail. A hangout-and-wait hunter, its eyes set high for good vision, it lurks innocently in the shallows. When it sights a good meal it slams into the side of an unsuspecting fish and impales it, one of the stream's top predators. Big Darby boasts eighty-six fish species in its seventy-eight miles, of which a dozen such species are rare or endangered. Since man's advent around 1750, most Ohio creeks have become silty and only host fish able to tolerate polluted water. Big Darby's unique fauna flourishes because it still has its clear water and clean substrate. Like the freshwater bivalves, the fish have delightfully descriptive names. Madtom may be so called because of the venomous spines in the fins which, if grasped, deliver a very nasty sting.

This morning the creek is muddy from big storms upstream and it's useless to try to see fish, yet I keep hoping to spot the bright slivers of color of Big Darby's darters. Members of the perch family, many are brilliantly hued. Tippecanoe darters (an endangered species) are brilliant yellow-orange, dorsal fin a screaming red, a color scheme that sobers to black when two males confront each other, as does the coloration of the variegate darter. The blackening appears and disappears quickly, and seems to pair with aggressive defense of territory. Banded darters are teal blue with a golden yellow iris around a big black eye. Darters' coloring is on their flanks, so that a predator, like a green heron or kingfisher, looking down into the water, simply sees a thin gray line that blends in with the background.

The redhorses, genus *Moxostoma*, are very sensitive to water quality, and Big Darby Creek is one of the few places the silver redhorse lives. The common name may have come from the broad back configuration of the fish and their coloring. The five redhorse species here, all of which need clean water, are specialized insectivores. The black redhorse is a very intolerant species and abundant in Big Darby, as is the shorthead redhorse. All find shelter in the stream's underwater meadows of water willow and arrowweed.

As important as what's here is what's not here. The usual trash fish are uncommon. Common carp and flathead catfish are introduced species that do not do well in high-quality streams. Big Darby's are caught only in limited areas of logjams and backwaters. Nor are there colonies of bloodworms or fat muckets.

At the edge of the creek a tiny fluttery blue butterfly samples the mud at river's edge beneath a piece of Big Darby "slump prairie." Above it, flowers confetti the steep slope with color, lavender and yellow and white, plants typical of midwestern prairies. Prairies are few and far between in Ohio now, and some exist in odd places and flaunt the concept that prairies are flat. This four-acre patch hangs on the steepest imaginable riverbank. It grows on the outside bend of a meander where the current speeds up and undercuts the banks which, being fairly loose glacial till, "slump" into the river. Slumpage leaves a bare patch in which prairie plants, unable to grow in the shade of deciduous woods, successfully invade. If unstable enough, the slope remains open and inhospitable to shrubs and trees, but here some have already rooted and, as they shade the undergrowth, prairie plants will eventually disappear until another slump bares another patch of bank.

A prairie indicator, purple coneflower, blooms generously across the bank. The bristle tips of the disk flowers on the tall cone are an intense orange, almost iridescent, a glorious, startling juxtaposition against the drooping lavender petals. Purple coneflower was once widely used as a medicinal plant for all kinds of ills from snakebite to toothaches, burns to colds. Even today in Germany there are over two hundred preparations made from these plants, some valued for their cortisonelike activity.

Partridge pea is one of the first pioneers to come in on bare ground and to stabilize it. Small lavender thimbles of gayfeathers are perfectly named. A little white spurge that looks more like a white forget-me-not manages to dispense a meager and diagnostic drop of white sap out of a broken leaf vein. Whorled rosinweed, so-called because of its resinous sap, and black-eyed Susan, are opportunistic, also able to root on these unstable slopes before trees are large enough to shade them out.

The canoe brushes under the overhanging branches of a black walnut and they unload their inhabitants on me. A daddy longlegs parades my sleeve, countershaded brown on top, silvery beneath, long lunar-module legs that reach out and tap-tap feel, tap-tap pause. I watch it pace around my wrist, up my sleeve, a creature I remember watching as a child, searching its future with its second pair of legs.

The next day I explore Big Darby Creek on foot, enjoying its well-treed banks and fringe of meadows, frittering away the day in wandering and watching, luxuriating in midwestern summertime. In the middle of the path lies a fifteen-inch snake, the diameter of my index finger, tan stripes on brown patterned with darker brown triangles, all dark head, inquisitive little face. Its bright red-orange tongue, split and tipped with black, samples the air and an alien presence.

To someone used to sparser western landscapes, Big Darby's meadows are happily lush. The combination is perfect: enough familiar plants to feel at home, enough new ones to pique my interest. Flowers I never knew what to call as a child are in bloom here, and as an adult I relish the pleasure of knowing their names. Yellow moneywort weaves through the base of grasses and herbs, waxy five-petaled yellow flowers the size of a quarter named, I assume, because they look like gold coins scattered in the grass. White avens is in flower and seed, its seedhead a ball armed with stiff crochet-hooked pistils that latch onto my shirt. A little cinnabar winged moth, dragging its landing gear, feeds on the flowers. In among the head-high plants I stoop to look at a patch of corn salad, to me a new plant, an odd, weak-stemmed low herb with small entire and opposite leaves, finely white-haired, its minute, tubelike flower with a fringed lip.

Dock dangles green seeds, not yet turned mahogany. Garlic mustard in seed tilts up linear two-inch pods. Also called Jack-by-the-hedge and sauce-alone, it's one of the weedier mustards. Wild rose has yet to bloom, while red clover has heads as big as golf balls. Mullein, Queen Anne's lace, sweet cicely are all plants of damper ground. A matted place reveals where a deer bedded down. Timothy, fescue, and ryegrass grow as high as my shoulder.

As I approach the river, thimbleweed, an anemone, blooms in drifts in partial shade, the ecotone between open meadow and stream-side trees. Its white flowers light up the shadows. The spectacular fire pink, brilliant red, with starlike flowers and extra fringe at its throat, is also part of the assemblage. Each sticky red star is a Betelgeuse come to earth. For the first time in my life I find teasel in bloom, having hithertofore known it only from its familiar seedhead. The tiny lavender flowers form a narrow ring, proceeding downward on the thimble. The seedheads are still unsurpassed for raising the nap on cloth, the fineness of their spines producing an elegant surface. Ruellias bloom with big lavender flowers two inches across. Wild parsnip looks like yellow Queen Anne's lace. Blue-eyed grass raises little six-petaled blue faces from small irislike leaves.

To reach river's edge I negotiate a thicket of grass higher than my head, webbed with grapevines that grab and snatch, so dense I can't see my feet. Multitudes of tiny caddis flies waft up out of the grass and as quickly settle, the adults of the larvae that live in Big Darby Creek. Caddis-fly larvae, along with riffle bugs, are among the least pollution-tolerant creatures. Caddis-fly larvae fashion tiny cylinders of pebbles or twigs or shells, each species with its own architectural style. They need highly oxygenated water circulating through the tubes where they spend the preponderance of their lives.

At water's edge I watch the flat current of Big Darby spin by at my feet. The creek's sound is modest, demure, like a cat lapping milk. White violets flower in the thick shade and a lovely big patch of jewelweed comes into bloom. The tangerine-colored flowers hang hidden beneath leaves bejeweled with drops of water. A proven folk remedy, both the crushed leaves and the juicy sap ease poison ivy rash. Some people freeze the pulverized leaves in ice cubes and rub them on the itchy areas.

A hackberry tree stands in water up to its ankles. Its finely toothed leaves are beset by pinhead galls. I count eighty-three on one leaf, about as many as a three-inch leaf can hold. The galls are made by psyllid flies that look like very tiny cicadas, less than an eighth-inch long. Females lay eggs on the trees that hatch into larvae in the fall and overwinter in the bark. They emerge as the new leaves appear in the spring, ready to attack the leaves, impeccably timed to the tree's cycle of life.

I find a boulder in dappled shade on which to sit and write. Beside me the creek garbles and gushes over a willow limb arched out into the water. The currents saunter and swirl, swizzle and ruffle. Blue-black damselflies skate through the air, fluttery and skittish. A white dot at the wing tip makes a distracting flashing during flight. Another damselfly, its protruding eyes giving it a hammerhead shark aspect, alights on a jewelweed leaf. The puzzlement is: with all these damselflies, where are the dragonflies? An ecologist suggests that the high, fast water has discouraged the usual dragonfly hatch and that the nymphs have taken cover in the interstices of the gravels in the stream until the flow quiets, whereas damselfly larvae are more likely to be cosseted in vegetation roots and so less likely to be buffeted by the high water on emergence.

A small shiny black fly alights on my page and explores my thumb as I write. The buzzing of summer's cicadas vibrates the air. A huge yellow and black bumblebee drones from one white clover blossom to another, faithfully pollinating, one by one. A mourning dove bemoans its lost loves. I could sit here for hours, listening, watching, pondering, relishing.

In this speckled shade Big Darby Creek anneals past and present, alerts me to a landscape heritage that ballasts my life. Here on this quiet summer morning, the first day of summer, Big Darby weaves together a lifetime, a then and a now. I feel as if I have rounded out a childhood, canoed the stream I never got to canoe as a child, filled in some of the blanks, interwoven past and present and future. I have visited with the scenes of my childhood, brought my adult knowledge to focus as I could not do then, tied up some frayed and raveled ends of memory, pleasured by this summer stream that is cared for as the one of my childhood was not. Big Darby Creek speaks in the accents of my native land, running water with a midwestern accent.

A filamentous spider silk tightropes between two grass stems. It billows and gleams in the soft air currents. This busy, ticking, little world that surrounds me says Big Darby is a good place to siphon if you're a northern riffle shell, a good place to warble if you're a yellowthroat, a good place to flow if you're a creek, a good place to swim if you're a redhorse, and a good place to breathe if you're a human.

Thomas Wolfe was wrong.

Ann Zwinger, who lives in Colorado Springs, is the author of a dozen nature books, among them *Beyond the Aspen Grove*, *Land Above the Trees*, *The Mysterious Lands*, and *Run, River, Run*, for which she received the 1976 Burroughs Medal.

PHILIP CAPUTO

Martha's Vineyard and Nantucket, Massachusetts

No Space to Waste

❖❖❖

Ever since the pilgrims stood on Plymouth Rock face to face with a green new world commensurate with man's capacity for wonder (to borrow Fitzgerald's lovely phrase), a dichotomy has dwelled within the American soul. On the one hand, we are romantics awed and enchanted by vast, pristine wilderness; on the other, we are conquerors roused to possess and exploit it.

The Puritans peopled the New England forests with devils and witches; at the same time, the more adventurous among them shed their dour broadcloth for buckskins and pushed into those forests to build new lives. The North American wilderness thus became the province of wickedness, to be combatted for moral reasons, a land of opportunity to be conquered for political or economic reasons, and yet the realm of freedom and natural beauty where a new race of humankind was born. It's been observed, by historian Frederick Jackson Turner and novelist Wallace Stegner, among others, that our national character was formed and periodically renewed by a confrontation with the uncharted and unknown. And so the paradox was established at the very start: we had to devour that which nourished us and our boundless American dreams.

I was thinking about this contradiction as I sat, late one windy, overcast afternoon, atop a hill on Martha's Vineyard. I like islands. I lived on one—Key West—for eleven years. Islands are worlds unto themselves, where the larger dramas of nature and civilization can be observed in microcosm. Our North American islands, the inhabited ones, that is, are also places where the dichotomy in our collective soul becomes more apparent than it does in the immensity of the mainland. And they are the stages where the last act in the drama *between* nature and civilization, between our love of wilderness and our compulsion to own and tame it, may be holding its dress rehearsals. If you want a forecast of what might happen in, say, New Mexico, Montana, or Alaska fifty years from now, take a look at the Florida Keys, Martha's Vineyard, or Nantucket today.

The reason is simple enough: the finiteness and preciousness of land is far more obvious on an island. Even on a large one like Martha's Vineyard, the limiting shore is never more than a long hike or a short ride away.

Sitting on the hill in the island's Waskosims Rock Reservation, a nature preserve the size of a large farm, I recalled a horsepacking trip my wife and I took in New Mexico's Gila Wilderness in the summer of 1992. We rode for eight days through fenceless, unpeopled mountains, encountering only a handful of backpackers and few signs of man's intrusive hand. One day, resting our horses and ourselves on a mountaintop, we looked westward more than eighty miles into Arizona, southward for two hundred miles into Old Mexico, and saw nothing but more mountains and mesas and the red and brown expanse of the Rio Grande basin. The Big Open.

The Gila rolls and soars over an area the size of some New England states. It's one of those places, which still can be found in the West, that nurtures one of our most cherished illusions: that we have, even in the late twentieth century, room and resources to spare, even to squander.

The belief, founded upon the sheer size of this country, that there is always someplace to go, someplace to which one can escape, is as fundamental to our national creed as the Declaration of Independence. The escape might be a two-week camping trip, or a flight to a new place where one can start life anew. The covered wagons of the Oregon Trail vanished in the 1860s, but the faith that things will be better beyond the horizon has not. We pursue that dream today in U-Hauls and Ryder trucks on paved trails called Interstates. And in that pursuit, we continue to gobble up what's left of our wild forests—those new starter homes, bigger second homes, and vacation homes need lumber. Our unspoiled coastlines have become picketed by summer getaways on stilts. In the deserts east of L.A., the concrete tide is washing over the last stands of Joshua trees while golf courses and retirement communities in Arizona suck the Colorado dry to feed these developments' insatiable need for water and power.

But what the hell, there are thousands of miles of coastline in America, millions of acres of forest, deserts the size of small countries, right?

As the century draws to a close, maintaining that illusion is getting harder and harder. There is a nervous recognition, just beneath the surface of our consciousness, of a truth that ought to have been obvious long ago: America is finite after all. And the fact that we are running out of room and resources flies into the face of another of our cherished beliefs: that growth and expansion can be and should be unlimited.

The heightening awareness that the American pie is shrinking accounts, I think, for the Manichean nature of the debate between development interests and environmentalists, with each demonizing the other. Whether for the purposes of preservation or of exploitation, Americans seem desperate to grab what can be grabbed now. Sometimes, listening to radical environmentalists, I get the impression that they won't be happy until everything we've come to call progress is wiped away and we all go back to living in log cabins, maybe even in wigwams. Sometimes, listening to laissez-faire capitalists, I get the impression that *they* won't be happy until every hillside in the Northwest has been clear-cut and every open space transformed into a mall or golf course.

Isn't there some sensible middle ground where the works of man and those of nature can coexist in harmony?

Look to our islands . . .

Martha's Vineyard and Nantucket are good ones to choose; their European settlement dates back almost as far as the founding of Plymouth colony. They have known every kind of civilized activity except heavy industrialization; but the natural world still thrives there, although tenuously and in domesticated form.

The Waskosims Rock reserve, in the narrow, western half of the Vineyard, is owned by the island's Land Bank. It gets its name from a large granite boulder that crowns a hill dominating a range of smaller hills and an oak-covered basin created by receding glaciers some twenty thousand years ago—a tick on the geological clock. On the spring afternoon I sat musing, the scrub oak were not yet fully leafed, the Nantucket shadbush were just beginning to throw out their white blossoms, and the wind made the air hazy with blowing sand from the shoreline only a mile or so away, beyond the last line of hills. Off to the right, a house and pond peeked through the trees, while behind me an old stone fence walled off the reserve, which is open to the public, from the Frances Woods wildlife sanctuary, which is not. Clearly, it was no wilderness I was looking at, but the sort of tame, pastoral landscape that used to inspire romantic poets. Yet even this rustic scene was almost lost in the 1980s, that decade of greed gone amok. A developer planned to fill the woods near the reserve with townhouses, but Martha's Vineyard residents managed to block the project, forcing the developer to sell the property to the Land Bank.

Not all the residents were overjoyed at this turn of events. On Martha's Vineyard, as in other places where environmental and economic concerns clash, there is a class-warfare element to the debate about what shall be preserved and what shall not. Martha's Vineyard being rather genteel, the dispute wasn't as nasty as elsewhere, but it wasn't without bitterness. The fantasy that there is room for everyone cannot be sustained on an island that covers only one-third the area of New York City, yet everyone wants a piece of it, each for his or her own purposes. It has been a summer resort for decades, mostly for the well-to-do. The island's year-round inhabitants—shopkeepers, carpenters, contractors, and fishermen—have seen public access to shorelines severely limited by beachfront community associations, woods and wetlands where they once walked or hunted fenced off as sanctuaries. I've always found it difficult to wax righteous about conservation when it creates difficulties for ordinary people. Yet the truth is that prosperity, as we've come to know it, carries the well-known prices of pollution, overcrowding, cluttered landscapes, and the Kmart tawdriness of the concessions one sees at popular national parks.

To gain broad support, conservationists cannot ignore human material and economic needs, but can preservation be made compatible with social democracy and free enterprise? The predicament strikes me as fundamental.

A kind of truce has been called to the land wars on the Vineyard, an armistice that owes as much to the current recession as it does to hard-won compromises between the forces of economic development and those of conservation.

I toured an area where cooperation brought about a happy ending. This was the 180-acre Katama Park, which has been an airport for the town of Edgartown since the 1920s, but also contains one of the last patches of sandplain grassland on the planet.

When Dutch and English settlers set foot on the New World in the early seventeenth century, sandplain grasslands covered hundreds of thousands of acres from Long Island to Cape Cod. These rare ecosystems came into being during the last ice age, when the glaciers reached the limit of their advance and melted. Countless tons of earth were released from the glaciers, creating flat outwashes of sandy, dry soils that became covered with grasses related to those of the short-grass prairies in the Midwest. The coastal plains flourished through all the millennia between glacial recession and the arrival of the first white people in America. In 1602, an explorer named Bartholomew Gosnold reported discovering vast prairies on the islands off present-day Massachusetts.

In contrast to their midwestern cousins, the prairies of the East weren't congenial to agriculture. The topsoil was too sandy and shallow to support large-scale farming; but the grasses proved ideal as sheep pasturage. Despite heavy grazing, the grasslands continued to thrive, and were prevented from natural succession by periodic floods, fires, and storms.

They have barely survived the twentieth century. Since the 1950s, relentless development has caused the sandplains to suffer ecological cataclysm. From Massachusetts to New York, the grasslands and related heathlands now cover approximately fifteen thousand acres on three islands. The designation of the Katama Plains on Martha's Vineyard as one of The Nature Conservancy's "last great places" is literally true.

That phrase—last great place—suggests the breathtaking, a natural wonder like Mount McKinley or Big Sur or the Everglades. There is nothing awe-inspiring or charismatic about Katama Park. A townhouse development is clearly visible from it, and it is in the middle of an airport that services the private planes of visitors who fly in and out on weekends. The airport has its charms—its grass runways and small hangar and "terminal" recall the days of biplanes and barnstormers—but strolling through swales of false indigo, blue-eyed grass, and sandplain flax while Beechcrafts and Cessnas land and take off doesn't exactly make you feel you are in the wild.

Like a lot of people, I want to be stunned by natural grandeur. My guide introduced me to the quieter rewards of nature in miniature. The small purple flowers at my feet were bird's-foot violet, a food source for the regal fritillary butterfly, one of the rare creatures of sandplain habitat. The trilling coming from a huckleberry hummock nearby was the call of the grasshopper sparrow. Although the Katama grasslands are a little contrived—they're in the middle of an airport, after all—it was inspiring to see such small creatures surviving in such a civilized environment. It proved that we and our works can reach an accommodation with those of God.

The contrivance extends to the ways the Katama grasslands are maintained. To keep them healthy and free from succession by pitch pine, scrub oak, and huckleberry, biologists stage periodic controlled burns, replicating what nature used to do on her own.

But preservation brings costs of its own.

My guide is a descendant of settlers who came to Martha's Vineyard three hundred years ago, yet she has to struggle in an environment of soaring costs and real estate prices.

"I was priced out of this place the day I was born," she says.

But she's lucky. Many of her contemporaries have been forced to seek livelihoods on the mainland.

There are other costs . . .

After leaving Katama, we hiked through what must pass for wilderness on a place like Martha's Vineyard: the Frances Woods wildlife sanctuary, 500 pristine acres of scrub oak savannah and wetlands adjacent to the 145-acre Waskosims reserve. I was enjoying a rare privilege. Access to the reserve is restricted; it is papered with No Trespassing signs. Given the lack of space on the island, wildlife does need a refuge from human intrusion, even the benign intrusions of bird watchers and nature lovers; but putting myself into the shoes of a resident, barred from beaches where his or her grandfathers launched fishing boats, barred from pastures where his or her ancestors grazed sheep because those pastures are now filled with vacation homes, I could understand why the signs and fences must rankle some island residents.

We crossed into the Waskosims reserve by climbing over a low stone wall erected hundreds of years ago to divide the Vineyard's Indian lands from those set aside for white settlement. The Indians must have been as rankled by that wall as today's inhabitants are by the barriers of restrictions and regulations.

Later, I went back to the reserve on my own to sit and think and explore some of its marshes and woods. It's a lovely spot, a sanctuary in which the soul can be renewed and the body exercised with a vigorous walk. But it is a tight little place on a tight little island, biologically managed, the trails well-marked and maintained, and, considering the crowds that pass through it during the tourist season, exceptionally tidy. Signs ask visitors not to leave the trails because the reserve contains rare and endangered plants.

Again, such restrictions are necessary in a place where space is at a premium and human activities have to be controlled if wildlife and its habitat are to be spared. I realize that, yet as I walked through the scrub oak, pitch pine, and juniper, I found myself irritated by the little colored arrows telling me which trail I was on, by the marker posts that told me when I had come to the boundaries of the reserve. I began to feel claustrophobic, and, having something of the American anarch in my character, I ignored a boundary post and hiked into private property. The trespass was rewarded. I saw a wild turkey and a couple of shy scarlet tanagers.

The next day, I explored the Miacomet Plains on Nantucket with Peter Dunwiddie, an Audubon Society biologist, and Elizabeth Bell, a land-acquisition specialist for The Nature Conservancy. Nearly a third of the island's thirty thousand acres have been set aside for conservation. As on Martha's Vineyard, they are carefully managed by controlled burns and with restricted access trails and roads. These protected areas also were threatened in the 1980s, when genealogist-entrepreneurs traced the descendants of the island's original European settlers, cleared up fragmented and legally clouded land titles, then bought the property cheap and began selling it to developers for up to $100,000 an acre.

Had this gone unchecked by conservation groups, the Miacomet Plains might well be townhouses and vacation homes today. Precious habitat for the endangered short-eared owl and the northern harrier hawk would have been lost. Now you can stand on a height in the plains and look over rolling, somber, windswept expanses that recall an English moor. If you are lucky, as we were that day, you'll get to see a harrier soaring on the thermals, diving with talons extended to capture a field mouse or sparrow.

Watching the hawk swoop toward a clump of bearberry, I was reminded once more that I was enjoying a privilege. Most of Nantucket's ordinary people have had to leave the island, except for those who cater to the tourist trade. The combination of high real estate prices and preservation efforts have turned the island into a complete resort, its economy almost entirely dependent on tourism and the trade of the "summer people."

"The last commercial fishing boat left here five years ago," Dunwiddie said.

Although some small-scale commercial fishing and scalloping operations continue, the big trawlers that used to sail from Nantucket are now almost as bygone as the whalers of Melville's day. And a Nantucket without working seamen seemed as strange as the West without cowboys. Biodiversity is being spared, but a kind of human monoculture seems to have been created.

Hiking past a pond, Dunwiddie told me that the future of conservation on Nantucket lies not in acquisition but in management. Is that another price we will have to pay to save our wild places and wild creatures from oblivion? Isn't a managed wilderness an oxymoron? Of course, true wilderness vanished from Nantucket and Martha's Vineyard long ago. Environmentalists seek to preserve biodiversity, not the wild.

Thinking of the wild places I had been in—the Gila in New Mexico, the Absaroka Wilderness in Montana, the Minnesota boundary waters, the Upper Peninsula of Michigan—I recalled hearing wolf howls and wildcat screeches, the sight of a grizzly's claw marks on a tall pine tree, and the time I waded a bonefish flat in the Florida Keys, near a spot where an eleven-year-old boy had been killed by an alligator only the week before. With the dangers came freedom, the freedom to wander more or less at will without bumping into a sign or fence every half-mile.

Much of New England is already that way, except for the northern reaches of Maine and New Hampshire. It's beginning to look a lot like old England, where the woods, streams, and heaths are the private preserves of the rich or the restricted refuges of conservation organizations. To put a literary spin on the ball, this is not nature as Jack London liked it, but as Wordsworth did: defanged and declawed.

I wondered if, some day in the not-too-distant future, as population and competition for space increases, much of the lower forty-eight will be like a gigantic Martha's Vineyard, an enormous Nantucket. I would hate like hell to ride up to the mountaintop in the Gila where my wife and I rested our horses and see subdivisions spreading across the Rio Grande basin. I would hate equally to run into a park ranger telling me that I can't enter a certain valley because it's habitat for some endangered butterfly or bird.

"Managed wilderness" may be the only way to resolve the dichotomy in our collective soul, but if all of our last great places become so managed and regulated, so fenced in and signposted that they are turned into outdoor zoos, we will lose something as valuable as the spotted owl, old-growth firs, and grizzly bears. A sense of adventure, the excitement of encountering the unexpected around the next bend, the awe that comes when standing face to face with nature in the raw, with all her teeth and claws and majesty. We will miss running into the interesting people who earn their livelihoods in re- mote places—cowboys and loggers and miners and backcountry ec- centrics. No human surprises, just a lot of people like us, with predictable outlooks and opinions, predictably dressed in Lands' End shirts and Timberland hiking boots. And we will lose the exultation of unrestricted space. The Big Open will be closed up and we'll all be required to stay on the marked trails, please, and turn back when we bump into a sign that warns No Trespassing—Wildlife Sanctuary.

Philip Caputo, a Pulitzer Prize winner, is the author of *Indian Country, Means of Escape, DelCorso's Gallery,* and *A Rumor of War,* which won the Sidney Hillman Foundation Award. His first novel, *Horn of Africa,* was a National Book Award finalist. He lives in Connecticut.

JILL NELSON

Block Island, Rhode Island

A Place of Grace

❖❖❖

Here, honking is not the horns of cars beneath the hands of impatient motorists, but a goose in a garden on Grace's Point, strategically placed and guarding its turf from hungry deer.

Likewise, the ever-present roar is that of wave against rock and sand as the Atlantic Ocean pummels the circumference of this tiny island, not of too many voices in too small a space raised in complaint or anger.

The soft, constant whispering is not of people asking, imploring, suggesting, but of the wind off the ocean as it whips across this island of few trees, rustling the gold-red leaves of shadbush, the gray bayberry, jingling the bright red berries that adorn the shiny-leafed black alder as Indian summer melts into fall. The wind provides a cushion of air for the northern harriers, peregrines, monarch butterflies, gulls—island residents—and dozens of other birds who stop off on the long migration south.

For a city woman, this is a place first of absence. Of people, of the familiar noises and odors of the town or metropolis, of all the things there are to do demanding to be done. It is, at first, disconcerting, this natural silence that seems somehow unnatural. But not for long. In no time at all I am amazed, awed, and seduced. Without distractions, I fall into the rhythm of the island, the water, the land, the animals: being an animal too, it is not very long before my human rhythms fall into step with those that preceded me.

Perhaps it is as it should be that for the insects, birds, and plants that thrive here, some of them endangered species, Block Island is a place not of absence, but of presence. A place where nature and human nature conspire to make survival possible.

Surely the trip to Block Island, twelve miles off the coast of Rhode Island, should have forewarned me. The trip, a bit over an hour, is about separation, isolation, distance. There is something about islands, about being on a piece of land in the middle of water, that simplifies everything: desires, yearnings, thoughts. Once arrived over a roiling sea, the bow of the boat drenched with spray, my stomach slipping slightly, ears cold and face red from the chill wind of late October, there is a sense of finality, commitment, surety. Islands do not suffer well the antsy or indecisive, means of escape being few and far between. Better to submit to the will of the island, relax, and enjoy it.

Everywhere, there is the feeling of absence. It is late fall and the summer people, fifteen thousand strong, are mostly gone, returning the island to its winter population of eight hundred. The bars, restaurants, and dockside souvenir shops are shuttered for the winter. Nearly everyone goes to the same restaurant for lunch because it's the only one open. Still, it is not simply the absence of summer and people, but of structures. In a nation where it often seems a dominant credo might be summed up, "If it's beautiful, we will build," on Block Island beauty still outweighs buildings. This is, as you might figure, by design.

There are about 1,200 houses on Block Island, double the number there were twenty years ago, but not nearly as many as there legally could be—2,400—or would be if development were allowed to go unchecked. Those who grew up here, the old-timers, asked to point out buildings that weren't on the island twenty years ago, insist it's easier to point out the few that were. Guided by their mind's eye it is possible to see the island as it was: sparsely populated, the rolling, treeless hills dissected by stone fences, farmland looking like the English countryside on an island in New England, sweeping vistas of grassland, fences, cliffs, straight across to the sea.

Even so, in the here and now, many of the vistas remain. Walk up a rise on the 274-acre Lewis-Dickens Farm and you look dead across farmland to the ocean sparkling in the distance, the view unbroken, by choice and sacrifice.

Or stand at the overlook and gaze down into Rodman's Hollow, its carpet of burnt orange, red, green, an occasional yellow as fall orchestrates its colorful symphony, unbroken by condos, quaint summer cottages, Dairy Queens, or fast-food joints. It was here, in the early 1970s, that the conservation of Block Island began, hastened by the arrival of developers and spearheaded by the commitment of local working people.

The spirit began much earlier, spearheaded by Elizabeth Dickens, island resident and lover, who from 1909 until her death in 1963 kept daily records of bird sightings, who for decades taught schoolchildren what she knew about birds, nature, respect for the island. Absent for twenty years, her legacy remains present.

It seems that around every bend in the road there's a pond, "kettle holes," as they're rightly called, formed by the movement of glaciers. People here like to say there are 365, one for every day of the year; others, splitting hairs and dismissing the poetic hyperbole, say 360 is a more accurate number. The largest is Great Salt Pond, but there is Fresh Pond; Deep Pond; Sachem, Harbor, and Middle ponds; ponds everywhere. Good fresh and saltwater fishing too, clams, lobsters, an abundance of seafood almost begging to be eaten.

In the morning I drive past Seal Cove, where northern seals spend the winter, on my way to Mohegan Bluff. Illuminated in the glare of the car's lights are clumps of seaside golden rod, swamp rose, high-tide bush with its fluffy, tiny, white blossoms, salt-marsh hay. Rounding a bend, two deer stroll slowly, gracefully into the undergrowth, unconcerned. Nor am I startled, so fully has the natural beauty of this place, the juxtaposition of absence and presence, overtaken me.

Mohegan Bluff is where the original inhabitants of Block Island, the Manisse, fought off a party of fifty Mohegans in 1590. Little good it did them when the Europeans arrived. Like the Mohegans, the Manisse are long gone. But though absent, their spirit pervades in respect for the land, nature, a sense of balance.

It is cold up here on the bluff, the sky blue-black, the wind whipping off the ocean. Slowly, the sky moves from darkest to less so, peeling back layered shades of blue to reveal yellow, orange, purple, red. A single star stands sentry against the night.

The sun is a long time coming. Gulls swoop low against the ocean, settle confidently on water textured by the wind, their shrill shrieks breaking the silence as they swoop up and away.

Once the sun comes it is immediate: pale blue, yellow, purple, red, orange—*voilà*! It is risen. It moves fast, a red-orange ball on a pedestal. Ascending, it turns pale, illuminating grasslands, dunes, rocks far below on the beach drenched by sea spray, houses in the distance, showing something where, under cover of darkness, there appeared to be nothing. This is the delicate balance of absence and presence, of the important seen and equally crucial unseen, of peaceful coexistence between nature and people that Block Island struggles to achieve.

A city woman, warming up, can dig it.

Jill Nelson lives in New York City. She is the author of *Volunteer Slavery: My Authentic Negro Experience.*

JOHN JEROME

Lake Wales Ridge, Florida

Scrub, Beautiful Scrub

❖❖❖

Geographers say that what defines a place—what makes it, finally, the place it is—are four properties: soil, climate, altitude, and aspect, or attitude to the sun. Florida's ancient scrub demonstrates this principle more acutely than any place I've ever seen. Its soil is pure silica, so barren it supports only lichens as ground cover. (It does, however, sustain a sand-swimming lizard that can't live where there is moisture or plant matter in the soil.) Its climate, despite more than fifty inches of annual rainfall, is blistering desert; the plant life it can sustain is only the xerophytic, the quintessentially dry. Its altitude is a mere couple of hundred feet, but it is high ground on a peninsula elsewhere close to sea level, and its drainage is so critical that a difference of inches in elevation can bring major changes in its plant communities. Its aspect is flat, direct, brutal—and subtropical. Florida's surrounding lushness cannot impinge on its desert scrubbiness.

This does not sound like a great place. It doesn't look much like one either: shrubby little oaks (which don't resemble oaks but do have acorns), clumps of scraggly bushes, prickly pear, thorns, and tangles. "It appears," said one early naturalist, "to desire to display the result of the misery through which it has passed and is passing in its solution to life's grim riddle." By our narrow standards, scrub is not beautiful; neither does it meet our selfish utilitarian needs. Even the name is an epithet, a synonym for the stunted, the scruffy, the insignificant. What is beautiful about such a place?

The most important remaining patches lie along the Lake Wales Ridge, a chain of paleo-islands running for a hundred miles down the center of Florida, in most places less than ten miles wide. It is relict seashore, tossed up more than a million years ago when ocean levels were higher and the rest of the peninsula was submerged. That ancient emergence is precisely what makes Lake Wales Ridge so precious: it has remained unsubmerged, its ecosystems essentially undisturbed, since the Miocene.

As a result it has gathered to itself one of the largest collections of rare organisms in the world. Only about seventy-five plant species survive there, but at least thirty of these—40 percent—are found nowhere else on earth. Eleven are now federally listed as endangered, two threatened, a total of thirty-three under review for future listing. The concentration of rare plants is so significant that U.S. Fish and Wildlife biologists propose to make the ridge the first federally designated sanctuary for endangered plants.

As habitat, Lake Wales scrub is doubly threatened: bulldoze it and you're left with well-drained land attractive for both citrus farming and housing developments. When freezes wiped out more northern groves in the 1980s, the industry moved south, buying up scrub. Now a citrus glut makes the land more profitable for RV parks, and some landowners are bulldozing even the groves.

Before European intrusion, ancient scrub covered 80,000 acres or more; less than 13,000 remain, most in patches of less than 200 acres, some of the most important less than 50 acres in size. "It may take five scrub sites," says biologist Steve Christman, "just to have one population each of the rare and endangered species we know about."

Not all scrub vegetation is rare. Most of it is stunted trees, palmettos, and cactus. Slopes tend to be dominated by evergreen scrub oaks, crests by Florida rosemary—not the spice but a relative of the pineapple—that forms the distinctive semi-open parks known as rosemary balds. Scrub hickory, bay, and holly are common, along with tillandsia, gopher apple, wild olive, hog plum, and staggerbush. In some places there is a sand pine overstory, albeit a spotty one.

The critically imperiled plants are much more exotic. One is Florida jujube, recently rediscovered after being assumed extinct since 1948. Another is Sebring scrub mint, a newly discovered species that when crushed releases a distinctive "Vicks VapoRub" odor. The source of the fragrance warrants investigation: a similar plant, Lake Placid scrub mint, contains a powerful natural insect repellent. That one is imperiled too; so is scrub blazing star, whose worldwide distribution is limited to a thirty-mile string of patches of scrub. The other threatened plants—scrub lupine, yellow scrub balm, Carter's mustard, wedge leaf button snakeroot, scrub plum, pygmy fringe tree, and Highlands scrub Saint-John's-wort—need not only protection but more study. We've only begun to understand the adaptations that allow them to thrive in scrub and nowhere else.

Lake Wales Ridge therefore represents a kind of museum of strategies, mostly for dealing with xericity. Small, divided leaves reduce surface area. Silvery or light-colored foliage reflects the blistering sun. Deep tap roots search out water—or, conversely, shallow, fine-haired root systems just under the surface grab the rapidly draining moisture before it can get away. Leaves and stems grow hair that traps moisture, provides shade, protects against drying winds. Curled leaves not only reduce the surface area exposed to sun but also help collect condensation. Thick, waxy coatings resist evaporation. Aromatic leaves—mints, bays, rosemarys—generate a haze that helps prevent drying out.

Plants may be the scrub's exotica, but its symbol, its "flagship species," is a bird, the Florida scrub jay—which, like the plants, is also threatened. The jay's complex adaptations vividly illuminate how scrub works, making the canary-in-the-mineshaft metaphor inescapable: the best measure of the health of a given stand of scrub, say the biologists, is the presence of Florida scrub jays. Slightly smaller than the common blue jay, with no crest and blue, brown, and gray plumage, the scrub jay is a close relative of the western scrub jay but a distinct species endemic to Florida. The threat, simply, is shrinking habitat. Scrub jays are aggressively territorial, and each nesting pair needs twenty acres of scrub.

The birds are monogamous, mate for life, and can live ten years after reaching breeding age. When no new territory is available, off-spring remain at home, postponing breeding until an opening occurs. These nonbreeding young adults not only defend their parents' territory but even help raise younger siblings, improving family survivability. Upon the death of the parents, the territory often passes, in a kind of natural primogeniture, to the dominant male offspring.

Territory isn't limited only because of human encroachment: habitat for the jays must contain a preponderance of bushy oaks three to six feet high, with an occasional taller shrub for reconnaissance. Larger trees shelter too many predators; smaller oaks produce too few of the acorns by which jays supplement their diet. (Each bird buries six to eight thousand acorns a year—and recovers about half of them, thus helping propagate the oak cover they need.) The mechanism that keeps oak scrub at the height the jays need is fire, which must recur every ten to forty years. Because people feel compelled to suppress this natural occurrence, we may threaten scrub jays even when we "protect" their scrub—if we do so misguidedly.

Central Florida has the highest frequency of lightning strikes in the country, averaging fifty per square mile per year. Historical records show that Florida has always burned frequently. (A nineteenth-century English naturalist estimated that in the preceding year 110 percent of the peninsula had burned—because some parts of it burned more than once.)

Scrub burns only with difficulty, in part because there is so little ground cover. When conditions are not exactly right, it even acts as a natural firebreak. When it is ready to burn, however, those strategies for dealing with dryness—the waxy varnishes, the concentrated resins, even the volatile haze of the aromatics—turn it into pure fuel. When scrub burns it does so with ferocious intensity.

It regenerates quickly. Scrub oaks resprout from rhizomes—70 percent or more of their biomass is below ground, fireproofed—and produce acorns again within three years. Florida rosemary reestablishes from seeds whose germination is stimulated by fire. Jays will continue to use and defend burned-over territories, and can survive so long as no more than 35 percent of the territory is burned at a time. In existing scrub preserves, managed burning is now being used to keep the habitat healthy.

The proper length of the burn cycle is still subject to research, but scrub-jay populations have been found to decline if the scrub goes thirty years without a fire. The rare plants suffer too: if burns are too frequent, the plants don't reach reproductive maturity; if fire is withheld, understory seedlings get shaded out.

The analogy may be flawed, but what scrub reminds me of most is krummholz, that stunted timberline forest trimmed short by snow and freezing winds. Scrub is a kind of desert krummholz, sculpted by sun and fire rather than ice. Fire, at any rate, is a necessary ingredient. After rainfall, naturalist Steve Morrison told me, fire is the most profound element in the Florida ecosystem. Fire is the force that makes scrub work.

Steve Morrison manages Tiger Creek and other preserves from The Nature Conservancy's Lake Wales office, and introduced me to the ancient scrub. As we picked our way along on foot, Steve would say this is one of the endangered plants, this is one of the rare ones, showing me tiny plants with intricate little structures that I hadn't a hope of telling apart. Understanding scrub requires information, detail, background—and a kind of hands-and-knees biology, or what one researcher likes to call "an elfin point of view." That's when it becomes beautiful.

The lichen ground cover is curiously reminiscent of coral reefs (demonstrating once again how nature delights in repeating forms). The smooth white sand is a perfect surface for tracking, showing us among others the S-shaped wriggle of the threatened sand skink, the one that "swims" through dry sand. (It has tiny vestigial legs set in grooves, lives on ant lions, and is very seldom seen—so the tracks

are a comforting verification of its continuance.) We also saw tracks
we assumed were of bobcats, and either feral hog or deer; both are
present in the scrub, but because of the friability of the sand, even
Steve's trained eye couldn't tell the difference. Nor could we distin-
guish between fox, coyote, and domestic dog, all of which visit the
scrub, along with black bears and—rarely, perhaps only historically
—the Florida panther.

We were driving from one scrub patch to another when Steve
pulled over and said, "Let's see if we can call up a scrub jay." He
popped a tape into the dashboard player and turned up the volume;
a couple of taped screeches later—within, literally, about ten
seconds—a pair were examining us from across the road. They're
inquisitive creatures, perhaps inappropriately accepting of human intrusion. Some jays develop social relationships with the scientists who
are studying them, appearing regularly for hand-feeding, and generally
charming folks' socks off.

I'd been given permission to spend a no-impact night in Saddle
Blanket Preserve, a five-hundred-acre Conservancy acquisition near
the town of Frostproof. It was perversely amusing to camp there, in
solitary wilderness splendor on a sandy desert ridge, surrounded by
threatened species of both plants and animals, within half a mile of
U.S. 27—the major north-south highway past Disney World's western
entrance. I was never out of earshot of internal combustion engines;
in Florida, Steve said sarcastically, one almost never is.

February nights are long, but a full moon lit the scrub so brightly
that the difference between twilight and midnight was not of order
but of degree. Not that I wandered much. "You'll be in more danger
from prickly pear than rattlesnakes," Steve had told me. The vegetation reminded me of the catclaw acacia I've run into—to my
regret—in the western version of scrub. That landscape, called chaparral, is mother of the invention of the cowboy's "chaps." The more
time I spent in the scrub, the more apt the analogy seemed to grow.
As in chaparral, one does not brush aside anything carelessly. It is
not a comfortable habitat for large, clumsy, thin-skinned, essentially
hairless vertebrates. The desert motto, according to Diana Kappel-
Smith: "Trust nothing."

The next day I visited Archbold Biological Station, and strolled a couple of miles on a pleasantly warm afternoon, following fire trails while scrub jays followed me—passing me along, so to speak, from territory to territory. (The characteristic swooping flight pattern by which they patrol their turf is as quick an identifier as their plumage.) I lounged for a while in the sand in the middle of a rosemary bald, listening to bird life flutter through palmettos just out of sight, never quite finding the source of the sounds. The wandering stripes of white sand seem to isolate the tiny plants and other phenomena, drawing the eye. I actually did spend a lot of time on knees and elbows. You have to: in the scrub, detail is all.

As a place, scrub is a meditation on habitat. Only because the sand is so sterile can sand skinks survive in it. Only because scrub jays need twenty acres do young adults postpone breeding. Because xeric conditions concentrate flammables, scrub becomes good fuel— but because there is so little ground cover, it won't burn until a sufficiency of that fuel is collected. Because scrub is hard to burn, it grows high enough to support jays; because Florida gets so much lightning, fire keeps scrub from growing too high—or did until people began suppressing it. And so on: because of this, then that; because of that, something else. The word "because," here as elsewhere in biology, is a mockery, of course. Because the few linkages we see are just about all we know, or think we know, about all these irreplaceable—literally—creations.

What scrub seems to do is clarify the problem. It lays things out: these are the forms of life that have figured out how to make even this harshness work. Make the earth as inhospitable as this, and here is what will figure out how to live there. Pacific vents come to mind, another bizarre set of conditions for which biology, in its pressurized drive, has come up with unique solutions. Or as John Fitzpatrick, director of the Archbold Station, says of Lake Wales Ridge, "We're looking at a little Galapagos archipelago of sand."

If we don't preserve the Lake Wales Ridge, what it will become is yet another citrus monoculture, with the usual attendant chemicals in the soil and pollution in the air, and RV parks: an agricultural monoculture, and a human monoculture. We'll squeeze a few more human beings into the space and a few more dollars out of it. In the process we'll reduce it to the degraded state that we already know everything about except how to stop. If we do save it, we preserve at least some of the genetic richness available to us on the planet.

Meanwhile, where there might seem to be almost nothing worth saving, here is all this biology, working all these complex schemes to accommodate the geographical harshness that soil, climate, altitude, and aspect have dealt it. Creating, therefore, a place like no other. It is not exactly beautiful, but then nothing is beautiful in nature, just as nothing is ugly, beauty and ugliness being templates of our own imagining. What's so beautiful about scrub, you eventually come to realize, is that it works; that it simply *is*.

John Jerome has been a columnist for *Esquire* and *Outside* magazines. His books include *Stone Work* and *The Sweet Spot in Time*. He lives in Massachusetts.

PAM HOUSTON

Willapa Bay, Washington

On the Trail of Walking James
❖❖❖

There's a young man in Willapa Bay who goes by the name of Walking James. He's tall and lanky, young looking for his age— eighteen—and a little shy. He's famous among tree farmers in Pacific County because he's the only tree thinner who will climb all the way to the top of the Douglas firs and cut the double trunks off. Even more astounding to me is James's other accomplishment: in the last five years he has walked and mapped every square mile of five townships in the Willapa Bay area.

His maps are detailed and professional, indicating all the usual topographic features: buildings, roads, landforms, and bodies of water. But James's maps are unique because they include features that are of particular interest to him: the Roosevelt elk's winter grazing ground, a little-known waterfall on the Niawiakum River, a red alder grove where he saw a pair of chestnut-backed chickadees, and the magical remnants of old-growth forest that for one reason or another the chainsaws have missed.

You don't have to spend much time with James to realize that he is a walking computer: he knows every bird and plant and sub-species found in the area, knows every hill and slough and meadow, knows each indigenous animal's favorite habitat, knows by heart the elevation of every square mile of the places he's been. When he isn't working high in the tree branches, thinning the new forests, allowing more light, and therefore more species to thrive, he is walking and mapping, looking for rare or endangered species that live in the pockets of old-growth timber he loves. When I ask him why he's devoted so much of his young life to mapping he tells me he hopes to save the old-growth remnants. He says he has always been interested in exploring the unknown, in recording the things that have been, in the past, overlooked.

A desire to explore the unknown has taken young people away from their homelands for centuries, but for James, there is plenty of unknown in his own backyard. Two years ago, when his parents moved from the Willapa area, sixty miles north to Olympia, Washington, on the southern tip of the Puget Sound, James walked back to Willapa Bay three times before his parents gave in and let him stay in the forest he loves.

Today James and I walk through a young Doug fir forest, and I can't help thinking of "Star Trek," of Mister Spock, or his more recent counterpart, Data, as James plies me with information, hundreds of plant and animal names, life-forms he has seen in the area too fast and too numerous for me to write down. He interrupts himself only to impart more information, to name the Townsend's chipmunk who natters at us from a nearby tree, the Wilson's warbler several hundred feet above us, the western sword fern that suddenly lines both sides of the trail. It is clear to me that James adores this forest, that he adores every bit of flora and fauna like another man might adore his Mercedes or his wife, but when I ask him to talk about his emotional investment in saving the trees he looks at me, one eyebrow raised, like an android.

I rethink my question, asking, this time simply how it makes him feel to be inside the ancient forest and he lowers his head and says he has no words to describe that feeling.

He smiles, suddenly less alien, more boyish, and suggests that I go into the ancient grove and see how it feels for myself.

It is June 21, the longest day of the year. My husband and I are standing in the center of a 274-acre ancient cedar grove on 5,000-

acre Long Island, the largest estuarine island on the Pacific Coast, in the middle of the 680,000-acre Willapa Bay watershed, the most productive coastal ecosystem remaining in the United States. We have come a long way to be here: a thousand miles in a pickup truck, a four-hour paddle against the wind and the tide around the island in a very old and shaky fiber glass canoe, and a five-mile walk down a logging road to this large ancient grove which has been miraculously preserved. Lush rainforest vegetation covers the ground, and there are waist-high bushes with broad waxy leaves and red and white berries. Birds and birdsong are everywhere, and fallen trees in various stages of decay.

We have come to this place from the desert, where the magic comes from the spareness, the simplicity, the delicate balance between creatures that need almost nothing and a landscape that gives them only slightly more than what they need; but here in this rain forest there is a similar magic in abundance, in the way this forest teems with life, swarms with life, life piled on top of life, so many life-forms trying to occupy the same space.

The four-leaf clovers are as big as daisies, the first wildlife we see is a slug as big as a hot dog.

It is the longest day of the year and the late afternoon light seems like it will hang on forever, unwilling to begin its six-month-long losing battle with the night, which stays away, it almost seems, out of respect.

At this time between sunset and twilight there is magic in all wild places. In the desert, night falls silently and slowly in an explosion of color in the western sky. Here it comes secretly in deepening shades of gray and a cacophony of bird sounds, in the footfalls of deer, and in rumbles and whispers that come from the soft shapes just beyond my range of vision.

In the desert, you can watch the rain for miles as it comes toward you, watch it fall out of the sky and disappear, watch it evaporate before it falls far enough to hit you where you stand, on the ground below it. In the rainforest you can hear the rhythm of the rain on the canopy minutes before it saturates the leaves and breaks through, minutes before you feel it on your skin.

Under the canopy, it is either raining, or it has just stopped rain-

ing, or it is about to rain. And even when it is not raining the wind
will rustle the trees and drops will fall from the sky, and the only way
I can tell whether it is or is not raining is to measure the amount of
light coming under the canopy, and to wait for the clean-smelling
breath of air that rides on the cusp of the rain.

When Lewis and Clark arrived in the Willapa Bay area at the end
of their two-year journey, in the days when the whole region was
covered with this magical forest, the rain drove them halfway insane.
Their supplies turned to mildew and their clothes rotted to their
bodies and they finally retreated inland, and south, for the winter to
a region that was comparatively dry.

The largest tree my husband and I can find in this grove is a western
red cedar, nearly two hundred feet high and big enough around to
build a comfortable house inside. A 150-foot western hemlock grows
right out of its roots, the two trees entwined together like old friends
with different natures, the cedar branches and needles airy and hopeful, the hemlock's melancholy and sad. The roots spread their mossy
fingers across the path, over and under much younger trees, and
what's left of the daylight filters down through the multilayered
canopy.

Night is falling on the longest day of the year and I find myself
wondering how many summer solstices these trees have seen, how
many times the sun has risen and fallen in its yearly path, hitting
different branches from different angles, sending the trees messages
of reproduction, dormancy, and growth. I know the answer, for the
hemlock could be well over five hundred years, for the cedar, well
over one thousand.

And I wonder what lucky combination of inaccessibility and
placement and latter-day preservation has saved this tree, when 99
percent of the old-growth timber in the Willapa region has been
chopped down. I put my hand on the bark of each of the old giants.
They are mossy and damp and the hemlock is surprisingly warm.

When I look way up into the top of these two trees and ask, how
could anyone cut down one of these giants, it is not simply a question

of morality. This tree is so massive, so solid, so powerful and permanent that I can't imagine the saw that would go through it, can't
imagine the size of the machine that would remove it, can't imagine
the sound it would make as it fell, shuddering, can't imagine the size
of the hole it would leave if it was gone.

And I know then, that I am under the trees' power, because all
of a sudden I can't imagine the one thing about these forests I know
to be true: that thousand-year-old trees this size are felled in them
every day.

We have lingered too long in this magical forest, and we are in for a
dark walk back to the place where we have, hours before, made camp.
In the graying half-light we take the path out of the ancient grove
and into a grove that was harvested in the 1930s, when the loggers
were less efficient. Perhaps they didn't take the trees that were gnarled
and twisted, perhaps they understood the forest would be healthier
if not all the trees were of the same age and height, perhaps a few
trees spoke to them, as the one in the ancient forest spoke to me,
perhaps these remaining old trees asserted their power, and were
spared.

For whatever reason, the 1930s cut is an only slightly more dim,
only slightly less magical version of the old-growth forest. Because so
many of the replanted trees are the same age, less sunlight comes
through the canopy, and because of the more regular canopy, there
is less undergrowth, fewer birds, and fewer signs of life.

I climb up onto the trunk stub of a big cedar that was harvested
in the thirties, using the branches of a neighboring hemlock. It is
tabletop smooth up here, and, given sixty years in the rain forest, not
all that badly decayed. Four couples could dance comfortably on the
top of this tree trunk. Ten people could sit up here in beach chairs.
The canopy rustles above me in a light breeze it won't let me feel.
The rain has stopped momentarily, and for just a few moments some
bright color of twilight lights the sky.

Surrounding the 1930s cut is a 1960s cut which resembles the
ancient cedar grove not at all. It is a sickly little forest: thousands of

trees all exactly the same height—Doug firs I think, planted for their symmetry and short maturation cycle, though they are wedged so close and thick and branchless it is almost impossible to tell.

There is no light coming through the canopy, no ground cover, no bird song, and, except for the uniform trees that look as if they have already been harvested, that look, if I turn my head sideways, like they are already stacked in piles at the lumberyard, there are no recognizable signs of life.

We walk back the five miles along the logging roads to the camp we have made in a cedar grove on a high cliff overlooking Willapa Bay. On our walk to the ancient grove several hours ago, logging trucks rattled past us, louder than thunder, each truck loaded to capacity with sweet-smelling sap-dripping sixty-year-old trees.

Now, however, it is dark—rainforest dark—the logging ferry is put to bed for the evening, and we are alone with the creatures and the big trees, the only two humans on the island.

The forest leans over us on either side of the dirt road, and I clutch Mike's hand and swivel fast each time an animal crunches through the forest. In the desert darkness that disguises nothing I am never afraid, but these woods hold too many possibilities, there is too much room in the wet dark for my imagination.

I hear footsteps behind us, heavy and threatening, and I insist that we start singing—"My Favorite Things," "A Hundred Bottles of Beer on the Wall"—I move from one song to the next almost without breathing. When we see the yellow glow of our dome tent, I am delighted to shed my wet rain gear and crawl inside.

The trees around our campsite have been logged, but haphazardly and a long time ago, and the nighttime woods outside the tent windows feel more like the ancient grove than the tight, airless 1960s forest. The rain comes and goes and we sleep intermittently.

We are a few hours into the shortest night of the year when Mike touches my arm and points toward the tent's roof. A nose, blackbear size, is pushing itself into the tent and sniffing. We have brought no food into the tent with us, but in an instant all the bear etiquette I've practiced so diligently in grizzly country comes back to me.

I am suddenly conscious of my toothpaste and cough drops beside me, even my breath, heavy with lunchtime's fresh Dungeness crab, would be enough to bring a grizzly bear into the tent. We watch the nose as it makes one, two, then three circles around the tent, and then hear the soft falls of padded feet as the bear ambles away.

I am completely asleep again when the ground starts to shake and the sky splits in half and a rattling that is at the same time inside and outside of my brain awakens me. My first thought is "earthquake" but it is, in fact, only thunder.

Adrenaline washes through me and the rumble, louder and more powerful than the most spectacular summer desert thunderstorm, intensifies and diminishes, rolls over our tent like a big tympanic wave. I catch my breath as the sweet burned smell of wood filters through the fly screen. We wait for the crackle of fire, the orange glow of flame that will send us running out onto the tidal mud, but this is just another night in the rain forest and soon everyone has gone back to sleep.

We wake to a gray light not unlike the gray light of evening and the increasingly familiar sound of light rain. When we arrived by canoe at this bay-side campsite the tide was (necessarily) in, lapping at the deep soil of the high bank, leaving seaweed fingers plastered to the orange soil. At this morning's low tide there is mud as far as we can see, in every direction, mud that if we tried to walk on would suck us in above our waists and then some, mud that will keep us on this island until the next high tide.

If the mud were solid we could walk fifteen miles to the mouth of the bay and the Pacific Ocean, twenty miles to the north bay town of Tokeland, twenty-five miles to the bustling port town called South Bend. But we cannot walk on the mud so we are happy to play around its edges, picking up the tastiest, freshest oysters in the world in public tidelands as if they were pebbles, cracking them open, washing them in the clear Long Island streams, and throwing them icy cold and slippery down our throats.

Our dented yellow canoe looks lonely and ridiculous, beached as it is and miles from the nearest water. We make a futile attempt to dry our tent between rain showers, watch the hawks dive for tidewater animals, watch a pair of bald eagles make lazy circles in the sky.

At two o'clock the tide's first wave washes in like a thought and fills a long narrow channel between us and the Long Beach Peninsula to our west. The channel widens in what seems like time-lapse photography, in minutes the oyster beds where we feasted are covered, and after waiting all day for the tide to turn, our tethered canoe is up and floating before we can even pack our still-damp tent.

We ride the incoming tide to the end of the island, but then have to turn northeast, against the tide, and paddle back to the public boat ramp where we've left our truck. The two daily tides in Willapa are not equal; the locals sound Hawaiian when they speak of the tides which are either high-high, high-low, low-high, or low-low.

Yesterday we fought the high-low tide on the way out to the island, but today it's the high-high tide coming in on the added strength of tonight's full moon, and we make very little progress against the current.

Today, however, the prevailing wind is in our favor, and we hoist our tent's ground sheet, use our paddles as rudders, and sail the canoe somewhere between a run and a broad reach toward shore.

Later that day we paddle up the Niawiakum, an estuarine river a little farther up the bay. An estuary is, literally, a tidewater place where the fresh water and the salt water meet. We come into the Niawiakum on the saltwater tide, watch the blue tidewater mix with the brown river water a few miles upstream.

Niawiakum, in Chinook, means "slow-moving river," and it is, though unlike the slow-moving rivers I know in the desert, this river is constantly changing its direction, and I am dislocated by the contradictory marks of movement on the shore.

An estuary is also a breeding ground, as full of life as the ancient forest, and with plenty of magic of its own. It is a nursery that protects all varieties of young crustacean: shrimp, lobster, crab, and crayfish, protecting their larvae from battering surf and hungry pred-ators. It has plants, water lilies and others, that remove pollutants, taking them into their own systems and making the water more pure. It is the place where young salmon undergo the physiological trans-formations that allow them to make the change from fresh to salt water. Here they change color, they change the osmotic capabilities of their skin (what once only let fresh water in now must let salt water out), and they receive the estuaries imprint upon them, so that many years later, when they have calculated, using tide and temper-ature and daylight patterns, the right amount of seasons going by, they will smell the fresh water of their particular estuary, and know that it is time to come home.

The tides in Willapa Bay give life a constant rhythm, a daily sym-phony in four parts, and everyone who stays here—the tourists, the oyster growers, the fisherman, even the man who ferries the logging trucks, have to respect the movement of the tides.

We paddle up the Niawiakum as far as the now-outgoing tide will allow us. A field full of elk raise their heads at us, and we decide to listen as the water speaks to us and tells us it is time for us, too, to go home.

Tonight we will stay in Tokeland, at a friendly, weathered old inn that feels, I have to admit, as much a part of Willapa as the ancient trees. Tomorrow we will start the drive back to the desert, and our clothes, our tent, and our skin will dry in increments, as we leave this watery place behind. We'll tell our friends about the black bear's visit, the wild clap of thunder, the icy sweetness of the oysters, the serenity and power of the ancient trees.

We will be back home in the desert, but the rainforest, its watery raging fullness, will come to us, often, timeless, in our dreams.

In the ancient grove, the sun is filtering through the cedar branches like spider webs, a red-breasted nuthatch is collecting berries, the branches of the hemlocks are rustling lightly in an afternoon breeze. A small herd of Roosevelt elk are

*moving through the ancient grove to the meadows where they graze each evening.
A black bear argues the toss with a swarm of honeybees who have made their
comb at bear's-eye level. A pileated woodpecker rattles the bark of a grandfather
cedar. A dark-eyed junco sings from the branches of a Sitka spruce tree. Above
the symphony, above the canopy, thunder rolls in from the Pacific, louder now
than the thunder of the logging trucks, louder even than the crash of the falling
trees. Somewhere on the island, Walking James has just discovered a new species
of butterfly. Any minute now it will begin to rain.*

Pam Houston, a part-time river guide and hunting guide, is the author
of a collection of short stories, *Cowboys Are My Weakness*, which won
the 1993 Western Regional Book Award.

ANNICK SMITH

Dos Palmas Oasis, California

The Lost Land of Ka-Zar

❖❖❖

Yikes! Snow. Snow and more snow. I shovel a foot of new snow off my deck and look out at the muffled white Montana hills where I live. My mind fills with sundreams. I know the sun is shining somewhere.

The Nature Conservancy has a desert preserve in southern California called the Dos Palmas Oasis. Oasis is a magical sunny word. I imagine camels and caravans, jungle comic books and tall tales from *The Arabian Nights.* Oasis is hummingbirds and frogs and palm fronds in the sand. Oasis is the ancient water of life. I want to go where it never snows, and a few days later, I'm gone.

In a high wind, my friend Bill and I breach the pass that divides the coastal California mountains from the desert. Wind is always blowing as you enter Palm Springs from the west, there is always a sandstorm on I-10, and the thousands of gleaming one-legged wind generators that guard this natural entrance where the Mohave Desert meets the Colorado Desert whir like sci-fi creatures in a sci-fi landscape. We enter a fantasy of white hotels and villas, magenta bougainvillea, turquoise swimming pools, emerald golf courses, and streets named Bob Hope and Gene Autry.

This is not the fantasy we seek. Bill turns his Honda south parallel to the San Andreas Fault, driving down, down through Mexican farm-worker towns called Coachella, Thermal, and Mecca toward the below-sea-level desert that borders the Salton Sea. Sun glares, dust blows, and I think about disjunctions inherent in a place where for eons tectonic plates meet and crash. I am reminded of the comic-book heroes my boys cherished when they were eleven: the giant green Hulk plunging beneath the earth's crust to the primordial lost land of Ka-zar; and Ka-zar the Savage with his loincloth and blond surfer looks; and Zabu, his pet saber-toothed tiger; and red-tressed Shanna of the Jungle, whose mission was to save dinosaurs.

We stop at a roadside stand at the edge of an orchard where stately date palms diffuse the blazing sun. Green light filters through green fronds onto rows of orange trees heavy with orange fruit. Bill sips his date shake and I gulp my fresh-squeezed orange juice. This irrigated miracle in the desert is a thing of beauty, but I doubt if the land can stand it for long. We have seen the alkaline white fields in this valley, the soil denuded. Hulk's job was to save the natural world from a cockeyed atomic machine designed to skew the very rotation of planet Earth. In that comic-book story, a dark force in humankind wants to bring chaos by warming the earth, creating weather patterns that will flood the cities, destroy civilization.

Warm currents out on the Pacific have created the storm-bearing weather that has driven us to the desert this winter day. The snow of the century has swept across country from Oregon to Boston. It has rained for two weeks on the California coast, bringing floods after drought. Parked near the edge of the San Andreas Fault, I wonder if Los Angeles is worth saving. Or Palm Springs. I wonder what is worth saving, and what do we mean by "save"?

The Salton Sea is a deadly man-made mistake, but man had nothing to do with the Salton Trough. That's the work of plate tectonics, the North American Plate sliding northwestward above and alongside the Pacific Plate on the great rift known as the San Andreas Fault. When Baja broke away from mainland Mexico ten million years ago, the

Gulf of Mexico filled most of the rift with water. And if the Colorado River had not deposited a huge berm of silt at its delta, cutting the steadily sinking Salton Trough apart from the Gulf, Palm Springs would be a seaside resort.

The Colorado River system has flooded the Salton Trough periodically for about a million years, leaving behind the rich deep layers of sediment that support the agribusiness orchards in these California valleys. The last natural big flood occurred about two thousand years ago forming prehistoric Lake Cahuilla, which spread its waters and wetlands like a vast tree with branches from the Chocolate Mountains that border Arizona in the east to the peninsular ranges to the west. Upthrust reefs hold fossils of coral and shellfish. Paleontologists have found fossil bones of nearly one hundred land creatures such as turkey, ground sloth, horse, zebra, mastodon, musk-ox, rhinoceros, dire wolf, camel, and (yes!) even Ka-zar of the Jungle's dreaded sabertooth. Some of the fossils go back two million years. Some are as recent as ten thousand.

Native peoples lived well in the valley's splendidly populated semitropical world. The Cahuilla, for whom the lake was named, fished and hunted here. Overhead is the great Pacific flyway. Millions of migrating birds swept across the Cahuilla's skies, nesting in the marshes. Only five hundred years ago, the prehistoric lake still held water. Cahuilla fire rings and fish weirs attest to a life full of food and warmth. But the hot winds came, as they had come for centuries; the sun baked the land; the water evaporated. The cycle returned to desert and the nomadic hunters, decimated by white men's diseases and ambitions, moved on and eventually evaporated into the mainstream.

Bill and I look west from the modest adobe and plywood home that serves as headquarters for the Dos Palmas Oasis Preserve. The house sits ninety feet below sea level. In noontime glare the desert that slopes toward the Salton Sea is a dull gray brown, sand and rock dotted with dull green mesquite, creosote brush, and screwbean. Sun glints off the polluted lake that spreads before us across the basin.

At the turn of the century, a canal was built to divert water from
the Colorado River to irrigate the Imperial Valley. The river was forty
miles away from the valley and four hundred feet higher. A series of
floods in 1905 brought snowmelt roaring down from the mountains.
The great Colorado jumped its banks at the intake, and by August
nearly the whole flow of the river was running into the canal. Sand-
bags, brush mats, and other hand-labor efforts to return the river to
its channel were futile.

For two years the Colorado flowed into Mexico, slicing a fifty-
foot-deep chasm through Calexico and Mexicali, then turning north
into the Salton Sink. Water rose seven inches a day over an area of
four hundred square miles. In 1907, with the help of the Southern
Pacific Railroad, workers were finally able to fill the breach with
thousands of tons of gravel and rock. The river returned to its channel, but we were left with the Salton Sea—a body of water which,
after almost ninety years of evaporation, is still larger than Lake
Tahoe.

Given the desert climate, had nature been allowed to take its
course this sea, too, would be nothing but sinkholes. But Manifest
Destiny arrived on the tail of Spanish explorers and gold seekers from
the States. Settlers dug more canals to irrigate date palms, citrus, and
banana plantations. The irrigation water flows down across the tipped
sedimented earth of the Coachella Valley and takes the topsoil with
it to the Salton Sea. It carries toxic natural minerals such as selenium,
as well as herbicides, pesticides, chemical fertilizers.

The Salton Sea is dangerously polluted, but drying it up would
be even worse than letting it sit. With no water to hold them in
suspension, the toxic chemicals would disperse into the air, be carried
on the winds. For miles and miles all plants, animals, people would
be poisoned on contact. There seems to be no good solution. Hulk,
baby, where are you when we need you?

Cameron Barrows, The Nature Conservancy's area manager for
southern California, leads us to a reed-fringed set of ponds where
hope is being nurtured. A hooded scarecrow in white jeans, arms

outstretched, guards the ponds. A school of tiny desert pupfish scatters at our approach. This minnowlike fish is endangered. Originating in the Colorado River, pupfish have evolved to survive in highly saline waters. "We're trying to bring them back," says Barrows. "And we're having some success."

Cam Barrows wears jeans, drives a pickup, and sports sunglasses and a coppery beard. He is a wildlife biologist who has chosen to work in southern California because, as he says, "the work to be done here is the most challenging."

Dos Palmas in the 1860s was the first stop on the stagecoach route from the Arizona mine fields and the Colorado River to Los Angeles. There was, of course, an oasis. And two palms. We look around at hundreds of palms emerging from pools of clear water—an island of palms.

"These are desert fan palms," Barrows says as I vainly scan the serrated fronds for dates or coconuts. What I see are strands of fruit dangling in clusters like tiny, nutty grapes. The *Washingtonia filifera* is the largest palm in North America and the only native species. Palms need to be rooted in water while holding the hot sun in their topknots. These oases, Barrows explains, are formed by clear fossil waters bubbling up from deep springs along cracks in the earth's crust. They appear along the San Andreas Fault and other subsidiary faults in a rough line at about sea level and offer the perfect rooting places for fan palms.

"In the 1800s," says Barrows, "there were only the two palms. By the 1930s, when miners built sluice boxes here, there were one hundred palms." In 1940, the Coachella Canal was built at the base of the mountains, and of course it leaks, and that water, too, rises in the springs of the Dos Palmas Oasis. "Now we've got about two thousand palms," says Barrows.

Near the original *dos palmas* is a small fenced-off patch of bare gray sand holding two large oval rings of white quartz rock, and one small ring. "That's the graveyard," says Barrows.

The largest grave marks the resting place for a doctor named Ehrenberg (there's a town in Arizona called Ehrenberg), who was murdered by bandits while carrying gold from Arizona. A young

woman who died in childbirth while on a stagecoach journey, and
her dead infant, occupy the other graves.

Sitting next to the tangled green fan palms of the oasis and the
clear springs that rise and ramble in rivulets through them, are several
rectangular spring-fed ponds dug out of the sand by bulldozers. These
straight-line indentations seem out of place and crude among the
rounded and weather-blasted desert slopes. Farmers and investors
tried to farm this desert, but the earth was too salty for crops, so
they tried commercial fish farming. They stocked their warm-water
ponds with catfish, bass, and a North African cichlid, tilapia, which
loves to feed on the endangered pupfish.

The Nature Conservancy hopes to restore the ponds to a more
natural state, but restoration is a problematic, complicated notion, as
alien to nature's process in its abstractness as the bulldozed ponds
themselves. Recontoured, with sloughs, islands, and marsh areas, the
ponds will be used for conservation purposes: they can serve as lab-
oratories to propagate pupfish once the introduced predators are
fished out; and their marshy reed beds will continue to offer nesting
and feeding sites for the endangered Yuma clapper rail, as well as
rare black rails, leaf-nosed bats, and Colorado desert fringe-toed
lizards.

Barrows tells us the Conservancy is working with scientists, the
BLM, California State Parks, the Fish and Game, and other environmental groups to develop a comprehensive restoration plan. The goal
is to manage not just the few small oases that it owns, but a huge
region of twenty thousand acres checkerboarded with public and private holdings.

"What we have here," he says, sweeping his arm to encompass
the mountain ranges that rise to the east, and the desert with its green
splotches of palm oasis, "is a largely intact ecosystem." The system
includes the Orocopia Mountains with their herds of bighorn sheep,
the Chuckwallas with their rare tortoise populations, and the mountains called Chocolate, with their precious metals and military bombing range.

Fresh clean water is the most priceless and basic commodity in
any desert, so the plan's heart lies in Dos Palmas. Coyotes, raccoons,

snakes, lizards, the occasional cougar, and wandering bighorn sheep come to water here. And in season the palms sing with warblers, tanagers, flycatchers, and Abert's towhee. It's a big project, this process of restoration, one that will cost $500,000 to implement. If Cam Barrows wanted a challenge, he's certainly got one here.

The Indian fire rings, the settlers' graves, the miners' sluice boxes, the farmers' ponds and canals, the marching line of power poles, even the bombed-out Chocolate Mountains tell a human story of greed, mistakes, and aspirations. Strange how, when you look at the infernal spaces of this desert, there seems to be nothing but rock, sand, and sky; but when you look closely at any one spot you are able to see everything that exists now, and most everything that came before. That's what I love about deserts. You can see each thing clear.

Bill and I head down a sandy path toward a second oasis called San Andreas. A uniformed man in a bright green John Deere all-terrain vehicle passes above us on the road to the Conservancy headquarters. He is the armed guard and foreman for a crew of convicts that is weeding out tamarisk near the oasis. We look for a chaingang —the manacled men in black-and-white-striped suits who swing sledge hammers in old movies—but see no one.

Tamarisk is a more dangerous threat to the land than any convict. Imported from Africa in a futile attempt to provide shade, the tamarisk sucks up water, chokes out native species, increases salinity, and offers no nourishment to plants or animals in exchange. With no natural enemies, tamarisk propagates madly in desert wetlands and is a force in wetland destruction. The Conservancy has brought volunteers from the Youth Conservation Corps, the Los Angeles Conservation Corps, and local prisons to help clear out the pink-plumed stands of tamarisk in this oasis. The weed is so hardy the sunstruck volunteers must chop the brush down, then spray the rootstock with herbicide. The results are worth the effort. After one day, you can see water seeping up from the dry ground that has been cleared. In a matter of weeks there will be pools, then marshes. Someday soon, another oasis.

We step over sand fine and powdery as dust to the edge of a palm forest. It looks impenetrable. The fan palms droop skirts of dead fronds as they rise, and those heavy brown, saw-toothed limbs sweep to earth like the wings of giant prehistoric birds. The skirted palms rise seventy feet, a green patch of forest in the desert. Bill and I are hot and sweaty in the 90-degree noontime heat. We rush toward the shade. Snow is forgotten. I find what looks like a path. "Come on," I say. Bill shakes his head, doubtful (with good reason) of my urge to explore. There might be snakes. Stinging scorpions. Who knows what dangers lurk beneath the palms?

The path is not a path, just an opening. I enter the jungle. It is cool here, and dark. I find myself at the bottom of a huge nest of crackling fronds, running water at my feet. I look up to a ceiling of green-fringed fans, the distant sky pale blue above them. In the cool light, sun glancing off the spiny leaves of green young palms, I feel underwater.

Bill has taken another route and he stands across the trickling oasis stream, hands on his hips, a large man small as a dwarf amid the skirted palms. I beat my chest and laugh.

"Me Tarzan," I say.

"Me Jane," he replies.

I wish we had brought a picnic. A few cold Mexican beers. A ham sandwich. It would be nice to settle down here like children in a tree house and play at make-believe until night comes, and the beasts of the jungle, and the velvet desert sky jeweled with stars.

This is what I have learned about an oasis. First you must enter. You cannot comprehend an oasis from the hot sands that surround it. An oasis is a nesting place. Its clear waters rise from the center of the earth. Its scale is small enough to be human, yet immense and holy as a cathedral.

We will never know the sacred stories of the native peoples who gathered here and are gone, along with the mastodon and saber-toothed tigers. All we have of them is bone turned to stone. But we know that any culture survives on stories, and all true stories are rooted in place, as the palms are rooted in ancient water. Sacred, magical, life-giving places such as these oases must be preserved and nurtured until we, too, are bone and sand. That is what conservation means to me.

The old animal that lives in our genes needs a home. I look up through the green light for a vine to swing on. All I see is a strand of the palm's fruit, clusters of small seedy sweet nubbins dangling too high for me to reach. Above the palms the pale sky is streaked with lines of white. The geometric contrails of jet planes are man's hieroglyphics. The wispy clouds are nature's.

I think of Johnny Weissmuller and the words of wisdom he offered to all and any aspiring Tarzan. I think these words might offer encouragement to Cam Barrows and all the folks who want to save what can be saved.

"The main thing," said Weissmuller, "is not to let go of the vine."

Annick Smith is a writer and filmmaker from western Montana. Coeditor of *The Last Best Place: A Montana Anthology*, she was executive producer of the film *Heartland* and a coproducer of the film *A River Runs Through It*.

VICTOR PERERA

Sierra de las Minas, Guatemala

The Quetzal, the Parakeet, and the Jaguar

❖❖❖

My first night in the quetzal reserve of Las Nubes (The Clouds), nearly eighty-five hundred feet up in the cloud forest of Guatemala's Sierra de las Minas, we heard a thump against our cabin wall. One of the rangers, Horacio Marroquín, ventured out into the spooky dark, misty night to find a sparrow-sized parakeet lying in the mud, twitching. Horacio picked up the parakeet, which had apparently collided against the cabin in flight from a nocturnal predator, and placed it under a basket.

In the morning, the basket danced on the table as the revived parakeet tested its wings and chirped feistily, raring to go. A visiting conservationist, Paco Asturias, noted the bird's unusual dark green head and decided to take its picture before letting it go. (The only Mesoamerican cloud-forest parakeet listed in Roger Tory Peterson's field guide has light green plumage and bars on its wings.) The parakeet screeched indignantly when Horacio picked it up by both wings, biting his knuckle and thumb and then slashing at its own feet—anything to break free of his grasp.

"Let the bird go!" Paco yelled. "I'll take its picture as it takes flight!" Horacio placed the parakeet on a rail and it took off before

Paco could snap his picture; it flew straight as an arrow for a huge oak tree standing fifty meters from our cabin, draped with Spanish moss, orchids, and bromeliads. The dark green–headed parakeet with unbarred wings vanished into the upper story of the tree, taking its identity with it.

The no-name parakeet's fierce determination was a fitting introduction to my visit inside Guatemala's Biosphere Reserve of Sierra de las Minas, home to jaguars, mountain lions, tapirs, howler monkeys, harpy eagles, horned guans, and the majestic bird of Maya royalty, protagonist of the plumed serpent legend and Guatemala's national symbol: the Resplendent Quetzal.

I had set out with Horacio before dawn from his home base in Salamá, a Ladino, or non-Indian, trading town near the Sierra's western end. He drove the Jeep of Defensores de la Naturaleza (Nature's Defenders), the environmental organization that manages the Biosphere Reserve. The Sierra de las Minas climbs to nearly ten thousand feet and extends 137 kilometers along the southeastern spine of Guatemala's highlands. Its northern slopes descend into Lake Izabal, the country's largest, whose waters drain into the Caribbean Sea.

The director of Defensores, architect Andreas Lehnhoff, had sparked my imagination with his precise and at times lyrical depiction of the Sierra, which was designated a Protected Area by former president Vinicio Cerezo in 1989. A little less than half of the Biosphere Reserve's 583,000 acres lie in core areas closed to logging, hunting, and agriculture. The remainder are divided into a multiple-use zone and a buffer zone that permit limited exploitation. Rising between two geological faults, the Motagua and the Polochic, "like an ocean storm breaking in great parallel waves," as a geologist described it, this mountain range is distinguished by a convergence of semiarid scrub with astonishingly diverse moist tropical and cloud forests. The Sierra's tallest peaks, Piñalón and Raxón, help create a rain shadow in the middle Motagua valley—sprinkled with cactus, aloes, and agaves—which receives only a tenth of the four thousand millimeters of annual rainfall on the Sierra's northern face. By any measure, water is the Sierra's most abundant resource. Sixty-three rivers irrigate the surrounding valleys and sustain nearly nine hundred species of mam-

mals, birds, and reptiles, or 70 percent of Guatemala's total. The
Sierra's conifers represent an invaluable reservoir of genetic germ
plasm for tropical firs, spruces, and pines. (The cones of one Guatemalan pine have been used to reforest tropical regions of Asia,
Africa, and South America.) A large percentage of the orchids, bromeliads, and reptiles found in the Sierra's six hundred square kilometers of cloud forest are endemic to the region, and contribute to
a biodiversity unsurpassed in the hemisphere.

As a native-born Guatemalan I had been imbued from childhood
with the legends of the plumed serpent god, known as Quetzalcoatl
to the Aztecs and Kukulcán to the Maya, who returns from exile in
the east to introduce poetry, the arts, and sciences to his people.
These legends drew me to the Las Nubes Reserve above Albores,
whose 675 hectares shelter the hemisphere's densest concentration of
quetzals. The survival of these three to four hundred quetzals is due
in large part to the reserve's relative inaccessibility. Not even the
government's imposition of a three-year jail term for killing a quetzal
prevented Guatemalans from hunting it to extinction for its meat and
its showy tail in most of the country's highland provinces.

So few of these magnificent birds remain in the wild that just to
see one is considered a great boon. I had enjoyed that privilege only
once before, in 1985, when a pair of quetzals flew over my head in
the Quetzal Biotope of Purulhá, on the Sierra's northwest border.
The larger male's crimson breast and three-foot-long iridescent green
tail feathers serpentining behind him made an indelible impression.
(According to legend, the quetzal's breast turned red from the blood
of its mortally wounded master, the Quiché king Tecún Umán, after
he was lanced through the heart by the conquistador Pedro de Al-
varado.) Apart from the Sierra and its adjacent forests, whose combined quetzal populations may total one thousand pairs, *Pharomachrus
mocino*, the largest of the American trogons, presently survives in sustainable numbers in the cloud forests of Mexico's southernmost state
of Chiapas and Costa Rica's Monteverde Preserve.

Getting to Las Nubes is half the adventure, as it sits at the end of
some of the steepest and roughest roads I have ever encountered.

The ascent begins in the lower Motagua River valley. At San Agustín Aguacaztlán, a Ladino farming community, we left behind extensive fields of cantaloupe and watermelon and started the long climb up to the crest of the Sierra. As the road deteriorates into broken lime-stone bedrock, the vegetation changes dramatically. Past the hamlet of Los Cimientos, avocado, mango, and banana trees give way to the first moss-covered oaks and cypresses. A spectacular turquoise-browed motmot sat placidly at the edge of a bamboo break, flicking its emerald green racket-shaped tail.

At fifty-five hundred feet, the ubiquitous milpas, or cornfields, become interspersed with coffee and cardamom plantations. The larg-est oaks, cedars, and other hardwoods start at around six thousand feet, wresting the upper elevations from firs, spruces, and native pines. The triangular leaves of the liquidambar, or sweet gum trees, are easily mistaken for maple, whose southernmost specimens can be found along the Sierra's eastern slopes. On this mountain range, remnants of Canadian and U.S. temperate forest cohabit with tropical hard-woods, conifers, and epiphytes from the Southern Hemisphere. In many more ways than one, the Sierra is a vital link of the Isthmian mountain chain Pablo Neruda called "the sweet waist of America."

Don Carlos Méndez Montenegro, the head ranger of Albores, awaits us in his home and rest house on a glade overlooking San Agustín's orchards six thousand feet below. The cloud forest of Las Nubes Reserve lies another two thousand feet above us and six tortuous kilometers of steep clay road.

"You will need chains and the winch to get up there today," Don Carlos counsels, after extending us a warm welcome. The stories I had heard about Don Carlos and his forty years in the Sierra led me to expect a rugged and colorful eccentric who is something of a recluse. His physical presence did not disappoint. At age fifty-six, Don Carlos is tall and slender and has the seignorial, Quijotesque air of his Castilian forebears.

I had been warned of the Sierra's dark side in the person of a local landowner who had threatened Don Carlos after he spurned the offer of a Jeep to permit logging inside the core areas of the Biosphere

Reserve. In April 1990 Don Carlos and his sixteen-year-old son Alex were ambushed and shot by unknown assailants on the road to Las Nubes. The bullets passed through Don Carlos's right arm into the stomach of Alex, who was the most dedicated conservationist of the Méndez family. Don Carlos had to undergo seven operations in Guatemala City before he was flown to New Orleans for reconstructive surgery on the nerves and muscles of his right hand and forearm. Alex, who had recovered sooner from the wounds in his stomach and intestines, developed spasms that may have been epileptic. After work one afternoon he dived into a cold water pool and drowned, apparently as the result of a cardiac arrest that Don Carlos attributes to his wounds. Alex Méndez became the Sierra de las Minas Biosphere Reserve's first ecomartyr.

"The doctor gave me five years to recover, but look"—Don Carlos flexed his hand open and shut—"I am well ahead of schedule. In another year or two, I may even be able to lift boulders again, but until then I am confined to this side of the mountain." *Montaña* was the word he used for the uncharted upper reaches of the Sierra, where only a few audacious souls like Don Carlos and his sons had ventured, and where Don Carlos swore he had encountered not only jaguars, pumas, and other large predators, but two wolves that preyed on his neighbors' cattle. If the tests Don Carlos will conduct on the animals' hides bear him out, then the Sierra may prove to be the southernmost range of the nearly extinct Mexican wolf.

Don Carlos introduced me to Doña Victoria "Toya" Méndez and four of their ten sturdy, fair-skinned children, who range in age from six months to twenty-eight years. The moment I spied forty-three-year-old Doña Toya breast-feeding her infant son Alex and coddling her infant grandson, also named Alex after their deceased elder brother and uncle, I stepped across a threshold into a realm of magic I have learned to associate with Guatemala's *campo*, or backcountry.

Nearly everything about Don Carlos and his family appeared larger than life. I could hardly believe my ears when he rattled off the surnames of neighboring cattle ranchers and coffee growers who had settled here as early as the sixteenth century: Toledo, Albizures, Aldana, Oliva, Morales, Vargas, Pérez, del Cid, were redolent of the

Jews, Mozarabs, Converts, and Marranos, or secret Jews, who had fled or been expelled from the Iberian Peninsula in the fifteenth and sixteenth centuries. I would discover that many of the family vendettas in older settlements of the Sierra de las Minas were rooted in old rivalries and feuds whose origins date from Spain's Inquisition. Saúl Toledo, a ranger in the neighboring reserve of Las Delicias, traced his "New Christian" lineage to our common ancestral home in Spain. When Horacio introduced us, Toledo spoke of the cloak-and-dagger ruses he'd employed to expel from the reserve a logger named Moisés Fialco, whose father and I had attended services in Guatemala City's Sephardi synagogue. Like most other controversies in Guatemala, environmental disputes can get very personal.

With Horacio driving and Don Carlos navigating, the Jeep bogged down several times and its front tires had to be lifted out of the mud with the aid of the winch. (The verb *winchar* has entered *campo* vernacular.) Under a steady rain, courtesy of tropical storm Gert, the road had been roiled into muck the consistency and color of mango ice cream. It took us two hours to cover the distance to the three cabins of Las Nubes's campsite, built with contributions from Swedish children.

We were greeted by Don Carlos's nineteen-year-old daughter Lilly, who gets her vivid red hair from a great-great-aunt. The other ranger was her twenty-three-year-old brother Juan Carlos, who was training two Quekchí Mayan rangers from a lowland reserve in Polochic. Their patrol route included the wetlands linking the Sierra with Lake Izabal, whose native green iguanas, turtles, manatees, and rare giant anteaters—Defensores's insignia—are being decimated by corn and rice farmers driven from their lands by Guatemala's thirty-year-old civil war. The slash-and-burn methods used by waves of starving refugees and seminomadic Mayan farmers who convert hardwood forest into milpa pose a major threat to the core areas of the Sierra's Biosphere Reserve. The few Mayas who train as conservationists shoulder a disproportionate responsibility. In the past ten years, the concept of human rights has taken root in the highlands, thanks in part to Mayan activists like Rigoberta Menchú, who was awarded the Nobel Peace Prize in 1992. It may take another decade for terms like "biosphere reserve" and "sustainable use" to gain currency in the Mayan communities.

The two Quekchí rangers had caught the flu, and wore on their backs every scrap of warm clothing they owned. To these dwellers of the Sierra's lowlands, Las Nubes might just as well have been the Arctic. And the coldest, wettest season was still eight weeks away.

A ghostly mist hung over the towering trees surrounding the camp, muting the bright colors of the orchids, tsilandias, and other epiphytes that repay their hosts with their gorgeous, inoffensive tenancy. The forest's dense, vibrant gray hummed with life. Along the edges of the road you walked on muddied beds of moss thick and yielding as emerald foam rubber. I marveled at the translucent green of the ten-foot-tall tree ferns—survivors from the age of dinosaurs—growing along the streams and ravines. Green and gray are the cloud forest's primary colors; a green so intense it illuminates the gray fog from within, and calls to mind Blake's forests of the night. Green too are the primary colors of the birds: the unnamed parakeet that collided with our cabin, the magnificent hummingbird feeding on red tsilandias, the emerald toucanet and the green of the quetzal's iridescent crest and tail that, under a magnifying glass, turns out not to be green at all, but an optical illusion created by a palette dominated by golden hues. And the orchids! The brightest crimson, white, and yellow epiphytes grow in the densest fog on the uppermost stories of towering oaks, spruces, and cedars, where there is no one to admire them save other orchids and the quetzals. Everything here is larger than life: conifers as wide around as giant oaks, oaks and Spanish cedars nearly the girth of sequoias.

Even the native pit vipers grow to incommensurate size. *Bothrops atrox*, known locally as *barba amarilla* and elsewhere as fer-de-lance, may grow seven feet long and thick as a firehose; *Bothrops atrox* is the largest venomous snake in Mesoamerica, and the most dangerous because it has no fear of humans. In southern Mexico's Lacandón forest, where it goes by the Maya name Nauyaca, more Lacandón Mayas died of its bite than from any other cause before the introduction of antiviperine serum. In my several eye-to-eye encounters with this daunting reptile, I have always been the first to blink and back away, very slowly. *Bothrops atrox* is believed to be the reptile half of the plumed serpent god Kukulcán, whose effigy graces the temples of Chichén Itzá, Uxmal, and Yaxchilán.

George V. N. Powell, the biologist and quetzal expert, had visited Las Nubes and radio-tagged three male and one female quetzals, in order to determine their range as well as their feeding and courtship habits. In Salamá the author Francisco Guzmán, known as the quetzal's poet laureate, had assured me that these birds were hidden from view between August and December, when they begin their elaborate courtship rituals.

"They may be hidden from Don Pancho, but not from us," Don Carlos assured me. With the aid of the radio transmitters, we traced the female quetzal to a tree of aguacatillo, an olive-sized avocado that fruits every three years.

A group of about ten quetzals were feeding when we arrived. They rose like large hummingbirds to pluck the fruits on the wing, and alighted briefly to gulp them down. Even with binoculars, the birds were gray, animated silhouettes; I had to conjure up their bright crimsons and iridescent greens from memory. On sensing our presence, the quetzals froze, becoming all but invisible in the dense foliage. The largest male was the first to sound the alarm, waving his two-foot-long twin tail—not yet fully grown—as he flew with a loud double whistle to a large oak on the left. One by one, the smaller males and females fled to neighboring trees. These quetzals, unlike the ones I saw in Purulhá, were still wary of humans, and that seemed all to the good. It started to rain, which rendered our binoculars useless, but we waited another half hour to hear the clarion call of the large male, answered by females who sent comforting signals to their chirping chicks, too scared to leave the shelter of the aguacatillo tree. I felt like a privileged intruder.

On our return, Don Carlos stopped to make quetzal calls at various feeding posts, but none came. Quetzals share their favorite fruit trees with the horned guan, a rare, turkey-sized bird whose single red horn gives it an antediluvian appearance. "We'll try again tomorrow," Don Carlos said. "Quetzals don't like to forage in the rain, so they should be here nice and early." On our walk he pointed out plants that had nutritional or medicinal value, like the quinine tree and the Pacific yew that is the source of the controversial cancer cure, Taxol. Don Carlos was familiar with trees and shrubs useful for every conceivable ailment, from balms for diarrhea, colics, asthma, and infertility to the exotic bamboo known as *cola de caballo* (horse tail), reputed to cure kidney infections. Don Carlos used the local Spanish or Indian names for most plants, and when he did not know them, he often made them up. ("Sylvan Warsaw" was his generic name for a variety of purplish flowers.)

Halfway back to the camp, he stopped to show me a hollow trunk with three woodpecker nests the quetzals would enlarge and take over to nest and bear their young. "The males sit on the eggs along with the females," he said. "It is quite a treat to watch them go in and out with their long tails, which they fold into themselves like green snakes." In April, during the short dry season, he had come upon a curious scene: two large male quetzals raising clouds of dust as they sparred on the ground like fighting cocks. "And it turned out to be over a worm," he said. "Of course, worms here grow to nearly a foot, and quetzals consider them a delicacy." Don Carlos's chance encounter had apparently settled three outstanding issues of quetzal behavior: contrary to popular belief, quetzals do alight on the ground on occasion, they do include live prey in their vegetarian and insect diet, and the males do fight over prey or females, particularly during the mating season.

In his book *Bird of Life, Bird of Death*, Jonathan Maslow speculated that the cult of the plumed serpent may have originated during the quetzal's courtship season, when a male will dive headlong from the top of a cliff to impress his potential mate; with his sleek body and three-foot-long tail trailing behind, the quetzal eerily resembles a flying snake.

"Oh yes, I have seen a male fling himself from the top of a giant oak," Don Carlos said. "There is no other sight quite like it. I don't know what effect it has on the females, but it sure impressed the hell out of me."

We took two more steps, and Don Carlos called out, *"Mire mire mire."* I turned to the left, and glimpsed a disturbance in the shrubbery.

"I saw its tail, it's the jaguar," he said. Two days before, on this very spot, a large cat had leaped across the road in front of Lilly, Don Carlos's red-haired daughter.

"It seemed to be flying," she said. "And it happened so fast I could not be certain if it was a jaguar or a puma."

Instead of putting distance between us and the jaguar, Don Carlos charged into the undergrowth to follow its trail. I had heard not a sound, and the thick layers of wet leaves left no prints. And yet, the cat's presence was palpable. Jaguars, Don Carlos claimed, rarely show themselves to men. In his forty years here he had seen only a tail or part of a head, or glimpsed jaguars in shadow, in silhouette, or as a receding blur. But they are less wary with women, which may account for the jaguar's—or puma's—spectacular leap in front of Lilly. Only after the initial excitement wore off did my knees buckle. What if we had startled the jaguar, or gotten between a mother and her cubs? In Yaxchilán years before, I had heard the soft cough and moan of a mating jaguar. The following day we had discovered its tracks on the banks of the Usumacinta River. But this was no chance encounter. The jaguar was checking out the new intruder on its turf, and letting him know of its presence.

Andreas Lehnhoff had shown me a survey taken by Defensores in the Sierra's three main Ladino settlements, asking which animals the settlers considered the most dangerous. Although the most harmful by far were the raccoons, coatis, and collared peccaries that devastate their milpas and orchards, the farmers invariably named the jaguar as the animal they feared most, because "they eat people."

When asked to describe an incident of a jaguar actually attacking a human, the respondents became evasive. No one had personally seen a jaguar or mountain lion attack humans, although on rare occasions they made off with a goat or calf. It was the "tiger burning bright" in their dreams that they feared, Lehnhoff concluded.

I dreamed of that jaguar nearly every night for two weeks. He will walk in my subconscious probably the remainder of my life, just out of view as he leaps soundlessly into the undergrowth.

The following day Don Carlos showed me some of the illegal deforestation carried out by loggers inside core areas of the reserve. The swath of devastation left by the bulldozers was similar to scenes I had witnessed in Mexico's Lacandón forest and Guatemala's adjacent Petén Biosphere Reserve. Each felled oak, spruce, or cedar brought down a half dozen smaller trees as it crashed to the ground. And worse still, dozens of large hardwood logs lay rotting on the ground, abandoned when the bulldozers could not make a road wide enough for the skidders to take them out. "Greed and ignorance are the two chief enemies of the Sierra," Don Carlos said solemnly. "We have made progress teaching settlers that water does not appear miraculously from the ground when they cut down the forest, as many of them believe; instead, they are destroying their chief source of water." A look of infinite sadness clouded Don Carlos's eyes. "I fear it will take longer to convince landowners that their trees are worth more when they are left standing—in the long run—than after they are converted to lumber."

When Don Carlos and I visited the aguacatillo tree early the next morning, the quetzals were not so quick to abandon their feeding. When they did leave, they deployed in the same order as the previous evening, but their departure was more orderly. We stayed for half an hour, listening again to the orchestrated bird calls, from alarm signals and territorial whistles to the mothers' soft chirping to calm their young. Don Carlos thought the birds were becoming accustomed to our presence.

I caught a glimpse of the female with the radio pack and small antennae, and wondered how this encumbrance affected the quetzal family's internal dynamics. Of the three males George Powell and his assistants had tagged, one had left his pack high in the forest canopy, whence it continues to transmit its signal. Although the probability is that the quetzal had fallen prey to an owl, a scissor-tailed kite, or some other predator, it was also possible it had managed to remove the transmitter and two antennae, which are attached with degradable cotton thread. One other tagged male had wandered away and was living alone in a lower part of the reserve. Questions about the use of radio telemetry inevitably cropped up, and led to intense discussions around the dining table. Had the encumbrance of the pack made the quetzal an easier prey to its enemies? Could it adversely affect its chances of successfully courting a desirable female? Paco Asturias, one of the founders of Defensores, was of the opinion that no self-respecting female would have anything to do with a male carrying on his back an unsightly rucksack that impairs both his courtship display and his prospects for survival. Regardless of the answers to these questions, there is no denying that our presence alters the nature of our investigation, and this intrusion has to be factored into the findings. The quid pro quo in this experiment is the radio-enhanced information about the quetzals' habits that may help the conservationist devise better ways to protect them; but they will no longer be the wild quetzals we came here to observe. Like the creatures confined to U.S. federal and state parks, the quetzal will have entered an involuntary Faustian compact with humans, surrendering a part of its innate freedom in exchange for our protection. The quetzal of legend that dies when placed in a cage will have to learn to survive in a larger, more benign, and irreversible confinement.

In the afternoon I followed Don Carlos up a forty-foot escarpment called Angel Rock for a panoramic view of the Sierra, only to find it socked in with clouds. During the half hour I spent at the top, clinging to the sides of the huge boulder as I remembered my susceptibility to vertigo, I reflected on my brief visit to Las Nubes. I had not caught even a glimpse of the sun, and yet my eyes were filled with a whole spectrum of muted greens, crimsons, and yellows nurtured by the moisture-laden clouds. No lowland rain forest preserve I had visited, not even Tikal, abounded with the diversity of life and colors I had encountered here.

Many of the forces that would destroy the wild, pristine beauty of the Sierra de las Minas Biosphere Reserve are already at work. But it will remain a place of hope, at least for a while longer, thanks to the dedication of Defensores's rangers, and to Guatemalans' growing attachment to their dwindled population of quetzals. The very notion of a "shadow" separating the Sierra's moist, fecund side from its dry, semidesert face had both literal and metaphoric implications, bolstering the suspicion that this mountain has a soul, a *genius loci* that is both definer and protector of its remarkable treasures. My travels in Mesoamerica have taught me that even the sturdiest *genii loci* are vulnerable, mortal presences. In the end, a place like the Sierra de las Minas is only as wild—and as safe—as its inhabitants' determination to keep it so.

"Listen, it's the howler monkeys," Don Carlos called out, as he danced on the top of Angel Rock like a goat, while I clung to its sides, disoriented by the enveloping gray void. I listened closely and finally heard the distant howl of the monkeys carried in the wind.

"They are singing," Don Carlos said. "That means the clouds will lift."

Victor Perera is the author of *Rites: A Guatemalan Boyhood* and *Unfinished Conquest: The Guatemalan Tragedy*. He teaches journalism at the University of California at Berkeley.

DOROTHY ALLISON

ACE River Basin, South Carolina

Promises

❖❖❖

My son Wolf, sixteen months old and fearless, loves nothing more than running off under the redwood trees down the hill from our house. The puppies chase after him barking joyfully, determined to catch the ball he waves above his head. I follow behind, just far enough back to give the baby a sense of freedom, not so far back that I can't rescue him when he falls over his own stumbling gait. "Mama!" Wolf shouts, and I find myself laughing. Hearing him call me Mama is almost as unimaginable as living in this landscape of rolling hills, redwood trees, and January camellias blooming as if it were spring. There is a river down the hill, a California river with a rocky bottom, docks, and summer bridges put up in May and taken down each October. It is beautiful and strange, as far from my childhood as I am. Even near the ocean where this river pulls in marsh birds and fishermen, there is no swampland like the ones I remember as a girl, a landscape so ripe flowers burst out of the brown-and-black-spotted muck, and promised vindication even as it threatened our white cotton socks.

When I was eleven my mama and stepfather took their one and only true vacation, driving us south to the coast below Charleston for a week away from work and school. We spent three days on Folly Beach and another three guesting at a bedraggled trailer loaned to us by one of the men who worked for my stepfather. The trailer was parked on a tiny plot just a quarter of a mile from the ocean, sur-rounded by old rice plantation property, flat damp grounds thick with mossy gnarled oaks and an impossibly dense lattice of old-growth grasses. Our uncle, Beau, Mama's brother, joined us with a tent draped in mosquito netting and a truckload of fishing gear.

"We'll catch enough fish to pay for the trip and then some," Uncle Beau swore. He sent my stepfather back to the highway for a load of block ice, and dug a pit to keep it a while. My sisters and I baited hooks and hauled buckets of water up to hold the fresh-caught fish. Mama stretched out on a plastic foldout lawn chair with a John D. MacDonald mystery.

"I want you to know right off," she announced, "I'm on vacation, so I an't gonna clean no fish I personally an't gonna eat." The men just laughed. My sisters and I were scandalized, and immediately be-gan to beg to learn how to clean fish.

The men caught very little as it turned out. The fish were plentiful but wise. It didn't matter to us girls. We had stopped paying any attention to them anyway. We took off on our own, walking the raised dirt platforms that set off the old rice fields and inspecting the locked-down wooden frames that were used to direct the tides into the various rice fields still intact. The remains of that old plantation were laid out like a giant chessboard, designed so that we could walk the border of each rough square, cleared enough that we could see the snakes sunning themselves in the grass before they heard you coming. Where the deeper water came in, the trees stood like the legs of fossilized Clydesdales, spindly and fine at the top, wide and swollen at the base. Where the trees parted, the grasslands went on for miles, stretching to the sea, here and there spotted with islands of maple and straggly palms, ringed with slow-moving creeks and rivers. We raced each other along the dikes and ate peanut butter sandwiches in the shade of stunted pines. Startlingly beautiful white birds called out as we passed, osprey, ibis, egret, ducks, and wood storks. Some lifted their enormous wings and swung up into a sky so blue and pure it made my heart hurt to stare up into its reaches.

Mama told us that Indians—Cherokee even—had lived in those swamps once, and runaway slaves and poor whites had come there, the latter fleeing sheriffs who would have locked them up for debt. All of them passed through carefully, leaving no mark, and that was what we were to do, carrying out everything we carried into the swamp. We peered through screens of ferns and wild ricegrass, and played at being runaways hiding in the tall clumps of grass. We tied our hair up in handkerchiefs, put rubberbands around the cuffs of our jeans to keep out the bugs, and brought back gifts of wildflowers and broken shells for Mama to admire. We would have brought her lily pads, but pulled free of the water they stank and shriveled. Instead, we searched out glittery feathers from those big white birds.

Back at the trailer my stepfather and Uncle Beau had cursed their luck with fish, given up, and gone off to get a bucket of spiced shrimp from one of the highway stands. Mama had put her paperback down and was lying quietly, staring up into the clear blue sky. "You come here," she called to us, sitting up and pulling me close to her hip, a story already shining in her soft brown eyes. I picked leaves out of my sisters' curls and listened to Mama while watching the sky myself.

"This is where things begin," I heard myself say. Mama sighed with pleasure and agreed with a quick affectionate hug. The sound of my uncle's truck growled off in the distance.

"We'll come back," Mama promised. But we never did.

The last time I went home to South Carolina, my cousin B.J. drove me around Greenville in her faded green Buick. We headed out to the western edge of the town, avoiding the new butterfly overpasses that channel traffic out to the Interstate. Our goal was to locate a house we both remembered well, a two-bedroom wood-frame cottage, memorable for the peach trees in front and back. There, I had turned a moody thirteen listening to the music playing at the old Rhythm Ranch dance barn half a mile away. There, B.J. had fallen in love while staying with us, spending her evenings curled up on the kitchen floor with the phone pressed to her ear so that her boyfriend could whisper his own lyrics and promises. We had talked about that house the night before, the way that place had marked us both. We remembered that it had been set on the far side of a huge open field choked with high grass and patches of blackberries. Near there, past the peanuts and the pines, the wetlands began, acres of swampy forest, thick with short pine and stunted dogwood, muscadines hanging in sheets off dark trees and birds rising in clouds off the intermittent stretches of grassland. It had seemed then that the wild places were close in and mysterious, opening off the backyards of the widely spaced old rented houses. Now my youngest cousins live in apartments and condos, drive out to the country only on weekends, and couldn't spot a muscadine if their lives depended on it. When B.J. and I talk about the old days, they smile and turn the television up louder.

"There were all those trees," B.J. kept saying, as we drove one suburban blacktop after another looking for that house. Acres of tract houses, barren of trees or blackberry bushes confused and saddened us. Earlier, we had driven past the old Greenville County high school. It was stark and mostly boarded up, the two-block stretch of dirt playgrounds pressed down to a concrete finish. All the windows that were not covered in plywood were shattered and gaping. We had driven around it twice looking for the road where at one time the school buses would come in to turn around. Both of us were growing tired and frustrated.

"I know it was around here somewhere." B.J.'s voice was strained and bewildered. I leaned my cheek against my palm and pushed my hair back out of my eyes. "Things change," I told B.J. as we drove away from the school. I was remembering a morning when I had missed the schoolbus and walked the two miles into that school. Once there, though, I had spent the day hidden under the extensions— temporary classes set up in mobile units on blocks. All afternoon I had watched the sunlight move across the banks of windows, turning them to mirrors that reflected the warning lights at the railroad crossing and the occasional passing clouds. At 3:00 P.M. I had skipped the bus and walked home again, cutting across the peanut fields on the other side of the railway line, arriving home as my mama was turning up our driveway. She had smiled at me and handed me a wrapped package of leftovers from the diner where she was working the day shift. I had taken the package with a guilty smile, expecting that at any moment she would recognize my crime from something in my eyes. But she had seen nothing and no one had called. It was the first time I ever skipped school, the first time I ever lied to her, if only by my silence. Not being discovered changed everything, and after that I skipped school whenever I wanted, wandering in the woods and swamps past our house, finding a peace and comfort out there that was not possible in our cramped and moody house.

"Do you remember when we'd all drive up into the hills?" B.J.'s voice was pensive.

"With Aunt Dot and Uncle Bill?"

"Yeah, in the back of the truck with watermelon on ice in tubs."

"And buckets to gather berries for Dot to make pies later."

"She never made pies. Didn't have enough berries left by the time we got home to flavor a cobbler."

"Well, think how many of us there were. Berry-eating kids leave little behind."

"But everything was so close and beautiful."

"Yeah."

Is it memory that feeds us as we grow older? Is it memory that houses all our dreams? The landscape of my imagination is all memory and passion, the wetlands where I wandered as a child, the hidden places where I birthed my stories, widened my vision, and plotted my escapes. That we were poor made no difference in that beautiful place. The flowers bloomed for us as thickly as for others, the breeze came in at evening and cleaned the heated atmosphere. We could run out into those woods and know that hope is everlasting. What feeds

children who never run there, never discover anemones under rotted
waste or startle birds so beautiful they hurt the heart?

B.J. and I drove back to the school and worked our way out for a
third time, tracing where the old railway line had been torn up and
buried, the highway that intersected just below where the old Rhythm
Ranch had stood alone in an open parking lot of rutted dirt.

"You remember the music?" B.J. asked me once, and I laughed
in reply.

"Bass guitars played off-key and drunken men singing heartbreak
songs."

"Honey, don't hurt me more than I can stand."

"Yes, Lord. They don't make music like that no more."

"No, Lord. Thank God, they don't."

Her hand slapped the steering wheel hard, but I remembered following her out in the evening to hike up the road toward the Ranch. We
would huddle there and listen to that music drifting out over the grass,
the lure of the grownup world irresistible. Broken-down old trucks
parked end to end next to rebuilt sedans and ancient convertibles with
ragged canvas tops. Half-drunk musicians were always wrestling near
the back door beside the stage, trading drags off cigarettes and curses
for the poor wages they were paid. Men and women would come out to
stand under the cedar trees that edged the parking lot, hugging and
whispering, and telling lies we could almost understand. Sometimes,
they would sneak off into the woods so close onto the lot that leaves
drifted down into the backs of the trucks.

"Honey, don't hurt me more than I can stand."

None of that remained. Twenty years had obliterated the county
roads. Where once the woods had been wild, now there were only
manicured lawns and quick-stop milk stores. Shopping centers stood
where there had been a landscape a child could explore but never
exhaust. Set off by arc lights and hurricane fencing, a discount center
and a massive concrete parking lot had replaced the dance barn. We
stopped at a shiny new Biscuitville for a Coke and spoke to the
waitress who told us, yes, she remembered the Ranch from her girl-
hood, and yes, it had been right there.

" 'Bout where the delivery vans park now," she told me.

I looked back and narrowed my eyes to remember the cedars with pickup trucks pulled up underneath, stooped men in cloth caps passing paper bags and laughing softly under the sound of steel guitars. Bullfrog voices thudding in the night, nightbirds screaming, the sky so close you could almost smell the stars.

"Progress," the woman said, and I nodded. B.J. wiped her eyebrows with her thumbs and shook her head. She had been a girl in love here. I had been a terrified, stubborn child. None of that was left, and neither of us knew how to speak about what we felt about losing the landscape of our memories.

"It's like it was another world," we told each other driving away. "And now it's gone. You'd think something so good, people would save a piece of it."

There is a smell that has stayed with me all these years, a haunting smell of dusty moss, damp split cedars, stagnant creeks, and salt-flavored evening breezes, that dreamlike landscape below Charleston, the wild open land around Greenville. When I went to Charleston this past fall, I smelled that landscape again, the landscape of memory and dreams. I had been sick for a week when I arrived, still sweating out fever, but determined to see what a handful of stubborn people were trying to save from progress and neglect. At the ACE River Basin project I saw the same lands where once my mama had told stories, where my uncle had laughed at the unpredictable nature of fish, where my sisters and I had run off into the wild to see whatever hid there. Unchanged, lush, and safe, those old rice plantations still lay sheltering birds and wild grass and childish dreams.

"I thought all the places like this were gone," I told the friends I saw there.

"Would be if we didn't work to keep them," I was told.

Exactly so, I agreed, and looked back twenty years to the landscape where I had been a girl.

❖ ❖ ❖

I live now in northern California close enough to the coast to bicycle over in the evening. Salt comes in from the ocean and stirs up the long grass, draws my eyes back toward the redwoods beyond the low hills. It is not the landscape of my childhood but always brings that memory back to me. If I close my eyes I can remember a place where the water was almost sweet, standing brackish around sunken trees and the half-buried nests of wood storks. The approaching twilight brings back the smell of shallow water darkened by tannic acid, mud-stained tree roots, and glistening full-bellied frogs. Over there, live oaks, sycamore, and palmetto shelter fern and Spanish moss. Ash trees and maple stand out against the occasional hickories and dogwood. Honeysuckle, day lilies, and anemone throw up brilliant sprays of cool glossy green and hot bright color. Sometimes where the river meets the ocean, I experience again that waking dream. I become again eight years old and running with my cousins, canvas shoes squeaking in the muck, and the sounds of the shoes pulling free echoing the frogs and crickets and fast-moving nightbirds. The sky above us filters pink and purple. Ducks and wood storks lift their wings over the still water of the deeper marsh. Squirrels, rabbits, raccoons, and their predators push through the brush. A car radio plays softly in the distance and the smell of unfiltered cigarettes drifts down with the music. My aunt Dot calls our names with weary patience. In a while, my uncles come stumbling back out of the night with buckets of bullfrogs and deep grunting laughter. By then we are all lying around on blankets eating from bowls of buttermilk and cold corn bread, watching the stars blink out above us, and listening to my aunts whispering gossip and lies. It is a dream full of safety, love, sheer physical pleasure, and the scent of a ripe and beautiful landscape, a landscape that has all but disappeared. Only for the duration of the dream does it become again painfully real. If that landscape were not safe somewhere, would my dreams survive? Could my stories live in a world where children never ran free in that place where all my hopes were first shaped?

When my son runs down the hill through the trees, shouting for Mama and laughing as freely as only a baby can laugh, I cup my hands in stubborn hopefulness, making to him the promise my mama could never keep to me. I will make this place safe for him, bring him back to this landscape throughout his life, this wild country of beauty and hope and mystery. Every time he calls for me from those trees in the dusk, I promise again, every time hoping I can keep my promise.

Dorothy Allison is the author of *Bastard Out of Carolina, Trash, The Women Who Hate Me*, and *Skin: Talking About Sex, Class, and Literature*. She currently lives in northern California.

Upon This River

❖❖❖

The San Pedro is the only river of consequence that rises in Mexico and flows *north* into the United States, where it cuts a hundred-mile course toward the Gila, which it joins at Winkelman, Arizona. It begins near the little mining town of Nacozari, Sonora, crosses the border a few miles west of Naco, Arizona, then runs down a broad-bottomed valley lying between several huge rocky outcrops: the Mule Mountains, the Huachucas, Whetstones, Dragoons, Rincons, Santa Catalinas, Galiuros, and the Tortillas. Some of these small ranges are so separated from their neighbors that their plants and creatures are unique to that single range, a phenomenon creating the so-called sky islands of Arizona. Ramsey Canyon in the Huachucas has a subspecies of leopard frog, for instance, that ribbets to a mate from underwater, whereas its cousin eight miles east in the San Pedro River uses the more common means of airborne songs.

This green riparian corridor, isolated as it is by the fierce exigencies of the Sonoran Desert, is another kind of "island" where particular species may differ from their close kith in neighboring tributaries: Lemmon's fleabane, to name one, apparently occurs only in the San Pedro Valley. What's more, this river, in places disappearing under its bed of gravel as if to escape the sun, is the heart of one of the longest undammed watersheds in the Southwest and holds fifty-five *globally* rare or endangered species: fine little creatures like the loach minnow, spike dace, Gila chub, the Huachuca tiger salamander, and plants like lemon lily, Canelo Hills lady's tresses, Tepic flame-flower.

But the valley is not just a place of rare things; even more it's a vale of richness: four hundred some species of birds (over half the number on this continent) are residents or migrants. Bird-listers come here to see a northern beardless-tyrannulet, an Abert's towhee, an eared trogon, or some of the fifteen kinds of hummingbirds. On the ground and in the waters live eighty species of mammals (occasionally a transient ocelot or jaguar), forty species of amphibians and reptiles, and the largest number of native fish in the Southwest. A visitor soon understands that raw numbers are part of the poetry of this arid landscape.

A valley so abundant in beast and blossom will surely attract humankind as well. Indeed, archaeologists have discovered more than two hundred fifty prehistoric and historic sites along the San Pedro, the earliest dating from at least eleven thousand years ago, an age that places the upper valley among the oldest known sites in the contiguous states. Around 9000 B.C., people of the Archaic Period— a time here of camels, horses, tapirs, giant bison—hunted mammoths with spears tipped with beautifully fluted Clovis Points. Only a few hundred yards from where the San Pedro enters Arizona is a "mammoth kill site" that incontestably establishes a community of hunters along the river six millennia before the Great Pyramid of Cheops existed. Recently, far-seeing and generous ranchers Ed and Lynn Lehner gave the site to the American people, a gesture that reveals how many San Pedro residents increasingly want to help preserve the valley.

Within view of the Lehner Ranch, possibly right across it, Coronado led his 1540 expedition searching for the Seven Cities of Gold. A year earlier, Father Marcos de Niza, perhaps the first European to see the American Southwest, likely traversed this valley, and a century and a half later, another famous Jesuit, Eusebio Francisco Kino, traveled the region for thirty years to establish missions.

Chiricahua Apache leaders Cochise (his stronghold lay in the Dragoon Mountains) and Geronimo (his, just to the east) made their names indelible during their struggle to keep the San Pedro Valley. For purely Anglo history, the infamous Tombstone is only seven miles from the river.

In the watershed farther north, in 1982, The Nature Conservancy bought the old Muleshoe Ranch along with its hot springs and grazing lease to begin cooperatively overseeing it with the U.S. Forest Service and the Bureau of Land Management. Six years later the success of the endeavor encouraged Congress to designate forty miles of the upper San Pedro as the first riparian National Conservation Area in order to protect and enhance this finest remaining riverine artery of what was once an extensive network of such systems. Today, you can walk along the rocky upland of the valley with its sere and thorny beauty of saguaro, acacia, and cholla; you can descend toward the river with its cienegas (natural bogs) and mesquite bosques, then continue to the thicket banks of Fremont cottonwood, Gooding willow, netleaf hackberry, and Arizona ash; if you do, you'll see why Congress chose the San Pedro as the initial riparian Conservation Area.

Just south of Fort Huachuca, close to the border, the first National Natural Landmark in the country lies near the river: Ramsey Canyon, a splendid preserve owned and managed by the Conservancy since 1974. The canyon, holding the largest number of threatened species of any Conservancy reserve in the country, in 1980 had only about a hundred lemon lilies, a globally endangered plant; six years later fewer than twenty remained; by 1990 there were but two flowering plants. Conservancy manager Tom Wood, in an inspired bit of "forensic ecology," reasoned that a recent severe wild burn was the result of long years of fire suppression creating a dangerously combustible "fuel load" on the ground, a condition uncommon in a natural system where more frequent small blazes control the thatch; when the big fire happened, it so denuded the slopes that following rains ran off rather than penetrating the earth, and little Ramsey Creek poured violently down the canyon, washing out lilies, cutting different channels that left surviving plants too far from the stream that carries their seeds to new soil. The two remaining blossoms were far enough apart that it was difficult for a hawk moth, their natural pollinator, to find both flowers. In a long and difficult canyon hike, Tom Wood acted for the moth by carrying in a cotton-lined box the anthers from one lily to the other. When, to his joy, both produced seeds, he sprinkled some near each parent, others in creek edges farther away, and sent the remainder to a national seed bank in Flagstaff. By 1992, about a hundred plants were again alive. His effort is one a federal agency is unlikely to accomplish; without his insight and dedication and the protection afforded by the Conservancy preserve, the lemon lily—*along with its dependent species*—would be that much closer to extinction.

Given this much good news of informed concern and progressive action by private and public groups, why is the San Pedro one of the first dozen sites in the "Last Great Places" campaign? (Considering all these firsts, you may see an irony in calling the river the San Pedro if you remember Jesus's play on the apostle's name in Greek: "Thou art Peter, and upon this rock I will build my church; and the gates of hell shall not prevail against it.")

Why?

• Mining has occurred in the San Pedro area for the last one hundred years, and more new open-pit mines loom.

• Some of our nineteenth-century attitudes and laws almost guarantee that cattle and sheep will overgraze public lands. The incredible changes—losses—in the Southwest since the introduction of ranching only a hundred fifty years ago make it difficult today for us to see the West settlers first encountered. To compare early-day photographs with present scenes here is often heartbreaking. Clearly, we must do certain things differently across the Rocky Mountain West, where grazing occurs on seven out of ten acres (a percentage even larger if you exclude towns, roads, and dry lake beds). To see the effect of wasteful grazing on this fragile topography one has only to walk the uplands of the Muleshoe Ranch where native vegetation still struggles to return six years after the removal of cattle, animals John Muir called "hooved locusts."

• Our growing populace often behaves like wheeled locusts. In our easy autos, we have a penchant for letting cities and towns sprawl willy-nilly across the countryside, a process evident around Sierra Vista, a San Pedro Valley strip-development founded in 1958 next to the expanding army base at Fort Huachuca. Today even the creosote flats near the river at Sierra Vista get bulldozed for trailers and cheap modular housing. It's a measure of our delay in committing ourselves to real conservation that we are down to protecting creosote brush instead of the original native bunch-grasses Anglo settlers found.

Even to speak of "last great places" reveals how pressing the need, an urgency resulting from a most uncharacteristic national slowness, to respond to immediate threats to our abundant land. If a foreign power tried to take from us a mere square yard of American soil, we would answer with arms. Yet, when our own outdated policies and attitudes work for an even greater loss, our response too often is a despairing, "What can *I* do?" The Nature Conservancy specializes in answering that question.

I am a Missourian living far from the San Pedro River, but I believe this emerald strand, still strung precariously with the iridescence of hummingbird bellies and the scintillance of clear waters and the glow of cactus blossoms, is something that does not belong to me although I belong to it: its beauty, its history, and most of all, its significance.

William Least Heat-Moon is the author of *Blue Highways* and *PrairyErth*. He lives in Missouri.

The Betrayal of Jack

❖❖❖

Morgan Bottoms, much of which is the old Carpenter family ranch, is an eleven-mile stretch in northwestern Colorado just east of Hayden where the banks of the Yampa are dominated by cottonwood forests. These groves cover hundreds of acres of land, mostly along the south bank but sometimes enveloping the river by spreading over areas north of it as well.

Each of the cottonwood groves at Morgan Bottoms is tall and dense. The canopy is multi-tiered, with the upper reaches composed of narrowleaf cottonwood trees, whose thick roots pump up huge amounts of water to keep the giant trees alive. Midway, a graceful story of box elders spreads out its many wings. Lower down, you see red-osier dogwoods, with their brilliant flame-colored bark. Various shrubs and forbs, including serviceberry, hawthorn, squawbush, and goldenrod, form a tangled ground cover, with coyote willows thick near the river. The forest floor is within the Yampa's floodplain and the river waters it during the high runoff in spring and early summer. Gnats, mosquitoes, and other insects swarm in the marshy reaches, as does an unbelievable array of bird life: great blue heron, great horned owls, golden eagles, even an occasional bald eagle; mergansers, wood ducks, mallards. Morgan Bottoms is a crucial place for sandhill cranes, part of their only breeding ground in Colorado and one of the state's three staging areas, where they fatten up before migrating south.

Yet this profusion of vegetation and wildlife habitat was alien to my eye. Across the whole arid West, cottonwoods run along nearly every low- and middle-elevation river, stream, and creek, but the trees form thin ribbons, two or three deep, not unlike the buffer strips of Douglas fir or ponderosa pine that the Forest Service so assiduously leaves along highways adjacent to clear-cuts. Out here, cottonwoods come in thin strips, not forests, so Morgan Bottoms takes on a surprising, almost suspicious, cast.

For we all perceive the natural world in layers. We may take in nature in a literal way—vegetation, animal species, waters, soils, land formations—but we overlay those facts with our own memories, imaginations, fears, and dreams, and for us those overlays are as complex and real as the natural facts themselves might be. There are many layers, some personal, some held by the public at large, over this part of Colorado.

To me the most haunting overlay on Morgan Bottoms, on the Yampa and on the White, on the whole Colorado Western Slope, will always be the experience of the Utes, how they lived and loved and worshiped and how these horse people rode this terrain for so many centuries.

The tenure of the Ute people in the region traces back farther than we can fully imagine. Some anthropologists think that they migrated into the Colorado Plateau region between A.D. 1000 and 1300. Others believe that the modern Utes emerged from the Fremont people. The Fremont, whom we date back to about four thousand years ago, lived both in villages and on the move, hunting and gathering, and leaving behind housing sites, baskets, pots, and magical pictographs and petroglyphs. In turn, the Fremont probably evolved from hunters and gatherers who lived on the Colorado Plateau beginning about 10,000 years ago or more.

The Utes themselves seem disinclined to join the debate of non-Indian scholars. They hold by their own explanation. At the beginning of time, Sinawauf, the Creator, had all of the peoples of the world in a bag. He opened the bag and placed the Utes in their mountain, plains, and desert country. By any account, the current of Ute blood runs very, very deep out here.

A dominant event in Ute history took place in the early 1600s, when tribal members acquired the horse from Spanish explorers. Vastly increased numbers of horses were later freed up by the Pueblos' revolt against the Spanish in 1680.

The Utes took immediately to this fantastic new animal and became extraordinarily mobile. Bands of Utes ranged from the Wasatch Front all the way to the Colorado Front Range—from present-day Salt Lake City to Denver. They established a lasting trail system, which included what is now Trail Ridge Road through Rocky Mountain National Park, the highest paved road in the United States. With the horse, the Utes traversed all the territory they could wish, speeding across open plains, ascending to the high plateau and mountain hunting grounds, shooting down into steep washes, draws, and canyons in that rough country. They were master horsemen. Just as a virtuoso pianist blends with a piano, a Ute rider became one with his horse.

To be sure, in many ways life was hard. The winters, even in the lower-lying valleys, were brutally cold. A head injury, broken leg, or serious tooth infection could be a life-threatening event. Loved ones were lost in battles with the Shoshone, Navajo, and Plains tribes to the east. The Utes signed a peace treaty with the Spanish in the 1600s, but a treaty was of no use against the smallpox, measles, and other diseases.

Yet the horse shut down so many threats and opened up so many options, so many freedoms. The curse of hunger, or outright famine, was essentially eliminated by the large-area hunting now made possible. Relations with other tribes and the Spanish took a new posture. The horseback Utes could escape, pursue, and fight so effectively that the other cultures conceded the central Rockies to the Utes as their mountain stronghold.

This was especially true for the Northern Utes, who lived in the

Yampa and White River valleys. The mountain buffalo inhabited the high parks across the high Flat Tops and mountain spine to the east. With the horse it became such an easy matter to reach all the best hunting grounds. Other than parts of the Pacific Northwest, Ute country held more kinds of mammals, and in greater numbers, than anywhere in western North America.

The hunt was a time of heightened excitement. Ute hunters were splendidly decked out in buckskins adorned with beads, fringe, paint, porcupine quills, and elk teeth. Eagle feathers would flow from their braided hair. Some of the hunting was done from stationary positions, behind cover, but when necessary the athletic hunters worked at top speed, united with their horses, using bows and arrows and, later, rifles. The whole community celebrated when the hunters returned in glory from a hunt, their pack horses trailing behind, weighed down with buffalo and elk meat.

What prizes the mountain buffalo were. They made a wonderful food—meaty, nutritious, delicious—whether cut into thin strips, smoked, and dried for the winter or put right on a spit. Their huge bodies yielded thick, versatile hides, which the Utes used for teepee exteriors (about ten hides were needed) and personal clothing. Sleeping robes made from the shaggy animals, along with the teepee fires, kept away the winter's bitter cold.

The women tanned the hides. They scraped the fat off the fleshy side with a deer-bone knife, soaked the skin overnight, applied a mixture having a base of boiled brains, sunned the hide for several days, soaked it again, stretched it (a difficult and tedious job), smoked one side over an open fire, and then finished the hide by softening it through vigorous rubbing with a stone or rope. These hides were warm, pliant, durable, and handsome when decorated with paint, beads, and fringe. Buffalo hides were also valuable in trade, allowing the Utes to obtain items from the south, such as clay pots, pipes, and bridles from the Apache and Navajo and steel fishhooks and brass bracelets from the Mexicans. The Utes preferred mountain buffalo, but the abundant deer, elk, antelope, and mountain sheep met the same needs.

The Utes made use of virtually the whole land, and the vegetation at Morgan Bottoms had many uses. The center pole for the Sun Dance was a young cottonwood. For fuel, the Utes preferred cotton-wood, especially in the summer when light, rather than heat, was the main objective and the cottonwood could throw out its bright flame with few sparks and relatively low heat. The cottonwood was also best for smoking meat since the smoke, not the heat, dried the meat. Cottonwood leaves were the best wrap for tobacco as the smoke coated the throat and added flavor to the tobacco smoke. The cot-tonwood smoke on the singers' throats enhanced the quality of their voices, giving a stronger range. An important Ute food, found near Morgan Bottoms, was a succulent tuber of the carrot family that grows only in northwestern Colorado and that gave the valley its name: the yampa plant.

Morgan Bottoms, then as now, was spectacular wildlife habitat and the Utes hunted the deer and elk that wintered there. Black bear used the thick underbrush as cover. Ute dancers wore the bearskins during the Bear Dance, the major festival held in the early spring when the leaves began to turn green in order to celebrate a new, hopeful year and a good hunt. The Yampa and White River Utes had relatively little to do with fish since the big game was so plentiful, but they did take some cutthroat trout, suckers, whitefish, and chub with spears, weirs, and their Mexican-made fishhooks. Although un-interested in the long-leggeds, they sometimes hunted ducks and geese. The Utes prized eagles for their feathers and bones, which they used as whistles in the Sun Dance.

So Morgan Bottoms was one of hundreds upon hundreds of places integral to the Utes of northwestern Colorado in their intricate life. They camped there for extended periods and also used it as a stopover point along the thoroughfare that was the Yampa corridor on the way to and from the mountain hunts. A vivid reminder can be found just upstream from Morgan Bottoms. On a vertical cliff up above the river floor is a panel of Ute pictographs with many burnished-red figures, including a rider on horseback.

This horse tribe controlled its domain, apparently with little com-petition, for more than two hundred years. Then events beyond its boundaries began to take a toll. Americans discovered gold in faraway

California, and in 1848 the United States immediately wrested territory
that now comprises all or part of seven states, including much of the
Yampa and White country, away from Mexico. In 1859 and the early
1860s, gold was struck all along the Colorado Front Range, drawing
would-be miners from the east and from the mining camps in California and Nevada. By the late 1860s, the Utes were in a vise.

Ouray is renowned as the great nineteenth-century hero of the
Utes, praised in all of the history books, honored in all the lists of
leading figures in Colorado history. Raised partly in an Apache family,
he came to his own tribe as a young adult and quickly assumed
leadership in the Uncompahgre band, which was located in the Gun-
nison and Uncompahgre valleys south of the Yampa and White. In
time, he came to be tacitly acknowledged as a spokesperson for the
seven bands at treaty time. Federal officials respected him as an able
diplomat, a man of transcendent judgment, skill, and reliability. Ouray
was quadrilingual, fluent in Spanish, English, and his two Indian
tongues.

In 1868, despite the most relentless pressure for Ute land, Ouray
was the principal negotiator in perhaps the most favorable Indian
treaty in the history of the country. The Ute domain recognized by
this treaty encompassed 16 million acres, one-fifth of Colorado, 120
miles west to east, 200 miles south to north, from the New Mexico
border nearly all the way to Wyoming. Most of the high mountains,
the place of the summer hunts where the animals must have seemed
limitless, were included. So were the lowlands, where the Utes and
the big game wintered. The government assured the Utes that they
could hunt on aboriginal lands that lay outside the reservation, which
included the White River watershed but not the Yampa. The Utes
held the whole reservation in absolute ownership, guaranteed by the
1868 treaty—and by settled principles of United States real property
law—forever.

Forever would not last long. The fury on the White River in 1879
made that impossible. "The Utes must go!" the newspapers shouted.
Even at the late date of 1880 and even under the most difficult circumstances, Ouray negotiated a far better resolution than seemed
imaginable. The two reservations in southern Colorado and the one

in northern Utah are just remnants of the old lands but still they amount to nearly two million acres. Ouray earned all the accolades.

Although a master hunter and horseman, after the 1868 treaty Ouray gradually began to take on many of the trappings of the whites, their dress, wines, and cigars. He acquired a Mexican servant, worked at a formal desk, and took rides in a carriage given to him by General Edward McCook. He encouraged his people to farm. Ouray felt that coexistence with the whites was essential and wanted to demonstrate some of the benefits of non-Indian society—but his assimilationist ways did not sit well with many Utes. Then, too, there were the inconvenient provisions in the Brunot Agreement of 1874, in which the Utes were forced to cede away most of the San Juan Mountains in southwestern Colorado, where silver and gold had been found. In a side arrangement, the United States guaranteed that Uncompahgre Park, where Ouray and his wife Chipeta lived, would remain Indian land even if, after the official survey was completed, the park lay outside of the redrawn reservation. The treaty also guaranteed to Ouray an annual stipend of $1,000 for "so long as [the Utes] remain . . . at peace with the people of the United States."

The pictures of Ouray display a figure of dignity and respect. His clothing is always neat and prim. Ouray's broad face is open and soft, welcoming. One can see how he drew in the Indian agents, the governor of Colorado, even presidents of the United States. Ouray inspired trust, affection, and comfort in the new people who were so keenly interested in Ute land.

Not Jack, the leader of the Northern Utes, who rode the Yampa and White River valleys. Jack was born Goshute and taken in for several years of his youth by a Mormon family in Utah. It was too shackling: the wrong clothes, the wrong schooling, the wrong God, the wrong land. He fled to the mountains in his teens and took up with the Utes, who were closely aligned with the Goshutes. In the early spring, just as the leaves were turning green, he lived the Bear Dance for days and a young Ute woman took him as her husband. He became a Ute: tribal custom was to take in Indians from other tribes and, if they became fully part of the society, grant them full tribal status.

Jack became so completely accepted by the Northern Utes, the most unrelenting Ute band, because his personality so completely matched. He loved the hunt. He rode with abandon. He was fierce: the photographs show a lean, leathery man with a hatchet of a face. Jack had no desire at all to be conciliatory. Yes, he had signed the 1868 treaty along with Ouray and seven other Ute leaders, but he did that out of strength: the treaty had set aside a reservation that included most of the hunting grounds and the United States guaranteed the Utes access to those traditional hunting areas, such as the Yampa and North and Middle parks, that lay outside of the reservation. And the treaty, which Jack knew cold, stipulated that no white people, except authorized federal agents, could enter Ute country without permission of the tribe. Jack had no desire to settle down and coexist with white people as a fellow farmer, which was what the white people wanted. He had the opposite desire. Ute country was for Utes and for Utes alone.

Some of the older Northern Utes, believing that cooperation with the whites was inevitable and necessary, thought Jack too abrasive, but the younger people, and most of the elders, idolized him. He became spokesman for the Northern Utes, the band most determined to hold on to the Ute way—the way of the horse and the hunt.

The tragedy that occurred in 1879, or something like it, became inevitable on May 10, 1878, when Nathan Meeker arrived at the White River agency as the new federal Indian agent, soon to be joined by his wife, Arvilla, and daughter, Josephine. Tension hung in the air like cottonwood smoke. The Utes felt violated by the 1874 Brunot Agreement, which had removed 4 million acres, including the San Juans, from the reservation. The Northern Utes did not hunt much in those southern mountains, but they knew that they were directly threatened by the precedent of ceding away Ute treaty land. They hated mining: it promoted a sedentary lifestyle and was an affront to the land they revered. Why should a whole mountain range be given over to such people? Then, too, the 1874 agreement seemed a clear threat to the status quo that Jack, Ouray, and many other Utes had tried so hard to achieve. How firm were the solemn promises made in the great 1868 treaty?

In 1876, Colorado became a state and the event of statehood seemed to signal to the non-Indian residents that local, rather than federal or Ute, prerogatives were paramount. Frederick Pitkin, who made a fortune mining in the San Juans, was the governor. Some people had been prospecting on the reservation, and others had come through to assess its worth for farming. Jack went to Denver on behalf of his people to meet with Pitkin. The governor's views were clear and oft-stated. He addressed the issue in his first inaugural address and regularly thereafter: Pitkin wanted the Utes out of Colorado.

In his own mind, Nathan Cook Meeker had nothing but the best interests of the Utes at heart. Idealistic through and through, Meeker became captivated by the Utopian agrarian communities and after the Civil War began writing an agricultural column for Horace Greeley's *New York Tribune.* With Greeley's encouragement and financial backing, Meeker went West and in 1869 founded Union Colony, one of the most famous communal farm societies. The nearest town was named Greeley, after Union Colony's benefactor. The colony's prospects were promising and irrigation canals were built, crops were raised, and produce was marketed in Denver.

Meeker's own star, however, fell. Horace Greeley died, and his estate called in as a debt the seed money that Greeley had advanced to Meeker. Soon thereafter, the members of the colony voted Meeker down as leader. He was out of a job and, as bad, bereft of a pulpit for his fervid views on the verities of farming and the hardworking, worthwhile communities that it built.

Senator Henry Teller of Colorado saw the right fit for Meeker and arranged for his appointment as Indian agent at White River. The sixty-year-old Meeker plunged in, full-spirited and determined to assist the Utes in the high-minded objective of making the necessary transition to a civilized, that is, agricultural, life. His way of using the land was better than the Utes' way and he would convince them of that.

Meeker's first move was to relocate the White River agency about fifteen miles downstream to a site (now the town of Meeker) where the valley widened out and the level ground and good topsoil would make for much better farming. There were political rivalries among Ute leaders, and Quinkent and Canalla, both older and more conciliatory toward the whites, were willing to move. Jack was adamantly opposed. The new location was further from the mountains and the hunt, and he argued strenuously that the treaty had mandated that the agency be at the existing site. The treaty had no such requirement on its face, although the provisions regarding the agency are sufficiently extensive (requiring, among other things, the construction of several buildings) as to suggest that the original site was to be permanent. Also, Jack was a treaty negotiator and may have known of assurances made during the negotiations. In any event, Meeker was not to be deterred. In an action that probably seemed to him routine rather than momentous, the federal installation was relocated.

The summer of 1879 came in hot, dry, and tense. Governor Pitkin was beginning his second term and Ute removal remained at the top of his list of priorities. Many fires broke out on the tinder-dry western slope of Colorado and homesteads were lost. Pitkin trumpeted as "facts" the complaints of settlers that raiding parties of Utes had set the fires.

> Reports reach me daily that a band of White River Utes are off their reservation, destroying forests and game near North and Middle Parks. They have already burned millions of dollars of timber, and are intimidating settlers and miners. . . . These savages should be removed to the Indian Territory, where they can no longer destroy the finest forests in this State.

Never mind that it was common knowledge in Colorado and across the West that the miners and loggers were notoriously careless and that their fires had ravaged the forestlands. Never mind that the reports of Ute aggression from white settlers were not substantiated (and never would be, even after federal investigation). At least one Ute hunter was shot down as an arsonist on suspicion only, the West's version of a lynching. Good. Fair recompense. The Utes did not belong in Colorado.

Nathan Meeker was growing increasingly jittery. The fires and the pressure from the governor and the settlers—which built up even more in the spring of 1879, when gold was discovered on reservation land to the south and miners promptly rushed in—were part of it, but there was more. He wasn't gaining the respect of the Utes. Moving the agency headquarters had caused deep bitterness. Quinkent and Canalla had relocated their camps to the new agency, but Jack and his followers had remained ten miles upstream. Further, the annuities—the treaty had elaborate provisions guaranteeing annual shipments of food and goods such as blankets and clothing—were late. The goods were important to the Utes. Ute hunters could trade them to settlers for rifles and ammunition. The delay in the arrival of the annuities was not Meeker's fault, but he was tarred with the issue regardless.

Meeker's own personal foibles added to his problems. He insisted that the Utes call him "Father." Behind his back, and a few times to his face, they called Meeker—who to the white man's eye was handsome, erect, and dignified—an "old lady" because he seemed so out of place and inept in Ute country. Also, fearing conflicts with settlers, he told the Utes that they should not leave the reservation, which the Utes knew to be contrary to federal policy and assurances given at the time of the 1868 treaty. Meeker saw himself as a good man headed in the best direction for both the Utes and his own people, but he knew that his problems were spiraling and had begun to fear for his own safety and, worse yet, for that of Arvilla and Josephine.

The Indian agent had been able to have nearly two hundred acres put under the plow. In early September, he ordered two additional parcels to be plowed and made ready for irrigation the next spring. One of the areas was a track where the younger Utes raced their horses. The other was the field where Canalla, the old medicine man who had tried to cooperate with Meeker, pastured his ponies. Meeker's mandate threw the Utes into an uproar. They didn't like plowing to begin with—it tore up the earth and was a symbol of the new life the white people were trying to force on them—and these were not places where plowing made any sense. The races were good for the young riders and showed off the magical skills of the horse. Canalla needed the pasture for his many horses. Still, this was not a time to anger the white people. Danger was in the air. There was a great deal of talk among the Utes, some with Meeker, much more in the teepees with elder-stem pipes and the tobacco wrapped in cottonwood leaves.

Meeker decided to go ahead with the plowing. Canalla, who was not a volatile sort, went to the agency and confronted Meeker, who was having his lunch. Pushing and jostling ensued between the two older men. Canalla pushed Meeker through the open door and the agent landed in a heap outside the building. His body seemed not to be hurt, but his pride was. On September 10, 1879, Nathan Meeker shot out fateful calls for assistance to Governor Pitkin and the Interior Department. This is the telegram to Washington:

> I have been assaulted by a leading chief. . . . Forced out of my own house and injured badly, but was rescued by employees. . . . Life of self, family, and employees not safe. Want protection immediately; have asked Gov. Pitkin to confer with Gen. Pope.
>
> *N. C. Meeker, Indian Agent*

Interior referred the matter over to the War Department, which on September 15 ordered troops to be dispatched to Meeker's aid. The nearest installation was Fort Steele, where troops were under the command of Major Thomas T. Thornburgh. Thornburgh did not take immediate action. This was autumn in the central Rockies and the major was out on an elk hunt. The Indian forts in the West had become somewhat low-key operations in recent years. The Sioux and the Nez Perce had been put down and the operating assumption was that the last Indian war had already been fought.

But enough telegrams, reports, and rumors were flying around Colorado in general and Ute country in particular that Jack became concerned. He decided to travel north to Fort Steele to talk matters through. Jack and ten of his men headed up Coal Creek Canyon to the divide between the White and the Yampa. This divide, where Milk Creek begins to flow north, was the northern boundary of the reservation. When the riders dropped down into the bottomlands of the Yampa, they learned that federal soldiers were in the area and sought out Major Thornburgh's camp.

On September 26, Jack and Thornburgh met. Jack said that he and the Utes wanted only peace and to be left alone: "I told them I never expected to see the soldiers here. I told him we were all government Indians and soldiers, and that the government at Washington ordered us both; that we were brothers, and why had they come?" Thornburgh truthfully said that he, too, wanted peace and that his orders were to avoid combat. He related the federal government's concerns about the fires, concerns that had been aggravated by still more reports from Pitkin. Jack, exasperated because he thought he had cleared up the matter of the fires during a meeting just a few months earlier with the governor in Denver, explained that the fires absolutely were not set by Utes. Further, ever precise, ever focused on the hard-negotiated treaty, the Ute leader argued that any entry into the reservation would be in violation of the treaty and an act of war. Ute land was, according to the treaty, "set apart for the absolute and undisturbed use and occupation" of the Utes. The treaty also said that "no person . . . shall ever be permitted to pass over, settle upon, or reside" on the reservation.

Thornburgh had some treaty words on his side. There was an exception for "officers . . . of the government as may be authorized to enter upon Indian reservations in discharge of duties enjoined by law." Thornburgh showed Jack his official orders. Jack understood Thornburgh's point but pressed his own position that there was no reason that federal troops, for the first time ever, should encroach on Ute land. The Utes had never engaged in combat with the United States. The fires were not set by Utes. Canalla had done no damage to Meeker.

The next morning, Jack returned to Thornburgh's camp to offer a compromise. Leave your troops in the Yampa Valley at least fifty miles from the agency, well north of the reservation line, and proceed with just five men to the agency. You can investigate the circumstances and will see that there are no possible grounds for bringing in your army. Jack hurried back to the agency on the same day, September 27, and Meeker promptly sent Thornburgh a message by runner supporting Jack's proposal, urging the major to proceed with just five men, and saying that "the Indians are greatly excited" and "seem to consider the advance of troops as a declaration of real war."

Thornburgh initially acceded. He seemed satisfied with the talks with Jack. After their first meeting, the Major wired his superior:

Have met some Ute chiefs here. Seem friendly and promised to go with me to agency. Say Utes don't understand why we have come. Have tried to explain satisfactorily. Do not anticipate trouble.

On the twenty-seventh, Thornburgh wrote to Meeker that he would follow Jack's plan: he would camp down on Milk Creek, well north of the reservation, and then "come in as desired with five men and a guide."

But after discussions with his officers and scouts, Thornburgh's hierarchical sense of duty prevailed. He had been ordered to proceed with troops to the reservation. Leaving his army fifty miles distant did not conform with his orders.

On September 28, Thornburgh formally reversed himself and sent a letter by horseback messenger on to Meeker, saying that he would cross on to the reservation, leave the force "within striking distance of your agency," and then come in with a guide and five soldiers.

Meeker replied on September 29 at 1:00 P.M. It was an ambiguous response. He endorsed the march on to the reservation: "I like your last programme; it is based on true military principles." But he also downplayed any trouble and sent a clear signal that he was safe:

I expect to leave in the morning with [Quinkent] and Gerrick [another Ute leader] to meet you. Things are peaceful, and [Quinkent] flies the United States flag. If you have trouble getting through the canyon [on upper Milk Creek] let me know. We have been on guard three nights, and shall be tonight, not because we know there is danger, but because there might be.

Perhaps something in Meeker's letter might have caused the major to reconsider his decision to march his troops on to Ute country. We do not know, for Thornburgh never received the message.

A mixture of fear, despair, and determination had settled in among the Utes. No one knew what Thornburgh had in mind, but they did know from Jack's reports that he and his troops had reached the Yampa. And every single Ute knew in vivid detail, just as though it were yesterday, the horrors of the Sand Creek Massacre east of Denver in 1864 when Colonel John Chivington led his murderous, irresponsible, and unnecessary charge on Black Kettle and the Cheyennes. Two hundred Cheyennes, most of them women and children, were slaughtered. Thomas Thornburgh was not remotely a John Chivington, but the Utes did not know that. They knew only that he was marching toward their land and that there seemed to be no reason for it.

On September 27 and 28, young Ute men had begun to move up toward the headwaters of Milk Creek, at the north edge of the reservation, and made camp on high ground above the trail over which Thornburgh might be advancing his troops and wagons. Down at the agency, most of the old men, women, and children moved their camps out of the agency, south across the White River. Dancing and singing went on nearly all night.

Jack, who had spent the night near the agency, was on his way before first light on September 29. He rode up past the autumn-yellow cottonwoods along Coal Creek, as he had a few days before, but this was different from that exploratory mission. Jack's scouts reported that troops were moving up Milk Creek. The Ute leader could not be sure whether Thornburgh would honor his request to leave the troops on lower Milk Creek, but his approach remained the same as it had been over the past few days, over the many years that he had held responsibility for his tribe's future. Look for solutions but be firm. See that the treaty is honored. Preserve Ute land. Preserve the hunt.

Jack crossed over Yellowjacket Pass, rode through the narrow Milk Creek canyon, and arrived at the large bowl just below. He found, as he knew he would, some fifty Ute young men camped at the high edge of the bowl among the sparse junipers. Jack's wife and children had come over from their camp. The young men, many in their early teens, were singing solemnly. Most wore Ute war paint, yellow and black. They were edgy. Jack, the young men, and Colorow, another Ute leader, gathered. They talked, telling each other what they knew, and waited to see what would appear on the trail down below.

At midday, Major Thornburgh and an advance column broke into view on the sagebrush-lined trail at the far end of the bowl. They proceeded on, followed by a long line of soldiers. Now Jack knew that Thornburgh did not intend to abide by Jack's request. Jack directed his wife and children to return to the camp. Thornburgh waved to the Utes and Jack waved back. Wanting to confer with the major and slow things down, Jack told his men to hold their fire and moved his horse down the side of the bowl toward the troops. A shot—no one knows whose—exploded and filled the bowl with instant sound and history. Jack shouted out to both sides, "Hold on, hold on," but full-scale combat was already raging. Within minutes, Major Thornburgh was dead, shot in the head. The Utes kept his troops pinned for five days until relief forces rescued them. In all, twelve United States soldiers were killed and forty-three wounded. Thirty-seven Utes died.

At the moment firing broke out, Ute riders raced down Coal Creek to the agency to warn of the danger. At about 2:00 P.M., Quinkent and about twenty other Utes, furious at Thornburgh's march on Ute land and releasing more than a year's pent-up anger at Nathan Meeker, took immediate action. They killed Meeker, all six other agency employees, and eleven other white men. They drove a stake through Meeker's mouth so, they said, that his lies would finally cease, even in the afterlife. Twelve Utes, led by Quinkent, then kidnapped sixty-three-year-old Arvilla and Josephine Meeker and a Mrs. Price, holding them for twenty-three days. The hostages initially reported that their captors had treated them well. Later, Mrs. Meeker testified that Quinkent had forced her into sexual intercourse on one occasion. Josephine said that she suffered the same from a Ute named Pah-sone.

Outrage and panic over the battle, the killings at the agency, and the kidnapping of the women spread all over Colorado, on the front pages, in the public lecture halls, over the dinner tables. Governor Pitkin fueled the anti-Ute hatred. In the months to come, Josephine

Meeker made sure that the furor would not die down. She took to the lecture circuit and gave detailed descriptions, far more lurid than anything she said to federal officials would suggest, of the indignities she suffered during her captivity.

Federal hearings were promptly held in Colorado and Washington. Ouray, who had been at his home in Uncompahgre Park far to the south at the time of the battle and who had struggled to keep both sides calm during the ensuing days and weeks, acted as what amounted to chief counsel for the Utes. The proceedings, especially those in Washington, seem generally to have been open and fair, due in good part to Ouray's vigorous and skillful representation. Jack and the other Ute soldiers were exonerated (the Battle of Milk Creek was seen as a misunderstanding, ripening into combat, between two governments). The killings at the agency and the treatment of the three women were viewed differently, and Quinkent was sent off to prison for a year. But the investigations, which drew out all of the tangled circumstances of this clash of irreconcilable cultures and could theoretically have created the basis for an understanding and resolution of the Utes' situation, were of little moment. Passions—that is, the passions of the settlers, whose passions counted—were too high. It was impossible for the Utes to remain in Colorado.

When the Utes were beckoned back to Washington for the hearings in early 1880, they were told that they would have to negotiate still another "agreement." All the Utes knew what this meant. All the land—almost all of it, anyway—would go. So would the hunt. Jack balked. He considered traveling to Dakota Territory to join Sitting Bull. In the end, Jack did go to Washington.

The final 1880 agreement, passed by Congress in June, erased the treaty signed twelve years earlier. The Southern Utes were to be located on a strip of low-lying land in southern Colorado, adjacent to New Mexico Territory. The government would try to find unoccupied land for the Uncompahgre Utes in the Grand Valley (this arrangement proved unacceptable to the settlers and the band was moved to the reservation of the Uintah band of Utes in Utah). Years later, a reservation was set aside for the Weeminuche band in barren country in southwesternmost Colorado. As for Jack and the other Northern

Utes, the 1880 agreement was terse: "The White River Utes agree to remove to and settle upon agricultural lands on the Uintah Reservation in Utah."

Of course, for all of the Utes these terms were dictated, not negotiated. Jack was present but refused to sign. A photograph shows him gaunt and glowering, the leader of horse people who had lost the hunt forever.

In the spring of 1881, the despondent Utes failed to hold the Bear Dance for the first time since the Creator opened the bag. Talks were held during the spring and summer of 1881. General Ranold MacKenzie, who was superintending the removal of the Northern and Uncompahgre Utes to Utah, had two difficult jobs, marching the Utes out and, in the meantime, restraining the rapidly gathering numbers of settlers wanting to stake their claim on former Ute lands. The Utes wanted permission for one last hunt on the Yampa to put in meat for the winter. MacKenzie refused. The Utes needed to be on the Uintah Reservation before winter broke and the settlers needed to beat winter also.

On September 6, the Utes moved out. On the last day the sky was marked by two large, separate clouds of dust. One was created by the Northern and Uncompahgre Utes, the other was created by the land rush of anxious settlers, released from the soldiers' restraint by a bugle call, pounding into the Grand Valley, now free of the Utes, to open it for settlement and farming.

For the Northern Utes, who in their tenacious way have rebuilt their lives at the Uintah Reservation in Utah, the issue now is not the land or even the hunt, but rather the truth. They have not forgotten 1879 or the long glory time that came before.

In the fall of 1993, Ute people came back to the place of the Battle of Milk Creek to dedicate their own monument, which tells the story of 1879 as they believe it, and their monument now sits next to the one the non-Indians erected to honor Major Thornburgh and his fallen soldiers. It was a powerful ceremony that drew a gathering of more than a thousand people: Utes from Utah and southern

Colorado, National Public Radio and Channel 4 from Denver, numerous citizens from Meeker and the surrounding area, and many from around Colorado. Luke Duncan, erect and dark and in braids, said simply, "We were removed to a country not our own. We still feel that loss today. It was very cruel." Eight Ute men seated around a deer-hide drum pounded out an honor song and the old sharp sounds pierced the autumn air of the White and Yampa country once again, and the overlay of the Ute experience hung thick over the sagebrush and juniper bowl.

Kenny Frost, also a Ute, has said that the Utes have been pushed out of western Colorado but that "now it is your responsibility to care for it." The first settlers and those of us who followed have made many mistakes out here but we have done some things right, too. The mountains are mostly within the national forest system, kept open for the public. The White River National Forest was the second national forest ever created, in 1891, after the forest (now the Shoshone) bordering Yellowstone National Park to the east. In turn, major blocks of those national forests have become part of our wilderness system. These include the Flat Tops, the elevated plateaus where the Utes' hunting trails ran.

Then, too, there is evidence of our care for the land in the cottonwood groves at Morgan Bottoms, where some of today's old trees may have been alive when Jack still rode the Yampa. Those forests surprised me simply because they are so rare. We have taken out almost all of the cottonwood forests, all across Colorado, all across the American West. Farmers and ranchers cut and cleared many for hay meadows or cattle grazing. Livestock grazing has depleted the understory plants, and the animals' hoof action has checked the regeneration of cottonwoods.

But the biggest killer of the riparian areas held by the cottonwood forests has been our compulsion to manage the rivers through construction. Bank revetment (the installation of riprap) tames a river by channeling it and disconnecting its flows from the floodplain. The dams and water diversions that allowed farms to succeed the hunt in the West have been even more destructive to the natural river systems. The dams block the spring floods, store the water in reservoirs, and then release the spring water in the late summer when the rivers would normally be low and insufficient for irrigation.

The cottonwood forests need the high spring floods to survive. The swollen river brings sediment down, giving birth to sandbars. The river dances around, spilling over its banks, changing course again and again, nourishing a broad swath, creating marshes, delivering water to the big pumps of the cottonwoods.

Conditions must be exactly right for cottonwoods to regenerate. There must be new, open sandbars; cottonwoods are shade-intolerant and the young plants need a clear, sunny area to get started. A sandbar must be low enough so that the young trees can tap into groundwater, yet high enough so that the bars will not be washed away by floods in succeeding years. Cottonwood seeds have a short viability time, just several days, so the sandbars must be moist (the water must have recently receded) for the seeds to germinate. And the mature cottonwoods must themselves release their seeds at exactly the right time, when the sandbars are ready, usually a period of just two or three weeks. The spring warming, when the leaves turn green, sends a signal to the mature trees but so, too, does the dance of the river. These circumstances are rare—they coincide just once every thirty or forty years. The dams throw off the elaborate system and gradually kill off the cottonwood forests.

Why have these deciduous riparian forests survived on the Yampa? Why on the White, where there are a few other cottonwood groves, though not as many as at Morgan Bottoms? Part of the answer may lie with relatively good land practices in these ranching and farming valleys. The essential ingredient, however, is that the natural action of these river systems has been little altered by dams and revetments. The Yampa and the White still dance in the spring and give life to these forests.

Still, for whatever restraint we may have shown and whatever good we may have done, we must remember the betrayals. For we betrayed Jack and the Ute people in so many ways. We took away the land and the buffalo. We took away the hunt. We betrayed the trust lodged in the great 1868 treaty, a device of our making that embodies the solemn word of nations. Jack tried to hew to those words, those promises, in a precise and honorable way, but the promises were stamped out by an onrushing society that would not pause to negotiate.

In our stampede to assimilate the Utes, we changed nearly all the Utes' names, including Jack's. Nicaagat. It is a song of a name, with the "c" and the "g" pronounced with a soft guttural clip, with all the syllables pronounced equally, flowing like mountain water over pebbles. Ni-ca-a-gat. It means "leaves becoming green," the time when the cottonwood come out, the time of the spring Bear Dance when he met his wife. Jack. Nicaagat.

And, in the end, we betrayed Nicaagat by driving a wedge between him and his people. Back in 1879, at the end of the commission hearings in Colorado, General Hatch announced that there would be no charges with respect to the battle with Thornburgh's troops but that Quinkent and the other men involved in the killing of Meeker and the abduction of the three women must stand trial. Ouray, old and dying, outfitted once again in his buckskins in defiance of his former white friends, flashed out a last burst of rage. There would be no trial of Utes in Colorado. "All of the people of Colorado and New Mexico are our enemies." The government, on the word of Interior Secretary Carl Schurz, whom the Utes trusted, agreed to a trial outside of Colorado. But the Utes would have to produce Quinkent and the others.

The Ute leaders at the hearing went into council. They agreed to the trial. They selected Nicaagat and Colorow to bring Quinkent in, which they did.

Quinkent's followers never forgave Nicaagat. Most of the Northern Utes revered him, but Nicaagat would never again be safe among the Utes. Nicaagat struck out with his wife and children, probably for the mountains, never to return to his people.

Conquerors, as well as the conquered, are diminished when a trust is broken. We know now that we came on too hard and fast for the Utes. We could have accommodated settlement by non-Indians and also allowed for the Northern Utes to hold good land in the Yampa and White country. We could have allowed for the hunt.

Betrayals, and all the lasting things that we learn from them, die out when our memories die. This is why the forceful but careful and restrained, even gentle, reminders from the modern Utes matter so. So, too, do the high, wild Flat Tops and the green expanses at Morgan Bottoms tell it straight, that these are healthy natural systems and that our ethics must run to them as well as people. Those places hold our memories, they keep us fixed on truth, on Nicaagat, who may or may not still travel down the Yampa from the mountains, past the red horseback pictures drawn by his forebears, past the trees whose leaves turn green at the time of the Bear Dance, riding with precision, riding with his best eagle feathers and his finest pony, back from the hunt.

Charles Wilkinson, the Moses Lasky Professor of Law at the University of Colorado, is the author of *The Eagle Bird* and *Crossing the Next Meridian: Land, Water, and the Future of the West.* The recipient of the National Wildlife Federation's 1990 National Conservation Award, he lives in Boulder, Colorado.

HOMERO ARIDJIS

❖ ——————————————————————— ❖

Sian Ka'an, Quintana Roo, Mexico

Where the Sky Was Born

❖❖❖

(For Kjell Espmark)

Betty, my wife, César Barrios, our guide, and I drove to Sian Ka'an (Where the Sky Was Born) in a Volkswagen Beetle. We arrived on an October morning when the heat was not yet "halfway up the sky," as the Punta Allen fishermen say.

The Sian Ka'an Biosphere Reserve, consisting of 1,305,051 acres of tropical forest, savannahs, mangrove swamps, *petenes* (wetland islets), cenotes, keys, springs, and coral reefs lying in the state of Quintana Roo and the Yucatán Peninsula, is the third-largest reserve in Mexico. Of this area, some 296,400 acres are oceanic. The barrier reef, the second longest in the world, is over sixty-eight miles in length. The reserve contains 800 species of flora and 2,161 of fauna, which comprise copepods (619), coleoptera (74), dipterans (310), crustaceans (216), mammals (103), native bees (90), corals (84), marine turtles (4), and birds (339) of which more than 70 are aquatic. The initial impression given by this vast reserve is that, if its Maya name is to be taken literally, then the sky was indeed born of the water. In the wetlands, particularly, the swampy terrain is covered with water and life almost all year round.

Having left behind us the last of the restaurants and the archway at the entrance to the reserve, we watch a crossing of crabs so camouflaged that they seem made of sand. Momentarily surprised by the noise of the car, the crustaceans remain static in the dirt road before losing themselves in the dense vegetation.

We recognize various types of palm trees along the shore line, among them the *chit* (*Thrinax radiata*), with its fanlike leaves and ivory blossoms. In the jungle, fighting the other trees to reach the light, they grow to a height of between thirty-two and thirty-eight feet but on the dunes beside the sea, they are no more than twenty feet tall. Some specimens show the scars on the trunk left by the leaves that have fallen. These palms grow slowly in the jungle and at the seaside. The demand for *chit* has increased in recent years as a result of the burgeoning tourism in Quintana Roo because not only are the roofs and walls of traditional Mayan dwellings made with its leaves but hotel and restaurant proprietors use them for cabanas whose walls are built with *nakax* palm poles. Fishermen use poles of the *chit* to make lobster traps called *sombras*.

"That one is a *kuka* palm," César points out from the car. It is the *Pseudophoenix sargentii* and is found in the lowland jungle of Quintana Roo. "That one," he indicates, "is the *xiat*." It is a variety endemic to the peninsula.

We can see the holes made by golden-fronted woodpeckers (*Melanerpes aurifrons*) in the trunks of the palms, particularly those killed by the deadly yellowing, a blight which no one knows how to keep from destroying the coconut palms. "I know," José Luis Soto, of Cabañas Ana and José, told me a few hours earlier and confided the secret: "by rubbing sulfur on the trunks." A gray fox crosses in front of us. A bright green iguana stands as though rooted to the spot. A tropical mockingbird (*Mimus gilvus*), a bird with a talent for imitating the sound of chickens, parrots, and dogs, flies from tree to tree. We spot a vermilion flycatcher (*Pyrocephalus rubinus*), waiting to snare insects out of the air.

On arriving at the edge of the Boca Paila lagoon, we take refuge from the sun under an almond tree. Afterwards, we begin the tour of the canals in a boat. These are not the man-made canals of Amsterdam or Venice, but canals engineered by nature. Their edifices are not palaces but formations of mangrove trees, islets of *petenes*, and structures of a vegetation that has adapted to the extreme dampness. There are 16,300 acres of different varieties of mangrove swamp. Those of the Yucatán Peninsula are made up of four species of mangroves: the red, the black, the white, and the *botoncillo* (small-budded). The most abundant is the red mangrove, whose name in Maya is *xtapche*. In his study on the wetlands, Juan José Morales compares it to an immense spider because of its long, curved roots which, out of water and aerial, sprout from the trunk and branches in all directions. Fixed in the marshy soil with its multiple superimposed legs, the red mangrove seems a fantastic animal stranded in the water. As a fisherman of Isla Mujeres expressed it, "The mangrove swamps are the beginning of the sea." For it is on their biotic riches that life in the open sea depends in large measure.

The boat advances through the canals fashioned by the red mangroves. The dark-brown color of the water, as though steeped from tea leaves, is produced by the mangrove swamps. The bubbles upon the surface indicate that the water is breathing. We notice a blue-winged teal or *maxix*, its name in Maya. As soon as we approach it hides among the reeds. In the marshes of northern Yucatán, this duck is overhunted. The clouds on the horizon surround the lagoon like a ring of sheep. We come upon a great egret. It flies with its head tilted backward. In her book on the birds of Yucatán, Barbara MacKinnon wrote, "It almost became extinct at the turn of the century due to the popularity of its nuptial feathers, which were used for ladies' hats."

"There goes a kingfisher," César, the guide, points out.

We pause to listen to the song of a red-winged blackbird (*Agelaius phoeniceus*). The branches of the mangrove swamps in the water form webbings, reed sculptures, some crowned with leaves. Orchids and bromeliads come into view. A black vulture, *ch'om* in Maya, passes in search of carrion, or perhaps chicks of the ibis or heron. We view a white ibis, neck outstretched. And more birds: a green-backed heron, a kingfisher, a sulphur-bellied flycatcher. And, all at once, we come upon a mangrove trunk with a ball over a yard in diameter on it that seems to be an excrescence or mass of mud. It is a termitarium. An anteater (*Tamandua mexicana*) is trying to break apart the extremely hard nest with its claws and with its sticky tongue to get at the insects that eat the dead wood.

The vegetation changes and the grass cover that forms the savannahs begins. The landscape is filled with reeds. The depths of the water are green. There is a crocodile's nest in the pasture where its young were born a few weeks before. Tiny orchids appear. The florescence on the surface lasts all year long, the bulbs remaining submerged. A white heron flies between the *botoncillos*.

An oval-shaped *petén*, concentrically formed, stands out to the left of the boat. The *petén* is an islet covered with medium-sized trees that grow amidst reeds, grass, and mangrove swamp. The one now before us has on it palm, sapodilla, and breadnut trees, orchids, and lianas. Another smaller *petén* comes into view followed by a larger one. Some have a cenote at the center. The *petenes* are said to contribute to the biodiversity of the Espíritu Santo and Ascención bays, where lobster abounds, and to be essential for the survival of wild fauna which find their water, food, and shelter there in time of drought. Troops of spider monkeys find fruits all year round as well as protection from their natural enemies and from man. "Fires are set by poachers around here," César informs us, "to catch the white-tailed deer." His words remind me that the animals sought by hunters, some to the point of extinction, are: the collared peccary, the coati, the paca, the white-winged dove, the yellow-lored parrot, the keel-billed toucan, the ocellated turkey, the ocelot, the white-lipped peccary, the spider monkey, the jaguar, the American and Morelet's crocodiles, the jabiru, the great curassow, and the leatherback, green, hawksbill, and loggerhead sea turtles. In the water, the carp and permitfish flee us.

We enter a canal along which a heavier growth of red mangroves provides cool shade. Their branches, one after another, seem like pendant spears, orchids and bromeliads sprouting from them. We are able to drive a pole ten feet into the swampy soil. The water is tepid.

We are before a circular Mayan temple. This is the highest temple on the coast. Bats fly screeching out of the dark chamber. César informs us that no less than ten varieties of these creatures have been identified around the archaeological ruins of the Chunyaxché zone.

The warbling of invisible birds can be heard and we peer at the limb of a ceiba felled by lightning upon an orange tree.

Our return to Playa del Carmen begins at this point. We stop at the Muyil nursery where Don Cándido Ek, about forty-seven years old (so he says), and his wife, Delfina, about thirty-two, live.

Don Cándido had been waiting for us near his hut and now, with a marked absence of ceremony, he proceeds, his two sons, Ismael and Joel, trailing after him, to show us the native Sian Ka'an flora that he cultivates with skill and devotion. He tells us the names in Maya and Spanish (one of his sons helping him in Spanish) of some forty plants he intends to disseminate among the people of the region. "Here's the vegetation and along comes the wind and scatters the seed along the road and that's how they are propagated in Sian Ka'an," he explains to us as he stands amidst his plants, shrubs, and trees. "The palm is very slow-growing."

Don Cándido Ek also wants to produce honey from stingless bees, known as *melipona*. "It's a honey the Mayas use for a medicine," he explains. "It's applied when women give birth, when the children are malnourished, when the navel of the children pops out and they want to make it go back in."

"How many children do you have?" I ask. "Six," he replies, and observing his wife Delfina looking pregnant under her huipil, says, "seven." "All boys?" "Four boys and two girls," he says, his white teeth bared in a smile.

His grandfather Caamal Ek (*ek* means star in Maya), he tells us, "is ninety-five but I think he's older as he has no 'birth ticket.'"

On another day we go to Punta Allen by car. The sea follows us all the way on the left side of the road. A swallow flies over the car for a few moments. Many termitariums can be seen on the trees. Young palms are growing among the old ones that died of the deadly yellowing. A black hawk is to be seen standing on a trunk.

We arrive in Punta Allen toward midday. It is a fishing village which, at first sight, appears to be poor and ugly. Its beauty lies in Ascención Bay and El Ramonal tropical forest. It is the only town in Sian Ka'an that has a potable water supply and sewerage. The reefs are less than a mile and a half away.

"A barrier reef was badly damaged by Hurricane Gilbert," we are told by Victor Barrera, a fisherman from Campeche, who has lived in Punta Allen since the age of sixteen. "The most terrible thing that happened to us was the death of the coconut palms. The coconut palms have many enemies. Fourteen, altogether. The worst is the deadly yellowing. When I first came here the coast was filled with coconut palms. For me, the death of those trees is an agonizing thing."

" 'We're off to the river,' the fishermen say when they are going to the lagoon," Victor adds. He agrees, after striking a deal, to take us in his boat around Ascensión Bay, famous for its lobster.

The bay, whose waters are calm and not very deep, is located on the central coast of Quintana Roo. Its mouths empty into the open sea, it has a coral reef, and is surrounded by mangrove swamps and marshes. Once there were manatees, dolphins, and otters here, but now we don't see any.

"My twenty-three-year-old brother Eleazar died in one of these springs fourteen years ago. A Señor Rodríguez, who had the idea of harvesting black coral, was teaching him to dive. The weather was bad. He dove into the water and didn't come out. The others went for help but when they got back he'd already disappeared." Victor, upright in the boat like a Viking figurehead, tells us the story. There are many springs around.

We see five pelicans, a heron, a cormorant, and a barracuda. The white head of an osprey with the black band across the eyes protrudes from its nest in a mangrove swamp. We notice crocodiles at the edge. The sky has grown overcast.

We are now in a canal between mangroves. We see orchids, white herons, white ibises. The water has turned milky green. It starts raining.

"White herons on the right, an osprey on the left, a cormorant in the distance to the right, beyond, a yellow-crowned night heron, a tortoise, a shoveller, green-backed herons, a pink spoonbill, a gray hawk." Victor, accustomed to scanning the air and water, appears to see everything and very quickly.

We move toward the shore, the water is shallow, we are in Quitacalzón. Following a hawk, we enter Key Yuyúm.

"Many of the mangroves have died off, the swamps are badly deteriorated, many are dry. This here is full of shovellers. They raise their crests during the mating season." Victor stops the boat at a mangrove swamp. "You can hear the clucking and flapping of wings inside. Pelicans nest in here, too, and there are spoonbills in season. I was told that flocks of flamingos were seen in January."

The sky is black. A storm begins. Victor maneuvers his boat in an effort to evade the rainfall. Rays of sunshine filter through the darkest of the clouds. The vehicle that is to take us overland to Playa del Carmen is waiting on the farther shore.

Drenched by lukewarm, fat raindrops, the boat lifted by the swell, we are spectators of the storm. There is no lightning.

The wind carries the clouds off elsewhere. The rain stops. We approach the shore. The wondrous trip is over. The threats to Sian Ka'an are all too evident. But the possibility of keeping the reserve well protected still exists.

Ninety-nine percent of the area's land belongs to the nation. The surrounding *ejidatarios* (communal peasants) scarcely number more than five hundred. Chicle tapping had been one of the traditional activities of the zone, but private lumbering of cedar and guayacans was instituted in 1935 and by now those trees are in danger of extirpation. This experience should teach us not to issue permits for forestry operations, dubious "ecotourism" developments, and private construction. Currently, politicians and entrepreneurs are discussing plans for developing Sian Ka'an with the ever-present risk, however, of opening the door to undesirable tourism projects, as was the case in other parts of Quintana Roo.

Sian Ka'an is one of the last remaining glories of the earth and must be preserved as such. Today, man is tempted to make nature "self-sustaining" by designing very ambitious management plans which, when ill-applied, unleash destructive forces that can neither be controlled nor stopped by anybody.

I sincerely believe that no one can make nature more "self-sustaining" than it has already managed to make itself. Nature has been quite efficiently self-sustaining for millions of years without man's help. Never in history has it been so assaulted as at the present time, now that we are "developing" it.

—Translated by Asa Zatz

Homero Aridjis is the author of novels, including *1492: The Life and Times of Juan Cabezón of Castile, The Lord of the Last Days: Visions of the Year 1000,* and *Persephone,* and collections of poetry including *Exaltation of Light* and *Blue Spaces.* Aridjis is the founder and president of the Group of 100, an organization of writers and artists committed to defending the environment and preserving biodiversity.

PAUL THEROUX

Palau, Micronesia

The Rock Islands

❖❖❖

One night in Palau, camped under the palms of deserted Omekang, one of the many Rock Islands, I crawled out of my tent and was uplifted. In my entire life I have never felt a sense of such serenity in the open air. I had the strong impression of the physical world as a peaceful room. Perhaps because it was midnight, and I had just woken up, the specific image that came to me was an enormous bedroom. The night was dead still, and the full moon lighted the beach with a glow that was lovelier for its mild fluorescence. In the mass of bright stars the Southern Cross was distinct. I stood stark naked and marveled at my luck.

There was no wind—not even the slightest movement of air. The temperature was about eighty, or a bit more. There was complete silence: the birds were asleep, the insects were still. The sea was flat —not only no waves, but no sound of water lapping at the shoreline. No flies buzzed. There were—this still amazes me—no mosquitoes.

There are hazards in Palau: sea snakes, stinging jellyfish, venomous cone shells, poisonous lion-fish, crown-of-thorns starfish, stonefish, fire coral, crocodiles (*C. porosus*, the saltwater croc), sea urchins, sharks. There are drunks and bad drivers too. But if certain precautions are observed, it is possible to live more or less unscathed in this archipelago of 343 islands.

Palau is notorious for sharks. I saw my first shark in the Rock Islands on my first swim, while I was snorkeling at the edge of a reef called Blue Corner. It was a black-tipped shark cruising along the coral wall about twenty feet below me, intent and preoccupied. It looked wicked and sleek, like a live torpedo, and its unhurried air made it seem more confident and more lethal. We were both swimming in the same direction. I was so alarmed by the fact of the shark, that I hardly noticed its size. Only later I estimated that it was seven or eight feet long. I changed course, trying not to make much fuss, and swam away from it. And then I saw my second shark. This one was nearer, but similarly uninterested in me. I kept on, making for the boat and saw my third, fourth, and fifth sharks. These were resting, motionless, on a flat ledge of coral, close enough for me to see the texture of their skin. At last I was back at the boat. In his excellent account of the culture of fishing in Palau, *Words of the Lagoon*, R. E. Johannes writes, "Sharks are common in Palau and it is a routine experience to be approached by one while . . . in channels through the fringing reef or over the outer reef slope." True.

That was almost my first whole day in Palau: the placid sharks, the calm air, the sunshine, the tropical heat, birds, fish, and bats, the green islands, the lagoons, my happy camp.

Still standing under the moon, I heard the intrusive noise of rustling, like a person kicking angrily through dry fallen leaves. This grew to a commotion. I got my flashlight from my tent and turned it in the direction of the sound and saw ten or more rats, fat and black, with glittering eyes and raw pink tails, and twitching whiskers, not at all deterred by my bright light, moving through a mass of dead palm fronds.

So instead of sleeping on the beach I zipped myself into my tent and reflected that no place is perfect but that Palau certainly came close. The Rock Islands were as near as I have ever been to the Peaceable Kingdom of the natural world in which there was complete harmony.

❖ ❖ ❖

Palau is in the Caroline Islands, in the western Pacific, just north of New Guinea and east of the Philippines. It is just one constellation of islands in the galaxy known as Micronesia. From Honolulu it is a seven-and-a-half-hour flight westward to Guam, a large ruined island of fast-food outlets and shopping malls and bungaloid subdivisions. And then a two-hour flight southwest to the main island of Babel-thuap and the town of Koror, which is the capital of Palau (Belau in its revised spelling).

Sixty years ago, and roughly until the end of World War II, Palau was an important place, and Koror a large metropolis. The imperious Japanese wanted it that way. They had taken over from the Germans who held it until 1918. This archipelago was designated the hub of their Pacific empire, and Koror was its capital. There were forty thousand people in Koror, and that included geishas, samurais, servants, chefs, bureaucrats—even locomotive engineers. Amazingly, there was a railway on the main island, running straight through town from the harbor. Koror was the center of Pacific operations, and known for its modernity, its teahouses, and its tremendous industry. Palauans were either taught Japanese and made to serve or else they were ignored and left to get on with their lives of fishing and diving.

A number of ferocious battles (the rusty relics of planes, tanks, and ships are strewn through the islands) broke the Japanese military hold on Palau, and the end of the war broke its political grip. With the transition to American trusteeship—it is the last American Trust Territory in the Pacific—everything is changed. Palau's entire population is fifteen thousand. The railway and the teahouses and the modernity are all gone. The Japanese one sees in Koror are investors or honeymooners or scuba divers on package holidays. The town is tiny, and faintly ramshackle, and extremely friendly.

The people of Palau have the face and the physique of their distant ancestors the Indonesians, and many show a distinct resemblance to the various ethnics groups who have lived there—Japanese, Chinese, German. The Palauans are almost alone in the Pacific in their volatile politics; their recent history is full of skirmishing, including several political murders, a presidential assassination, and other forms of violence. You would not know it. Koror seems comatose and that is where most of the people live. The rest live in a handful of towns or villages on six other islands. If there is a common denominator in Palau, it is a passion for fishing and a profound understanding and love of the sea.

They are no longer the brilliant canoe makers they once were. Canoe-carving had stopped in about 1920, according to a man I spoke to, an elderly canoe carver, Ethalool Eungel, whose traditional title was *Elapsis*. The canoes he had made in his career were measured by the arm-span (*reyongola*). They were poled or paddled and called *barotongs*. He had once made a thirty-five-foot canoe, known as a *kebekala*, for twenty-five paddlers. Some outrigger canoes are still carved—Elapsis was carving one as a gift to the community center using only a simple adze as his tool. Old Palauans gathered to watch him hack at the hollowed-out log, admiring his work.

They are people of the sea—powerful divers and spear fishermen, wonderful swimmers and boatmen. This suffix "men" is unfortunate. The women here are equal to the men in most of these pursuits, active on the water, knowledgeable in marine lore, and skillful in fishing. Though the women rarely run boats in this matrilineal society, the Palauan woman is at the helm in almost every other sense.

My companion and guide in Palau, Chuck Cook, was one of Palau's protectors. An employee of The Nature Conservancy, he had been sent to the islands three years before to study the ecology of the islands and to advise Palauans on how to balance economic development with environmental protection. To this end, he had recruited botanists, ornithologists, marine biologists, even croc specialists.

"I brought a professor here from Australia, whose specialty is crocodiles. He took a census of the crocodiles. We found four hundred of them. Two kinds—estuarine and saltwater."

Just how do you conduct a crocodile census? I asked him.

"We went out at night, when the crocs are out, and we took our boat into creeks and along the shore and shined a powerful light into the mangroves. We'd see here and there a pair of red eyes and make a note of them. At the end of it all, the Prof did a calculation and estimated four hundred. It's not an exact figure—there might be more, there could be less. They were all saltwater crocs."

Chuck, from Tennessee, was forty-one, and widely traveled, knowledgeable about the flora and fauna of Palau, a passionate fisherman, an experienced paddler and camper, hearty, physically fit, and game for any excursion. A good companion, he and I, and all foreigners in Palau are known as *chadrangebard*. It is an expression which means "a man from the West." That word came into being at a specific time in 1783, when Captain Henry Wilson of the *Antelope* swam ashore, having crashed his ship into the western edge of the Palau reef.

In addition to his sea kayak, Chuck also had a twenty-three-foot whaler, with twin outboards. This helped us put together the perfect expedition. On the bigger boat, which we christened "The Mother Ship," we had a large cooler the size of a well-proportioned coffin filled with food and drink. Tied down on the deck we had the rest of our equipment—tents, cooking utensils, snorkeling gear, fishing rods, and all the rest, including our two kayaks.

We lacked nothing and it seemed to me that this was the greatest way of exploring a widely scattered archipelago. Our plan was to make for the outer island in the Rock Island group, which lies southwest of Koror; then anchor the large boat, make a base camp, and strike out from there, exploring the smaller islands through the narrow openings and coral reefs where the water was shoaly and shallower. In some channels the current ran very fast—four or five knots; or there was an open-water crossing that was subject to storms. The Mother Ship bore us across these tricky passages; and for the rest of it we had our kayaks.

The Rock Islands seemed to rise from the sea soon after we left the harbor of Malakal, near Koror. They are low and humpy limestone islands, several hundred of them, great and small. They are the structures of old coral reefs that were thrust out of the sea long ago by the forces of undersea vulcanism. They are covered with pandanus and palms. One of the palms is indigenous to the islands, a short tree with thick fronds like bristling feathers. The Rock Islands are known in the local language as *Ellebacheb*, which is also a synonym for small uninhabited islands of rocks and trees. The islands are very green, rounded, all sizes, from small green lumps in the ocean, to long rounded ridges. The sides are steep and unclimbable on most of them. Some have white sand beaches. Birds nest on their sides and one of the pleasures of paddling was listening to the screeches of these birds, the swifts, the finches, the swallows, the Palau fruit dove, the black Nicobar pigeon, the screech of the greater sulphur crested cockatoo, the white-tailed tropic bird that swoops and glides and makes a clicking chatter among the heights of the islands and never seems to come to rest.

We left the Mother Ship anchored in the small bay of an island, near a sandspit, and paddled our kayaks to a spot known locally as the Soft Coral Arches, and in the coolness of a sheltered lagoon I got my first look at the abundance of Rock Island fish life, and the swaying corals. Then we paddled to Eil Malk island and climbed to the center of it, to Jellyfish Lake.

"There is a small croc that lives here—I've seen it but he only comes out at night," Chuck said.

There are a number of these marine lakes in the Rock Islands. The lake fed by springs lies in a limestone bowl at the center of the island. Some are connected by caves to the sea, others are sealed. They are strange, with high sides and muddy, brackish water and mangroves. We swam through the brackish water where a mass of jellyfish lived and bounced through the water—millions of them perhaps. There was no question that the Jellyfiish Lake was a wonder of nature; in a previous incarnation these jellyfish were poisonous. Here they had evolved into a harmless species, and there was not one, but two—the first (a species of *mastigias*) like a large, soft polyp, orangey-pink, the second (*Aurelia aurita*) white and rounded and delicate, almost lacy, and when it filled to propel itself it resembled a white mobcap or a billowing hanky. They were so thick in the water that they softly crowded me and slid against my face and arms—my whole body. I found this a truly disgusting swim.

The marine lakes are found on the high humpback turtle–shaped islands. We were camped on one of the low islands, where there was a sandy beach, and easy access for our kayaks. Because of the fluctuation of the tides, a campsite in the Rock Islands has to be carefully sited. There is a six- to seven-foot variation, and so what looks like a lovely dry spot at six in the evening might be under water by midnight. There are very few long sloping beaches in the Rock Islands. They tend to be narrow and steeply shelving. We had left our Mother Ship anchored in a pretty bay, and we returned to this bay in our kayaks and made camp, choosing a spot well away from the tidemark. As we made camp, the fruit bats were jostling in the high trees, and taking off, leaving the islands to feed—then they were in the sky, great flights of these fat creatures beating across the channel to find food.

That was the night I made a Palauan version of spaghetti alla vongole, noodles with mangrove clams. That was the night I decided that I had discovered a Peaceable Kingdom. And then saw the rats. The cast-off shells of the mangrove clams attracted the rats.

It is rare to find silence anywhere in a natural landscape. There is always the wind, at least. The rustle of trees, of grass, the drone of insects, the squawk of birds, the whistle of bats. By the sea, silence —true silence—is almost unknown. But there was no lap of the water. The air was motionless. I could hear no insects. Perfect silence. A perfect place: the world as an enormous room.

Palau is famous for its quarter-ton giant clams (*Tridacna gigas*), but its undersea beauty is in its coral. "Get this. There are sixty-nine species of hard corals in the Caribbean," Chuck said, as we made our way out to the reef, a spot called Ngemelis Drop-off, a wall of coral plunging hundreds of feet into the blackness of the ocean. "There are four hundred varieties of hard corals in Palau."

In addition, there are two hundred species of soft corals: the merest glance into Palau's lagoons is a vision of abundance. Some corals look like flowers, but with more extravagant blossoms than ever seen on land; and under the sea they have the effect of a great embankment or bower, flowers clustered together in glorious profusion. Some corals look like miniature hot-air balloons, other like polyps, or grotesque millipedes or spiders, still more look like the Gorgon Medusa. Others like human organs, red and pulsing. These and hundreds more exist in the waters of Palau. I was especially struck by a gray and elongated type of coral which looked like a bundle of bones, the youngest varieties looking like ribs, the oldest like a cluster of femurs, a whole clutch of leg bones. The action of storms, or perhaps anchors thrown casually over the side of dive boats, had broken many of these corals, and I began to think of this particular spot as the Boneyard.

When I mentioned this name to Chuck he said, "You mean the Cemetery."

Later that second day we saw more sharks.

"Shark just under you," Chuck said, surfacing and then diving again. For him a shark was not an emergency. *They're well-fed*, he explained. *They're not hungry.* It was a bit like the dog owner who says of her mutt, *He won't bother you.* Perhaps not; nevertheless, you remain in a state of vigilant anxiety.

That was another blacktip, just swimming beneath me in the shadows beneath the reef edge. In the course of that day I saw a whitetip and then a gray reef shark. They ranged from four to seven feet. Two whitetips were sleeping on the bottom. None of them were aggressive. They swam among the schools of jack, the sweetlips, the tuna, and wrasse and surgeonfish.

"Small blacktip sharks, though harmless in the Pacific, are treated with respect by Palauans, and with good reason," R. E. Johannes wrote. There have been five documented attacks by blacktips.

Lemon sharks (which I did not see) are not feared, nor is there any irrational fear of sharks in Palau. But if there are more than three sharks, and only one diver in their presence, the diver usually retreats, and leaves the water. Johannes says that members of a group of sharks are less cautious than individuals, and switch faster from exploratory to aggressive behavior.

Divers have the most to be concerned about, since the act of spearing a fish, the sound of the spear gun being discharged, or the panicky fish vibrating on the spear "act as exceptionally effective shark attractants."

In the Trobriand Islands I had dived with spear fishermen who told me that they made a whooping sound underwater to frighten sharks away. In Palau this was also practiced with good effect, the diver shouting, "Woo! Woo! Woo!" underwater into the shark's maw. An old Palauan told me that a sudden scraping of coral irritates sharks and drives them off. And he went on, "If the shark is aggressive we say, 'It is your territory,' and we go away."

Some fish can also be beckoned. A spear fisherman seeing a school of jacks might purse his lips and blow noisily, to call the fish. Removing his snorkel tube, Chuck showed me how this was done. I saw about twenty jacks make a 90-degree turn into his face. If he had a spear he would have been able to nail a fat one.

From where we were paddling, we could see the larger southern islands in the Palau group, Peleliu and Angaur. Both have settlements on them. We had thought of visiting them but we decided to stay among the uninhabited islands.

One of the most beautiful island clusters in the Rock Islands lies in the southwest, and is called Ngerukewid and often referred to as "The Seventy Islands." In fact there are forty-six islands —very green and rounded and close together, and so strangely shaped that paddling among them in the limpid green water is as disorienting as paddling in a maze, among misleading shapes and bays and openings. Some have sandy beaches where the Micronesian megapode birds lay their eggs and leave, letting the eggs incubate and hatch in the heat of the sand. The foliage is thick and consequently the bird life more various and vibrant: noddies, terns, swallows, kingfishers. A variety of swiftlet that is endangered elsewhere in the Pacific is prospering here.

Although it was the lowest tide of the year—inches deep in some shoaly places—we were able to make our way to a cave entrance and paddle as far as an interior corner, because we had kayaks here in Ngerukewid. We drew our boats up on the narrow shelf of coral and climbed into the cave where we found a log platform, a rusted transformer and an old moldering radio. Without question it was an out-post of the war, but whether it was the haunt of a Japanese soldier looking for Americans, or vice versa, it was impossible to tell. Certainly no one else had left a mark there. It gave the impression of a gravesite, or more properly a burial chamber, another mausoleum of the war.

We paddled among these smaller, intensely beautiful and remote islands for a day and a half. Because there is no deep water or reef nearby they are ignored by divers and fishermen, and those are the people who most visit Palau. Some of them stayed in a small dive resort on Ngerecheu (Carp Island), making trips out to the reef to dive and take pictures underwater. On the far side of Carp Island, up a long path in the jungle, we found an enormous chunk of Yap money—like a gigantic millstone, about seven feet in diameter with a hole in the middle. This one had broken, and perhaps that was why it had been left. But it was hard to imagine the technology that enabled the Yapese to quarry something this size—perhaps a ton—two hundred feet up the side of the hill, and then sail it. They had thousands of other similar specimens—four hundred miles across the ocean to Yap.

We snorkeled and fished in the morning, snoozed under trees in the heat of the day, and set off again in midafternoon, looking for a camp around five or six o'clock. The coral was only one of the wonders of the Palau depths. The profusion of fish was another—and it was not their numbers, the schools of grouper and tuna and surgeonfish and barracuda; it was also their size. Thirty- and forty-pound groupers were not unusual, and the wrasse were the size of big dark pigs. Seeing some fish jumping beyond the western edge of the reef we headed out and saw a school of twenty-five or thirty dolphins surrounding a school of tuna, which themselves had been feeding on a smaller fish; a churning example of the food chain.

"I have always wanted to go up that muddy creek to the interior of that island," Chuck said, pointing to the mangrove-lined mouth of a creek. It was not named on any map, but a Palauan told us it was called Ngermiich (pronounced "Yermiha"), perhaps derived from the word *miich*, which meant nut tree.

"We never fish there at night," this man said. "Because of the crocs."

I wondered out loud whether a kayak trip was a good idea.

"They're just a lot of crab-eating crocs," he said derisively, with true Palauan contempt.

This creek lies on the southeast side of the large island of Uruk-thapel. We anchored the Mother Ship offshore and paddled in, through a narrow rocky entrance to a little harbor, where there was an abandoned fishing shack, and paddled up this tidal creek in about a foot of water. We would not have made it through the mud, but even so, paddling was difficult because of the knobby mangrove roots. It was dark. There were vines, but no insects.

"I wish we had come here when we did our croc census," Chuck said. The water was less than a foot in some places, and in other places we had to shove our boats across sandbars. After about forty-five minutes of this paddling up the narrow bottom-scraping creek, we entered a lagoon that lay in a valley with high sides, on which cockatoos screeched and flapped, waking the fruit bats which flew off and then returned to hang again. We could see fish flitting beneath us in the clear water.

It was a sort of fish nursery, Chuck surmised. The fish came here and laid their eggs, the eggs hatched, and when they grew large enough to fend for themselves they made their way out. We were eating our lunch in our boats—the sides of the lagoon were too steep for us to be able to land: we were surrounded by walls of rock and jungle hundreds of feet high. Then we saw that we were being drawn to the head of the lagoon, as though in a current. Yet there was no visible current. Nearer the edge of the lagoon we saw the reason: a submarine cave which obviously led back to the sea, and a strong current flowing through it and sucking our boats into it too until we paddled away. The fish could pass through that sea cave.

"I'll bet there are sharks here," Chuck said.

Not fifteen seconds later he called out "Shark!" and saw a blacktip shark speeding through the water past us.

There were two more lagoons farther on, connected by creeks, and the whole creek and lagoon system was about three miles long. It was a true wilderness of green shadows, very creepy and exciting for the way it was undisturbed.

We paddled back through the creek to the sea on the outflowing tide, through the mangroves, where there had to be crocodiles.

"So if a fourteen-footer leaps off the bank at us, what do you think we should do?" Chuck speculated.

His laughter echoed among the muddy trees, and he was still calling out, but it had begun to rain and his words were drowned by the falling water. We were by now bearded and sweating and stinking.

That day and other days, heading to a paddling spot or a campsite, we passed the rusted hulks of ships. They were not all war relics. Many were freighters or longliners that had fetched up on the reef and been abandoned. Seeing them, one is reminded of what a dangerous place Palau is for a ship or large boat.

Many of these islands are untouched and have a pristine look. But just as many are littered, and the obvious campsites contain cans and bottles and bits of plastic. It was paradise to me, but it would be wrong to portray it as unviolated.

Palau's remoteness, its small population, its numerous islands, and its abundance (more fish, more coral, more uninhabited islands than I had seen in three years of peregrinating in Polynesia—all this and dugongs too), have helped to make it special. Yet there are few places on earth where humans live that can be called unspoiled. Palau contains war litter and battle junk. It has been colonized. It is misleading to portray it as a wilderness of solely twittering birds and leaping fish, for there are people living there, and humans have a unique capacity for fouling their own nests. But violation is relative. Palau is one of the least-spoiled places I have ever seen. Since its waters are clean and it is teeming with fish and fresh air, its soul is still its own.

The convention is not to mention humans when someone is writing about a pretty place. The Palauans are fishing folk. They take what they need from the sea or amuse themselves in the water, and they are content. But they are careless campers, they litter, they leave garbage and cans behind them. Even on its outlying islands you might find empty Spam cans or beer bottles. The dive tourists are careless too. Some dive boats throw their anchors into coral, breaking it. Some divers break off chunks of coral to take home. It is against the law, but it is hard to enforce such laws.

Wondering whether Palauans had traditional beliefs about this issue of humans and nature, I had an audience with the *espangel* (high chief) of the Omrekongel clan. He was born, he said, in 1904, and so at the age of eighty-nine he had seen a great deal of Palauan history: the Germans, the Japanese, the Americans. He spoke Japanese, having studied it for five years when he was in school. He had been a turtle catcher as a young man, and had caught a famous hawksbill turtle that was six feet across, each shell scute, or scale (which is how they are described) eighteen inches wide.

"Our family tree starts here in Arakabesan," he told me, when I asked him about his family. "Our history says that we come from the spring water. A child came from the spring—a miracle child that was looked after by an old lady. His name was Dibech. It means 'origin.' "

Hadn't Palauans come from Southeast Asia?

"Other Palauans might have come from other islands or other places," he said. "But we come from here. And you can see that they are culturally different from us." He added with a laugh. "It is not proper to inquire into other people's origins. But sometimes a person's authority is questioned. We have a saying in Palau. 'Your feet are wet'—meaning you have just arrived."

And then, speaking about the future of the Rock Islands, we talked about environmental concerns.

"If we don't see a law enforcement officer," he said, and his "we" included the human race, "we are like monkeys."

No island is unsinkable, but any island can be ruined. The islands of Palau are under threat from many contending business ventures —golf courses and hotels are but two of the more recent ones. Palau's natural beauty does not only attract potential developers, agents, and impresarios; it also inspires protectors and defenders. One of the strangest of human paradoxes is that an innocent and pretty face attracts both the rapist and the father figure. Lovely landscapes can have that same effect.

Paul Theroux has published many novels and story collections, including *The Mosquito Coast*, *Saint Jack*, and *Millroy the Magician*. His nonfiction works include *The Great Railway Bazaar*, *The Old Patagonia Express*, and *The Happy Isles of Oceania*.

PETER MATTHIESSEN

Peconic Bay, New York

Great River

❖❖❖

Fishers Island lies at the far northeastern end of New York's Suffolk County, which surrounds the islands and strong tidal waters of Peconic Bay, and I went there first in 1927, when I was two weeks old. It is a high island of hills and bluffs, rich deciduous woods and freshwater ponds, more like a rock-girt fragment of New England than like the salt meadows and moorlands, scrub oak and pitch pine moraines of the glacial outwash plain known as Long Island. Indeed it lies closer to the coasts of both Connecticut and Rhode Island than to the North and South Forks of eastern Long Island that surround Peconic Bay.

I loved the quiet of the summer bay, the blue water and the hot sand shores with their acrid horsefoot smell and windrows of stout quarterdecks and light gold jingle shell that in other days was gathered up for oyster cultch; the gulls plucking scallops from the shallows, swooping upward, and dropping them on the old erratic boulders carried down out of the north by the great glaciers that formed the high moraines of "fish-shaped Paumanok"; the ospreys lugging glinting fish across the sky, the bright lobster buoys and white sails, the yelp and cry of nesting gulls, the screech of terns; the dull red shadow in the sea made by myriad gills of flat oily menhaden that turned to red purplish, so the captains said, when the school was thick; the phosphorous from the plankton in the night water that thickened in the boat's wake as it entered the warmer water of the outer harbors; the rising of the bow wave as the shallows neared, in warning to the boatman (baymen say that the boat has a natural pull toward the deep of the channel). On every shore were the long silhouettes of pounds or fish traps with their weed-hung mesh, looped up on the stakes for drying in the August dog days. On every stake perched a tattered shag, spreading its ancient wings to dry.

My father was a boatman and a fisherman—indeed, still is!—and I was not yet ten when he first took me deep-sea fishing, crossing Block Island Sound to Montauk Light at the tip of the South Fork, then southward on the open ocean in pursuit of tuna and swordfish. In those days, before World War II, the abundant swordfish came within a few miles of that coast, and one day, parting the smooth swells, we counted no less than eighty large oceangoing sharks, in addition to numerous sea turtle and great ocean sunfish and the gliding and flickering oceanic birds—shearwaters and petrels. Another day, I saw my first pelagic whales—finbacks or humpbacks, in all likelihood—and in my excitement, forgetting to balance as the boat rolled, very nearly fell overboard from my perch on the cabin roof.

At the start of World War II, Fishers Island, as part of the coast defense system, was closed to summer people, and for a few years, my family made summer visits to East Hampton, where my parents had friends and where my mother had summered as a child. In 1944, when I was seventeen, I joined the Coast Guard, and for part of that summer was assigned to duty on a picket boat out of Mattituck, on the North Fork. In those days, the East End of Long Island was a paradisal place for a young man in uniform whose life revolved around hunting and fishing, birding, tennis, hard drink, and the mysteries of young women, and since a number of East Hampton friends had kind and hospitable parents, I hitchhiked across the island by way of Riverhead and Flanders whenever I had a weekend liberty.

In 1950, on a last adventure before getting married, I had tried to sail a small rough cod boat—a double-ender with a mutton-leg sail and a one-cylinder engine—south from Bonaventure Island, in Quebec, and though the north leg of that voyage had come to an end in comical disaster, I eventually brought the boat south to Long Island, where friends had used her while I lived in Europe. A few years later, after college, marriage, and a few years abroad, I returned to the Hamptons to live all year around, settling with my young wife and our small son Luke in the pastoral community on Accabonac Creek known as the Springs. A year later, we moved to Amagansett, where my daughter Sara was born. I had published a novel and a number of short stories but was not yet making a living as a writer, and inevitably, feeling at home on the water, I drifted into commercial fishing.

In Indian summer of 1953, I became a part-time bayman, dredging for scallops in Three Mile and Northwest harbors, and along the western shore of Gardiners Island, and helping out occasionally on a small haul-seine crew, launching a dory from the ocean beach. The following spring, I joined Captain Ted Lester's seine crew out of Amagansett, and that summer, in Rockport, Massachusetts, I acquired a thirty-two-foot tuna harpoon boat, and turned her into a charter fishing boat in order to pay for her. For the next three summers, I was a charter-boat captain in the fleet at Montauk, fishing the Point for bluefish and striped bass and heading offshore in pursuit of tuna. Though tuna were abundant—there was no market for them then—the oceanic sharks and swordfish already seemed diminished, to judge from the few that were spotted even on dead-calm summer days when a fin might be seen slitting an oily silver sea two miles away.

In early autumn, I turned again to scalloping and clamming, and to duck hunting, all the way from the Flanders creeks at the head of Peconic Bay to the remote ponds in the walking dunes east of Napeague, toward Montauk. Except for Flanders, where a good friend had a blind, most of our hunting was jump-shooting from canoes in the long coves of Georgica Pond (no longer legal) or prowling the

shores of Hog Creek and Accabonac, or the dune ponds west to
Mecox, or the myriad sloughs and potholes in the Poxabogue–Long
Pond oak woods between Sagaponack and Sag Harbor, or in the
Northwest Woods, almost all of these waters lost now to develop-
ment. In the late fall, on into December, there was pass shooting for
sea ducks at Cartwright Shoals and in the channel between Cedar
Point and the Mashomack shore of Shelter Island—wonderful names!
Through hunting and fishing, and bird-watching, too, I came to know
almost every water, large and small and salt or fresh, on the South
Fork. Much more than the islands, these waters are my home.

In 1960, after a few years of world travel, I returned to the East
End, buying my first house (and doubtless the last) a few miles farther
west, in the farm village of Sagaponack. These days, a bomb dropped
in summer on a Sagaponack cocktail party might destroy nearly half
of the U.S. literary establishment, but in those days, downtown Sagaponack was a two-room red schoolhouse, a former farmhouse that
accepted boarders, and a one-room post office–general store with gas
pump run by the proprietor, Lee Hildreth, without undue effort or
assistance. In Sagaponack, I went surf casting and occasionally lent a
hand to the local haul-seine crew, and for a few years, before the
decline of wild birds made me give it up for good, resumed bird
hunting with farmer friends who maintained corn lots for pheasants
and a fine duck blind on Sagaponack Pond. In the first of a series of
small boats, I went fishing and clamming out of Sag Harbor, prospecting the shores of Northwest Harbor west to the inner reaches of
Peconic Bay and east to Montauk and Fishers Island. In this period
I wrote a book about the migratory shorebirds of North America,
and later another about the commercial fishermen of the East End,
from the early shore whalers to the present-day baymen, in the course
of which I had occasion to revisit most of my old haunts in what
was left of the once-prosperous waters of the East End.

As early as 1633, the bark *Blessing of the Bay* recorded the bountiful
marine life, both fish and shellfish, of the Great River, as the early
seafarers called the long sheltered reach of water—now Peconic
Bay—between the high moraines of the North and South Forks at
the east end of Long Island. The South Fork was settled just seven

years later, when a party from the Massachusetts Bay Colony was set ashore at what is now North Sea in Southampton Town. On the south shore—the glacial outwash plain—these settlers would discover a rich topsoil eighteen inches deep (the now-celebrated "Bridge-hampton loam"). On the north shore, where they had their harbors, the calm Peconic waters abounded with edible marine life. The biological plenty of this region must have seemed to the settlers almost unimaginable, not only the swarming fish and shellfish but the numbers of great whales along the ocean beach, pursued by the Shinnecocks in dugout canoes who first perfected American shore whaling. Today, of course, the bountiful farmland is ploughed under to accommodate the human swarm, and whales are seen only occasionally from the ocean beach. Certain fish species are much diminished, and the shellfish largely polluted or exterminated by wetlands deterioration and man-caused algal blooms, until now the bayman—the fisherman-farmer of former days—is following the wild species into extinction.

A few years ago, I finally gave up on my favorite clam ground off Mashomack, where a pair of osprey nested, and school bass came to where the tides chipped the water at the point, and deer would graze along the shore, unfrightened by a man waist-deep in water. The Peconic waters are by no means dead, simply out of balance due to our infernal meddling; one day, one hopes, the beautiful Northwest Harbor, crossed by the whale ships bound into Sag Harbor, and at one time the richest source of productive fisheries on the whole coast, can be restored to something like its former bounty, for its longest shorelines—Mashomack Peninsula, Cedar Point, and a part of the Northwest Woods—are largely protected from development.

My father, in his spry nineties now, still comes each year to Fishers Island, where he lives from late spring into early fall. I go there by boat two or three times every year, leaving northwest past the Cedar Point Light and heading northeast across Gardiners Bay toward the outer islands of the North Fork, passing the crumbling, ruined fort that lies off the long empty spit called Gardiners Point. The rip between has always been fine fishing ground, and the seascape here where the Great River meets Block Island Sound and the Atlantic, has many strong associations. One October, forty years ago, our scallop boat broke down, then broke her old mast when we tried to sail her back in a hard blow, and we spent a long cold night in that lonely bay.

> Eight miles to the northeast lay Fishers Island, the easternmost point of Suffolk County, where I had spent most of my first fifteen summers; five miles to the southwest lay Three Mile Harbor at East Hampton, where I visited first in 1942. Now it was 1953, I was in my mid-twenties, and had moved permanently to the South Fork. Thus I had lived in Suffolk County all my life, on or about the edges of these waters; this wild and lonely place where our small boat washed up and down on the high chop lay at the very heart of my home country.

Forty years later, it is still my "home country," it restores me still. North of the Ruin lies Plum Island, off Orient Point on the North Fork (before the land shifts of the last glaciers, which formed Long Island, the deep Plum Gut, which lies between these two, was the old bed of what is now the Connecticut River) and beyond Plum Island, the North Fork subsides gradually into the sea—Old Silas Rock, Gull Island (where the rare roseate tern, crossing the bow on its long silver wings, has made a nesting colony), and Little Gull, a foundation for the light that overlooks the swift deep waters of the Race, where Long Island Sound, on the ebb tide, empties out into the ocean. At the far end of the Race, three miles to the east, stands the old lighthouse on Race Rock, and just beyond it, Race Point on Fishers Island, which is separated from New England by Fishers Island Sound.

One July day, just a few years ago, with my son Luke and his son Christopher, I went by boat to my father's former house at Fishers Island, on a wooded hillside overlooking the little beach where I —Luke, too—had first learned about salt water. This broken coast and its offshore islets, with their many coves and tide pools, was where I was taught by my father to swim and fish and handle small boats, and where a lifelong fascination with wild birds and marine life had its start.

I was describing to my son and grandson how I'd loved to swim in the clear green inshore water over the white sand and how I dreaded the dark water where the white sand vanished, the unseen dangerous large sea life bound to be lurking where long straps of the great devil's tail kelp, swaying across half-hidden murky shapes of glacial boulders, marked the border of the deeps and the dread "blue water." But even as I told them about this, I realized that the blue water was gone, and the clear emerald water, too. In the half-century between Christopher's boyhood and my own, year by seeping year, the border between waters had disappeared. Even here in Fishers Island Sound, with its lack of industry and its strong currents, the fresh life-filled brine of those drowsy seaside summers was no longer a sparkling clear green and stone blue but a murky and amorphous olive-brown, straight across the whole three miles between Connecticut and Fishers Island.

> Today's voyager, approaching our shores through the oiled waters of the coast, is greeted by smoke and the glint of industry on our fouled seaboard, and an inland prospect of second growth, scarred landscapes, and sterile, often stinking rivers of pollution and raw mud. . . .

I wrote those direful words thirty-five years ago, when Luke, then five, was playing on this beach. If they seemed pessimistic then, they don't today. In the innocent presence of my son and grandson, I was filled with sadness and with shame. Thirty-five years hence (when Luke's round-eyed little boy might require a permit to father a child of his own), these coastal waters may be thick dead gray and lifeless, and dangerous to swim in, like the poisoned rivers of our cities. Already summer clouds over our coasts have a yellow cast, and even the sky is opaque by day and night, like the salt water. The sea is losing what the Japanese know as *inochi*—its "life integrity," its essential nature.

Perhaps it is not too late *if we mean business.* Our dread about our shrouded future could be displaced by a joyful new determination to clean up our once-splendid country and restore the wildlife of the

Great River to good health and plenty. Imagine swimming in the reborn rivers, fishing in them, drinking from them. In the exhilaration of renewal, even the corporations could celebrate, for there are profits to be made in whole new industries of returning the world to harmony and balance. In a respectful attitude toward Earth lies true prosperity; we are not separate from what we are destroying.

Peter Matthiessen is a founding editor of the *Paris Review* and the author of more than twenty books, including *In The Spirit of Crazy Horse*. Three of his books—*The Snow Leopard, The Tree Where Man Was Born*, and the novel *At Play in the Fields of the Lord*—have been nominated for the National Book Award, and *The Snow Leopard* won it in 1978.

BARBARA KINGSOLVER

Horse Lick Creek, Kentucky

The Memory Place

❖❖❖

This is the kind of April morning no other month can touch: the world is tinted in watercolor pastels of redbud, dogtooth violet, and gentle rain. The trees are beginning to shrug off winter; the dark, leggy maple woods are shot through with gleaming constellations of white dogwood blossoms. I'm driving through deep forest near Cumberland Falls, Kentucky, winding across the Cumberland Plateau toward Horse Lick Creek. My daughter is quiet beside me in the front seat, until at last she sighs and says, with a child's poetic logic, "This reminds me of the place I always like to think about."

Me too, I tell her. It's the exact truth. I grew up roaming wooded hollows like these, though they were more hemmed in, keeping their secrets between the wide-open cattle pastures and tobacco fields of Nicholas County, Kentucky. My brother and I would hoist cane fishing poles over our shoulders, as if we intended to be productive, and head out to spend a Saturday haunting places we called the Crawdad Creek, or the Downy Woods (noisy with downy woodpeckers), or—thrillingly, because we'd once found big bones there—Dead Horse Draw. We caught crawfish with our hands, boiled them with wild onions, and ate them and declared them the best food on earth.

We collected banana-scented pawpaw fruits, and were tempted by fleshy, fawn-colored mushrooms but left those alone. We watched birds whose names we did not know build nests in trees whose names we generally did. We witnessed the unfurling of hickory and oak and maple leaves in the springtime, so tender as to appear nearly edible; we collected them and pressed them with a hot iron under waxed paper when they blushed and dropped in the fall. Then we waited again for spring, even more impatiently than we waited for Christmas, because its gifts were more abundant, needed no batteries, and somehow seemed more exclusively *ours*. I can't imagine that any discovery I ever make, in the rest of my life, will give me the same electrified delight I felt when I first found little righteous Jack in his crimson-curtained pulpit poking up from the base of a rotted log.

These were the adventures of my childhood: tame, I suppose, by the standards established by Mowgli the Jungle Boy or Peter and the Wolf or even Laura Ingalls Wilder. Nevertheless, it was the experience of nature, with its powerful lessons in static change and predictable surprise. Much of what I know about life, and almost everything I believe about the way I want to live, was formed in those woods. In times of acute worry or insomnia or physical pain, when I close my eyes and bring to mind the place I always like to think about, it looks like a springtime woodland in Kentucky.

Horse Lick Creek is a tributary to the Rockcastle River, which drains most of eastern Kentucky and has won enough points for beauty and biological diversity to be named a Wild River. Horse Lick is sixteen miles long, with a watershed of 40,000 acres; of this valley, 8,000 acres belong to the Forest Service, about 1,500 to The Nature Conservancy, and the remainder to small farms, whose rich bottoms are given over to tobacco and hay and corn, and whose many steep, untillable slopes are given to forest. The people who reside here have few choices about how they will earn a living. If they are landless they can work for the school system or county government, they can commute to a distant city, or they can apply for food stamps; if they do have land, they are cursed and blessed with farming.

It's rough country. The most lucrative crop that will grow around here is marijuana, and while few would say they approve, everybody knows it's the truth.

Sand Gap, the town at the upper end of the valley, is the straggling remains of an old mining camp. "Gapites," as the people of Sand Gap call themselves, take note of us as we pass through. We've met up now with Jim Hays, the Conservancy employee who oversees this holding and develops prospects for purchasing other land to improve the integrity of the preserve. The three of us—Jim, my daughter Camille, and I—jostle in the cab of his pickup like pickled eggs in a jar as we take in the territory, bouncing around blind curves and potholes big enough to swallow at least a good laying hen. We pass a grocery store with a front porch, and the Pony Lot Holiness Church. "Jesus Loves You, Bond Baptist Church Welcomes You," declares a sign in another small settlement.

Jim grew up here, and speaks with the same hill cadences and turns of phrase that shaped my own speech, in childhood. Holding tight to the wheel, he declares, "This is the hatefulest road in about three states. Everybody that lives on it wrecks." By way of evidence we pass a rusted car, well off the road and headed down-hollow; its crumpled nose still rests against the tree that ended its life, though it's hard to picture how it got there exactly. Between patches of woods there are pastures, tobacco fields, and houses with mowed yards and flower gardens and folkloric lawn art. Many a home has a "pouting house" out back, a tarpaper shack where a person can occasionally seek refuge from the rest of the family.

Turner's General Merchandise is the local landmark, meeting place, and commercial hub. It's an honest-to-goodness general store, with a plank floor and a potbellied stove, where you can browse the offerings of canned goods, brooms, onion sets, and more specialized items like overalls and cemetery wreaths. We stop to buy a picnic lunch for the road. While we're waiting for our turkey sandwiches to be assembled, a pair of hunters come in to register and tag the wild turkey they've just killed this morning—the fourth one brought in today. It's opening day of turkey season, which will last two and a half weeks or until the allotted number of carcasses trail in, whichever comes first. If the season were not strictly controlled, the local turkey population would likely be extinct before first snowfall.

Nobody, and everybody, around here would say that Horse Lick Creek is special. It's a great place to go shoot, drive off-road vehicles, and camp out. In addition to the wild turkeys, the valley holds less conspicuous riches: limestone cliffs and caves that shelter insectivorous bats, including the endangered Indiana bat; shoals in the clear, fast water where many species of rare mussels hold on for their lives. All of this habitat is threatened by abandoned strip mines, herbicide and pesticide use, and literally anything that muddies the water. Some of the worst offenders are not giant mining conglomerates but local travelers who stir up daily mudstorms in hundreds of spots where the roads cross the creek. Saving this little slice of life on earth—like most—will take not just legislation, but change at the level of the pickup truck.

Poverty tends to run a collision course against the most generous human impulses, especially when it comes to environmental matters. Ask a hungry West African about the evils of deforestation, or an unemployed Oregon logger about the endangered spotted owl, and you'll get just about the same answer: I can't afford to think about that right now. Environmentalists must make a case, again and again, for the possibility that we can't afford *not* to think about it. We point to our wildest lands—the Amazon rainforests, the Arctic tundra— to inspire humans with the mighty grace of what we haven't yet wrecked. Those places have a power that speaks for itself, that seems to throw its own grandeur as a curse on the defiler. Fell the giant trees, flood the majestic canyons, and you will have hell and posterity to pay.

But Jackson County, Kentucky, is nobody's idea of wilderness. Who will complain, besides the mute mussels and secretive bats, if you muddy Horse Lick Creek?

Polly and Tom Milt Lakes settled here a hundred years ago, in a deep hollow above the creek. Polly was the schoolteacher at Bethel School. Tom Milt liked her looks, so he saved up to buy a geography book, then went to school and asked her to marry him. Both were in their late teens. They raised nine children on the banks of Horse Lick. In the truck we pass by their homestead, where feral jonquils mark the ghost-boundaries of a front porch long gone.

A part of their legacy is the Lakes family cemetery, hidden in a little glade. Camille and I wander quietly, touching headstones where seventy or more seasons of rain have eroded the intentions of permanent remembrance. A lot of babies lie here: Gladys, Colon, and Ollie May Lakes all died the same day they were born. A pair of twins, Tomie and Tiny, lived one and two days, respectively. Life has changed almost unimaginably since the mothers of these children grieved and labored here.

But the place itself seems relatively unaltered—at least at first glance. It wasn't a true wilderness even then, but a landscape possessed by hunters and farmers. Only the contents of the wildcat dumps have changed: the one I stop to inventory contains a hot-water heater, the headboard of a wooden bed, an avocado-green toilet, a playpen, and a coffee maker.

We make our way on down the valley. The hillside drops steeply away from the road, so that we're looking up at stately maple trunks on the left, and down into upper branches on the right. The forest is unearthly: filtered light through maple leaves gives a green glow to the creek below us. Mayapples grow in bright assemblies like crowds of rain-slick umbrellas; red trilliums and wild ginger nod from the moss-carpeted banks. Ginseng grows here too—according to Jim, many a young man makes his truck payments by digging "sang."

Deep in the woods at the bottom of a hollow we find Cool Springs, a spot where the rocky ground yawns open to reveal a rushing underground stream. The freshet merely surfaces and then runs away again, noisily, under a deeply undercut limestone cliff. I walk back into the cave as far as I can, to where the water roars down and away, steep and fast. I can feel the cold slabs of stone through my shoe leather. Turning back to the light, I see sunlit spray in a bright, wide arc, and the cave's mouth framed by a fringe of backlit maidenhair ferns.

Farther down the road we find the "swirl hole"—a hidden place in a rhododendron slick where the underground stream bubbles up again from the deep. The water is nearly icy and incredibly blue as it gushes up from the bedrock. We sit and watch, surrounded by dark rhododendrons and hemlocks, mesmerized by the repetitious swirling of the water. Camille tosses in tiny hemlock cones. They follow one another in single file along a spiral path, around and around the swirl hole and finally away, downstream, to where this clear water joins the opaque stream of Horse Lick Creek itself.

The pollution here is noticeable. Upstream we passed wildcat strip mines, bulldozed flats, and many fords where the road passes through the creek. The traffic we've seen on this road is recreational vehicles. At one point we encountered several stranded young men whose Ford pickup was sunk up to its doors in a "soup hole," an enormous pothole full of water that looked like more fun than it turned out to be. We pulled them out, but their engine only choked and coughed muddy water out the tailpipe—not a good sign. For the rest of today, their recreation would involve walking.

When Tom Milt and Polly Lakes farmed and hunted this land, their lives were ruled by an economy that included powerful obligations to the future. If the land eroded badly, or the turkeys were all killed in one season, they and their children would not survive. Rarely does an animal foul its own nest beyond redemption.

But now this territory is nobody's nest, exactly. It's more of a playground. The farmers have mostly gone to the cities for work, and with their hard-earned wages and leisure time they return with ORVs. Careless recreation, and a failure of love for the land, are extracting their pound of flesh from Horse Lick Creek.

A map of this watershed is a jigsaw puzzle of Nature Conservancy purchases, Forest Service land, and private property. The Conservancy's largest puzzle piece lies at the lower end of the valley. We pass through Forest Service land to get to it, and park just short of a creek crossing where several tiny tributaries come together. Some of the streams are stained deep, clear orange with iron. I lean against the truck eating my lunch while Camille stalks the butterflies that tremble in congregations around the mud puddles—tiger swallowtails. She tries to catch them with her hands, raising a languid cloud of yellow and black. They settle, only mildly perturbed, behind us, as we turn toward the creek.

We make our way across a fallow pasture to the tree-lined bank. The water here is invisibly clear in the shallows, an inviting blue-green in the deeper, stiller places. We are half a mile downstream from one of the largest mussel shoals. Camille, a seasoned beachcomber, stalks the shoreline with the delicate thoroughness of a sandpiper, collecting piles of shells. I'm less thrilled than she by her findings, because I know they're the remains of a rare and dying species. The Cumberland Plateau is one of the world's richest sites of mussel evolution, but mussels are the most threatened group in North America. Siltation is killing them here, rendering up a daily body count. Unless the Conservancy acquires some of the key lands where there is heavy creek crossing, these species will soon graduate from "endangered" to "extinct."

Along the creekbanks we spot crayfish holes and hear the deep, throaty clicking of frogs. The high bank across from us is a steep mud cliff carved with round holes and elongated hollows; it looks like a miniature version of the windswept sandstone canyons I've come to know in the West. But everything here is scaled down, small and humane, sized for child adventures like those I pursued with tireless enthusiasm three decades ago. The hayfields beyond these woods, the hawk circling against a mackerel sky, the voices of frogs, the smells of mud and leaf mold, these things place me square in the middle of all my childhood memories.

I recognize, exactly, Camille's wide-eyed thrill when we discover a trail of deer tracks in the soft mud among bird-foot violets. She kneels to examine a cluster of fern fiddleheads the size of a child's fat fist, and is startled by a mourning cloak butterfly (which, until I learned to read field guides, I understood as "morning cloak"). Someone in my childhood gave me the impression that fiddleheads and mourning cloaks were rare and precious. Now I realize they are fairly ordinary members of eastern woodland fauna and flora, but I still feel lucky and even virtuous—a gifted observer—when I see them.

For that matter, they probably *are* rare, in the scope of human experience. A great many people will live out their days without ever seeing such sights, or if they do, never *gasping*. My parents taught me this—to gasp, and feel lucky. They gave me the gift of making mountains out of nature's exquisite molehills. The day I found and with great care captured and brought home a luna moth, they let on as if I'd discovered the Hope diamond hanging on a shred of hickory bark. I owned it as my captive for a night, and set it free the next, after receiving an amazing present: strands of tiny green pearls—luna moth eggs—laid in fastidious rows on a hickory leaf. In the heat of my bedroom they hatched almost immediately, and I proudly took my legion of tiny caterpillars to school. I was disappointed when my schoolmates did not jump for joy.

I suppose no one ever taught them how to strike it rich in the forest. But I know. My heart stops for a second, even now, here, on Horse Lick Creek, as Camille and I wait for the butterfly to light and fold its purple, gold-bordered wings. "That's a mourning cloak," I tell her. "It's *very rare*."

In her lifetime it may well be true; she won't see a lot of these butterflies, or fern fiddleheads, or banks of trillium. She's growing up in another place, the upper Sonoran Desert. It has its own treasures, and I inflate their importance as my parents once did for me: she signals to me at the breakfast table and we both hold perfectly still, staring out the window, to watch the roadrunner raise his cockade of feathers in concentration as he stalks a lizard. We gasp over the young, golden coyotes who come down to our pond for a drink. The fragile desert becomes more precious to me as it becomes a family treasure: the place my daughter will always like to think about, after she has grown into adult worries and the need for imaginary refuge.

A new question in the environmentalist's canon, it seems to me, is this one: who will love the *imperfect* lands, the fragments of backyard desert paradise, the creek that runs between farms? In our passion to protect the last remnants of virgin wilderness, shall we surrender everything else in exchange? One might argue that it's a waste of finite resources to preserve and try to repair a place as tame as Horse Lick Creek. But I would not. I would insist that our love for our natural home has to go beyond finite, into the boundless—like the love of a mother for her children, whose devotion extends to both the gifted and the scarred among her brood.

Domesticated though they are, I want the desert boundary lands of southern Arizona to remain intact. I work and hope for their salvation so my daughter's dream-place, the land of impossible childhood discovery, will remain a place of real refuge. I hope she will always return to find the roadrunner thickets living on quietly, exactly as she remembered them. And someone, somewhere, I hope, will keep downy woods and crawdad creeks safe for me.

Barbara Kingsolver is the author of *Pigs in Heaven*, winner of the 1993 *Los Angeles Times* Book Prize for fiction. Her earlier novels include *The Bean Trees*, and *Animal Dreams*, which won the Edward Abbey Ecofiction Prize in 1991. She has published a nonfiction work, *Holding the Line: Women in the Great Arizona Mine Strike of 1983*, and a collection of poetry, *Another America*. She grew up in eastern Kentucky and now lives in Tucson, Arizona.

ACKNOWLEDGMENTS

So many people helped make this book possible. Above all, we thank the contributors, for the gift of their words.

We especially want to express gratitude to Scott Anderson, Susan Anderson, Joann Andrews, Marty Asher, Tim Barnett, Cameron Barrows, Terry Bronocco, Michelle Brown, Dan Campbell, Kelly Cash, Graham Chisholm, Mike Coda, Chuck Cook, Shelia Dennis, Anne Dubuisson, John Flicker, Carol Fox, Jane Fox, Dan Frank, Ron Geatz, Martha Hodgkins Green, John Hall, Bob Hamilton, Jim Hays, Bill Kittrell, Keith Lang, Bob Lindholm, Dave Livermore, Steve Morrison, Harvey Payne, Mike Provost, Joe Quiroz, Kathy Roush, Joe Satrom, Mary Sexton, Kelvin Taketa, Gordon Todd, David Unger, Nancy Warner, David Weekes, Jamie Williams, and David Williamson.

It has been a pleasure and a privilege to bring *Heart of the Land* to life.

JOSEPH BARBATO AND LISA WEINERMAN

THE NATURE CONSERVANCY
AND "LAST GREAT PLACES"

❖❖❖

Founded in 1951, The Nature Conservancy is a private organization widely recognized as one of the most successful in the field of conservation. Its mission is to preserve plants, animals, and natural communities that represent the diversity of life on Earth by protecting the lands and water they need to survive. Thus far, it has protected more than 9.3 million acres in the United States and Canada, and has helped like-minded partner organizations protect millions more in Latin America and the Pacific.

The Nature Conservancy's staff of 1,600, a national volunteer force of more than 20,000, and a membership of more than 833,000 have together created and maintain more than 1,500 preserves—the largest private system of nature sanctuaries in the world.

In its conservation program "Last Great Places: An Alliance for People and the Environment," the Conservancy is protecting outstanding ecosystems in the United States, Latin America, and the Pacific. At each site, the organization is working in close alliance with partners, both public and private, to demonstrate that economic, recreational, and other development can occur while preserving nature.

For information about the Conservancy and its work, call or write:

THE NATURE CONSERVANCY
International Headquarters
1815 North Lynn Street
Arlington, Virginia 22209
1 (800) 628-6860

ABOUT THE EDITORS

❖❖❖

Joseph Barbato is an editorial director at The Nature Conservancy and a contributing editor at *Publishers Weekly*.

Lisa Weinerman is a fundraiser in the Latin America and Caribbean Division of The Nature Conservancy.